THE COLD GATES OF HELL

Lorenzo Spencer, Sr.

THE COLD GATES OF HELL

Copyright © 2018 by Lorenzo Spencer

Some names and identifying details have been changed to protect the privacy of individuals.

The views expressed in this book are the author's views alone and do not represent the views of RiverHouse Publishing, LLC.

For all inquiries, please contact
LorenzoSpencer2018@gmail.com

ISBN 978-0-9988108-8-1

This book is dedicated to my lovely mother, Margaret King Spencer, who made me believe that I could be successful in life and be anything I wanted to be. No matter how hard life may seem, she always inspired me by telling me," son, you will make it."

This book is also dedicated to my two sons, Lucas Lorenzo Spencer and Lorenzo Montreal Spencer Jr. who I will always love.

Also, I want to give thanks to my brother Calvin Spencer for being there for me and for the prayers he sent up for me. I want to give thanks to Danny Spencer, who was there for me also. Special thanks to my sister, Brenda Spencer, who helped me through my time by giving me words of hope and love.

ABOUT THE BOOK

THE COLD GATES OF HELL is based on the true story of how Lorenzo Spencer, Sr. was called to preach by God but ran from his calling because of his lack of knowledge. Spencer believes that it was because of God's will that he was punished not only for the crimes he committed but also for his disobedience.

During his time in prison, Lorenzo fought many fights, which are detailed in this story. However, God still showed him favor by allowing him to win every single one.

Ultimately, Spencer was given a message by God entitled, "You Cannot Serve God and Satan." This message caused many incarcerated gang members to withdraw from their gangs and give their lives to God. Ultimately, gang leaders felt that Lorenzo was taking over their organizations, and ten gang members jumped him for preaching the gospel.

This story chronicles prison life from Spencer's eyes and explores the actions of some of the hardest convicts that came through the *dirty south prisons*. Spencer exposes corrupt officers and convicts who ran the jail with a heavy hand, sometimes leading to death and gives an in-depth look at the infamous 1991 riot that took place inside the Memphis jail located at 201 Poplar.

Read the autobiography of how God worked countless miracles through Lorenzo Spencer, which unto this day are hard for him to believe.

TABLE OF CONTENTS

WARNING

THIS BOOK IS RATED "R"

Due to the violent nature and offensive language of this book, children under the age of 17 are not to read it without the permission of their parents.

This book may not be reproduced rewritten or reprinted in any form or fashion without the written permission of the author.

INTRODUCTION

EZEKIEL 2:9
THE COLD GATES OF HELL

"Let's go! Let's go!" I yelled aloud, while pulling the Bible away from my own dead hands. Pulling it away caused me to fall backwards out of the doors floating and spinning.

At the same time, I held on to the Bible.

"Aaaahhhh!" I yelled out while awakening, lying back on my bed with a Bible in my hands. How it got there, I cannot remember...

CHAPTER 1:
WARNING FROM MOTHER

I can remember as clear as day. It was the summer of 1989. I was working for Airborne Express as a driver and delivery man. Before leaving the office, my boss told me to keep the truck overnight, after making my delivery and return it the next day.

While unloading in the AutoZone warehouse, I received a call in their office. It was my boss telling me to leave the truck out front of the office, and to drop the keys into the overnight box.

"So soon things change," I thought in the back of my puzzled mind.

"Lorenzo," my boss continued to yell over the telephone, "you have hit-men in the office looking for you!"

My brother and his Italian friend had come up to my job.

"I cannot have this around here," my boss continued, "don't worry about coming back, because you are no longer needed around here!"

My brother, Renard, had long hair, and greenish brown eyes looking over the top of his sunglasses. Both he and his Italian friend had on long trench coats, due to the fact that it was raining outside. Because of this incident, my brother had gotten me fired just for being cool. The boss had everyone go home, and he closed early.

My oldest brother, Renard, was living with our mother. I was sitting on his bed listening to some tracks that we recorded in our studio, 'Kelly's Productions,' when the telephone rang. It was Renard telling me that he had come up to my job to let me know that I didn't have to work there any longer, because things had worked out on getting our recording studio in business.

"Don't worry," I said to Renard, "I won't be going back, because you got me fired."

We recorded some of the most famous Hip-Hop Artists and R&B groups in Memphis.

While lying on Renard's bed, I heard a knock at the door. "Come in," I said.

A second later, I heard a soft voice say, "Hello son, how was work?"

My mother, Margaret, is 5 feet 5 inches, 160 pounds, with long black way hair, brown eyes, and a smile that would make the world smile back. She has a gold tooth with the initial M engraved inside it. She is the mother that everyone would love to have. There would be times when we would be low on food, barely making ends meet, and I would come into the house, and see strangers at our kitchen table eating, while she fed them the Word of God.

"It was okay," I responded.

"Here," my mother said, handing me a Bible. "This will take you a long way in life. It will help you through your ups-and-downs, and your ins-and-outs. There will be some dark days, some cloudy days, and some rainy days. However, if you only read this, you will see life clearer, and the sun will shine again, if you only read this."

I smiled and said, "Okay, Mama."

It was as if God had a way of pulling me into the words of my mother's wisdom, no matter how far away I strayed. I always ended right back up in her wisdom, which was more precious than gold. I felt that as long as I was by myself, I didn't have to hear her words, but when I closed my eyes, no matter where I was, her voice would always be there.

When she walked out of the room, I put the Bible under the bed. I began to tap around on the percussion function that was on the keyboard I had, while listening to some of the tracks. Moments later my mother came back into the room to see if I was reading the Bible that she had given me. I reached under the bed, grabbed the Bible and opened it as if I was reading it, although I could not read even if I wanted to, because I just didn't know how.

"Lorenzo," she said softly, pushing open the door. When she saw me reading the Bible, the expression on her face went from a concerned mother to a smile of relief.

"Son, I'm on my way out. That's good, I see you're reading the Bible. I'm going over to a friend's house, and I'll be back shortly."

"Yes, Mama," I replied, still holding the Bible as if I was reading it.

As soon as she walked out, I put the Bible back under the bed, and resumed listening to the music. After a while, I went into the kitchen to get a pop, and there was a knock at the door.

"Who is it?" I yelled.

"Ann," a sweet voice answered.

When I opened the door, it was as if Jet Magazine had delivered a large centerfold. She had the same smooth brown skin that my mother had.

"Hello, may I help you?" I asked in a low tone.

"I'm looking for Mrs. Spencer, is she here?"

I managed to regain the breath that her beauty had taken away from me and said, "No, I'm her son. Is there something I can help you with?"

"Not really," she answered.

Before she could open her mouth to finish speaking, I said in a gentleman-like voice, "Come in and have a seat; she will be back shortly." She had hazel brown eyes, thick red lips, and long wavy hair with a lovely smile. She was bow-legged with a large gap and six-pack-abs. "Thanks a lot," she said.

"My name is Lowe," I introduced myself.

"My name is Ann," she said, "I'm on my way to the pool, and I always stop to check on her when I'm passing through."

"Oh, that's good looking out," I responded.

She asked, "How would you like to go swimming with me?"

"Hell yeah! I mean, y-y-yes, I would love to. L-l-let me go get some swimming trunks," I said, stumbling over my words.

While we were walking in the swimming pool gate, there was a song playing on the radio called, "Zero in July" by "The Bar-K's". I trailed behind a few steps to get a good look at the Coca-Cola shaped body that Ann had. "Damn," I was thinking to myself.

As I looked around, I was not the only one that was getting an eye full. Everyone in the pool was looking at Ann as she unwrapped the beach towel from her Coca-Cola shaped frame. When I looked around, not only were men staring, but the ladies as well. I noticed a lady licking her lips as if she was licking ice cream. When Ann jumped into the pool, she swam like a beautiful mermaid. After seeing that, I was ashamed to get in. She was doing all kinds of sexy moves. Once I was in the water, Ann swam up to me, and pulled me deeper into the pool. After a while, I couldn't take all the attention that she was attracting.

"Let's go," I demanded.

"Okay," she responded. I had enough of everyone making passes at her. I had better plans, and this was only making me angry. I couldn't stand watching other people lust after a lady that was about to be all mine.

Don't get me wrong, I want someone that draws attention, and makes heads turn, not someone everyone wants.

While she was wrapping the towel back around her nice body frame, all eyes were on her. Knowing that we were about to leave released a lot of pressure from me.

"See you girlfriend!" One of the ladies said to Ann while we were leaving out of view. However, Ann kept her focus on me with lust gleaming in her eyes.

The basketball court was only 40 yards away, and it was some balling going on.

"You want to play?" Someone asked me, before I could even hit the court, knowing that I was a ball player.

When the game began, I glanced at Ann from the corner of my eye. I could tell that she was enjoying herself by seeing me winning. She was shocked to see me playing basketball the way I was. Once the other team started losing, the game was no longer interesting to them. I played everyone off the court.

While walking up to Ann, I threw the ball over my head in a cool fashion, and it went straight into the goal, hanging the nets. I could tell that today was my day.

"Damn, baby you are good," Ann said with both of her hands over her mouth as if she were seeing fireworks. She then began wiping off my sweat.

Hand in hand, we walked into the park talking and getting to know each other better. It felt like we knew each other all along. We sat on the bench staring at each other deeply in the eyes, while watching the sun set. I could tell that she wanted me more than I wanted her. I put the first kiss upon her lips, and things began to get intense.

"Let's go to my place," she demanded.

I didn't know what was about to happen at her place, but I was all for it.

"Okay," I said.

While at Ann's house, she cooked a candle-light-dinner. My brother was expecting me to show up for recording. "This is a way to pay him back," I thought to myself. I never thought that things could be so romantic at home, but Ann proved me wrong.

After dining, Ann and I sat on the living room couch listening to love songs. Staring into her eyes, I noticed that they sparkled like diamonds. I would say things just to see her smile light up the whole room as if the sun were shining. We must have kissed until our lips were numb. The situation was getting critical, and my third leg was running away.

"I have to go. It's getting late," I tried to explain, but she didn't want to hear it. She had a desperate look in her eyes.

"No, no, please stay," she begged as if her body hadn't had sex in years. "Would you take a bath with me?" She asked, while I had her embraced in my arms.

"Yes, I will," I answered, knowing that I needed this release.

Before getting in the tub, I was looking at her nude body like it was too good to be true. At the same time, she was looking over my body, biting on her lips as if she was eating chocolate ice cream on a stick covered in fudge.

I stood at 5 feet 10 inches and weighed 180 pounds. I was bowlegged with brown skin, and a low clean haircut. I was a little shy, but always dressed to kill. I could tell that I was the man that Ann wanted from when we were in the pool. She knew that everyone's eyes were on her, but I had her attention, and her eyes were on me.

The bubbling hot water heated things up the more. While sitting in the tub rubbing each other down in some hot oil, I could only think to myself, 'this woman has nothing but class.' She stood up with her hands in mine, pulling me up with her. Before I could place another kiss on her lips, she was going down to her knees. She wrapped her warm cherry lips around the head of my manhood and made my whole-body shiver.

"Mmmmm, it's good," she moaned softly. While she was enjoying her chocolate treat on a stick, my knees buckled as I looked down at her.

"Uh-uh-uh," I moaned, while the wonderful sensation went through me.

"Come on, this is too good," Ann whispered, pulling me by the hand. I could tell that she was the type of lady that liked to guide her man.

She took me into her bedroom. The scenery was romantic with moonlight shining through the window. On the radio, one of Janet Jackson's love ballads was playing, with a follow up by Luther Vandross.

While I was laying back on her bed, she caressed me all over. She began part two of licking with her ice cream. She tried to take my entire manhood down her throat, but she couldn't do it. She began to gag, but that only made her suck even harder as if she was trying to taste a delicious treat.

"Okay," I thought to myself while pulling her around onto the bed. I had full control from there on out. I began to please her by tasting the grapes on the end of her chest. As I sucked and licked my way down her honey brown skin, I could see my prize.

Just as I was about to taste it, she moved my head and said, "No, no, I want you inside of me."

I put the tip of my manhood into the entrance of her womanhood.

"Oh, oh my God," she whispered into my ear. The moistness and tightness made my manhood even harder. By looking into her eyes, and hearing her say that, made me want to give her everything I had, so I gave her my all.

When I began to push deeper into her, she assisted me by grabbing my back, and pulling me deeper inside. It was as if there was a war going on, and we were both fighting for ground. The more I pushed down into her, the more she pushed upward, asking for all of it.

"Oh my God; oh shit baby!" Ann said as she let out her first load of wetness, while licking me in the ear. "You have some good manhood. This is all mines, and you better never give it to anyone else."

"How is it?" I asked.

"It's good, and this is all yours," she responded. We switched all kinds of positions until our bodies couldn't move. From there, we slept the night away……

The next morning when Ann awoke, I was at home getting ready to go and do some recording. She called me, but I didn't have time to talk, although my plans were to be with her every day. I had just talked to my baby boy's mother. We were on bad terms, but I loved her, and I always will. We said our good-byes and see-you-laters, and it hurt me……

Before I left Memphis with my wife, I had some dark clouds over my head. I tried to run from them and God. I knew that I would have to face them eventually. My mother knew it as well, and she wanted it to be over. Once I was back in Memphis, Reynard told me that the cops came to my mother's house looking for me while I was in Michigan.

As I was in my brother's room, I could hear my mother talking to someone in the living room. The voices did not sound familiar. She came into the bedroom.

"Lorenzo," my mother began, "You know that God has a calling on your life. You need to slow down, and hear what he is trying to tell you, and do just that. You know the police have been looking for you, and they are at the front door. I told them not to hurt you."

'That was what the talking was about,' I thought to myself. I had heard her telling them that I was a good son. They asked her did I have a weapon. She told them no. The bedroom door opened.

"Step out Mrs.," an officer said to my mother as they moved in on me. I had my back turned so that they could cuff me, and to let them know that I was going peacefully, but one of the officers grabbed me with brutal force.

"Get against the wall!" he yelled as if there was a crime being committed.

"No, no, you said you wouldn't hurt him," my mother cried out in tears.

"I'm not going to tell you again! Get out of the way!" One of the officers yelled at my mother like she was a little child.

"Look sir," I said angrily, "I'm letting you put the cuffs on me! I could have jumped out of the window! There is no cause for all of this! I'm doing what you are telling me!"

The officers continued to slap and push me.

"You aren't letting me do a damn thing! Shut up, boy!" One of the officers yelled back at me.

"Please sir, you said you wouldn't hurt my son," my mother begged. She had a look on her face that I haven't seen since my father passed away.

"Get back now!" One of the officers yelled while raising his hand at my mother as if he was going to hit her.

"Man, let me tell you one mother-fucking thing!" I yelled out in anger. "My daddy didn't hit me, and if you didn't have that gun and these cuffs on me, I'll beat your ass!"

The officer responsible for most of all the brutality replied, "I don't need a gun. Take the cuffs off him." He told the other officer.

I felt like the happiest man in the world, because this is what I did for a living; knock men out. The officer pulled his gun out and gave it to the other officer. Before he could even turn around good, I hit him so hard that he was going down to the floor like a melted candle. As I stood over him about to land another blow, the other officer hit me hard in the upper left corner of my forehead with his gun.

"Hit him again, and I'll shoot you," the officer told me. I was looking down the barrel of the officer's gun with blood running down my face. Once they cuffed me again, and read me my rights, I was put into the back of the police car and taken to the Med to be stitched up. Afterwards, I was in the back of the police car on the way to 201 Poplar. The officer that hit me in the head with the gun said to me, "Along with your six charges, you know have one added to them."

"What for!" I exclaimed.

"Assault on an officer. You know if I wouldn't have stopped you, you would've killed him the way you were hitting him."

"Fuck you, bitch!" I yelled out. My whole life was flashing before my eyes. I knew that this was my last time seeing the outside world for a while.

CHAPTER TWO:
ENTER INTO JAIL

I t had to be a hundred degrees or higher outside. I was taken through a garage and patted down. Some doors were open with about fifty men packed like sardines standing and laying around. I just stood there looking.

"Step in!" The officer yelled at me.

While forcing my way inside, I had to cover my nose because of the odor. The smell was so strong it knocked me back.

"Step in, you heard me the first time!" The officer yelled once more.

The heat mixed with the odor really took my breath, and it had me gasping for air. The officer that was doing all the yelling looked to be about 6 feet 2 inches, and 300 pounds. I didn't want another fight, so I had to obey. The tank was only about 12 square feet. It looked as if it should have held only 10 or 15 men in it.

One of the officers' name was Ribb, and the other officer's name was Nelly. Both were some of the best comedians I had ever heard. They made fun of everyone who came through the jail. I stood there for a while laughing at their jokes about everyone until I realized I had a headache, and my knees were tired. I had just been brutalized by two police officers. Now, I had to stand up for hours and wait until my name was called.

I don't think so, I thought to myself, 'I hate to sit down in a place where drunk men had used the bathroom on themselves, but it was either that, or stand up all night.'

"Get your funky ass up! I wish you would, I'll stump a mud hole in your ass!" I yelled out at one of the white boys who smelled as if he hadn't had a bath in months. He flinched; I muscled up at him and said, "Don't think about it, I'll fuck you off!"

When he was lying down, he looked about my height, but when he stood up, I was looking at a tree. I started to think that I had bitten off more than I could chew. However, at the time, I felt like I was King Kong, and he got out of my way.

The other men in the tank had smiles on their faces as if this guy had been bullying someone before I came in. I sat with my back against the wall until I nodded off with one eye open and one eye closed.

"Spencer and Keith Sweat, come on out!" One of the comedian officers yelled out and didn't waste any time making fun of the man that came in under the A.K.A. of Keith Sweat.

Sweat could make jokes about people as well, but he couldn't hold up. While they were making jokes, I bent over laughing. Before I knew it, they were making fun of the three little stitches that were sticking out of the upper corner of my forehead; they made jokes about that. It didn't last too long. After they saw the change of my facial expression, they let up. It was very funny to me when they were teasing everyone else, but it's not so funny when the shoe is on the other foot. I held my peace as if I paid them no attention, and it didn't last too long.

We were stripped and waiting to go into the intake room for mug shots and fingerprints.

"You, you got some balls. I like the way you made that trick get up," Sweat said to me as a way of getting to know me. "I'm Keith Sweat. I have a Cadillac that's been dipped in gold, with gold rims, a jerry curl top, sprayed down with jerry curl juice, and dipped in stay-soft-fro," Sweat said trying to put a smile on my face. I

laughed and smiled only for a little while. After that, my mind reflected back on my mother, sons, and family.

"Lowe, Lowe, are you alright?" Sweat asked me, trying to get me back down to earth.

"Yeah. Yes, I'm okay," I answered snapping out of it. When he called me by my nickname, Lowe, I was having flashbacks of my brothers calling me.

After a while, we were moved into another tank where we could still hear the teasing going on. An inmate came in with an odor on him that knocked everyone out. This guy looked like he was up for years smoking crack and drinking. The officers told him to pull his shoes off, and it was as if his socks were glued to his feet.

"Man, hell naw, put that shit back on you! You just go on through, you don't have nothing on you but funk!" the officer said. They wouldn't even pat him down or touch him.

"Yes, it's me baby, the handsome one! The big M-Town trying to put a charge on me! I'm from the Big Apple; M-Town can't hold the handsome one!" a professional wrestler said. "I didn't rape her. She thought white guys had little cocks, but when she felt it running up her back, she hollered 'RAPE!' but it was too late, the handsome one had to get his rock soft! Yes. It's the handsome one, baby!"

I couldn't believe what I was seeing, but all of this and more was right before my eyes. There were homosexuals in one tank one called Nay-Nay and Shay-Shay.

"What's up big boy? Damn you are looking good. I'll suck you dry. I can suck a golf ball through a water hose. Mmmm, just look at you." Shay-Shay said while doing neck moves.

"Look man, keep that shit to yourself! You are in here just like me, so that makes you a man, so back the fuck off!" I said with an angry look on my face like I was about to knock his ass out.

"I'm a woman. My ass is a pussy, and it's good and hot."

"That's not a pussy, that's a booty hole! Look, don't mess with me! I don't play that gay shit!" I said angrily.

"Girl, he think he's all that," Shay-Shay said to Nay-Nay.

"Girl, he is all that and some more," Nay-Nay responded.

The two gay inmates began conversing with each other. There were so many inmates that they were lying on floors, up and down the hallway. While an officer was taking me to the mugshot room, he kicked a homosexual in the head and busted it on purpose. While I was taking a mug-shot, an officer was bringing an inmate into the Med room down from one of the courthouses. He looked like he had taken a couple blows to the face and had been a little banged up. He was holding his ribs in pain.

"Let me tell you one damn thing! You don't come in my courtroom getting smart! No one runs my court but me!" One of the black judges came out of the courtroom pointing his finger in the inmate's face and slapping him with the other hand. There were two officers with him, and they looked like they were the ones that put the first beating on the inmate. A judge's place was supposed to be in the courtroom, not on the inside of jail putting his hands-on inmates.

While I was being moved to what was called 'The Bullpen', officers were escorting inmates to the Med for all kind of holes and cuts to their bodies. Once I was locked into the Bullpen, I turned to look for the inmates that came in with me, and I realized I was all alone. Some of the inmates were being taken out while I was being locked in, because they were too buzzed or too drunk. They were taken to a second-floor pod where they could sober up.

"I got a gold straight shooter with rims on it, and I smoked the curl off my Cadillac." Sweat said while he was being taken to the floors.

When I began looking deeply in the eyes of the inmates that were in the Bullpen, I could tell that it was something wrong with this picture. It was like some of their eyes were saying please, please help me, and others were saying it's going down in here. It was so quiet, I knew something just wasn't right. Then as I looked closely, I put it together.

This was one of the most violent convicts in the Memphis jail. Everyone talked about how he could fight. His name was Barse. He kept looking at me as if he was sizing me up. I gave him a look back that said, *if you do, you had better kill me, because I'm sure as hell going to try and kill you. It's going down.*

"Go on finish him up, take care of your business, and if you don't, or if you lose, I will beat your ass!" Barse said to a big white boy that went by the name King.

"Come on, trick! It's going down!" King exclaimed as he started in on a black man.

I could tell from the look of Barse's hands that there been a lot of fighting going on, and that he had beaten someone. There were two guys lying out in the corner. I thought they were asleep, but when I got a closer look, I saw that they had been knocked out.

"Woo wee! Th-That hurt! Ah shit!" King said as he took a few blows to the face. Every time it looked as if King was going to lose, Barse jumped in to help him out.

I could tell from the way that Barse was talking to King that he was a mind manipulator. While the bloody beating was going on, Barse was looking over his shoulder as if I was going to get involved, or as if he wanted to try me.

It crossed my mind a hundred times to stop it, but I kept my back against the wall, and stayed ready for whatever came my way.

After they finished beating the man down, King got a good look at me. "Hey, you, I know you! What's up, you played football with me at Oakhaven!" King said.

"You sure did play with me!" I responded back with a handshake.

"What's your name?" King asked.

"Lorenzo," I answered.

"Show you right, I know you! I knew you looked familiar! They call you Lowe!" Barse said with a handshake.

Nevertheless, I kept a close watch on them both.

"Lowe, you want to get in on some of this?" Barse asked me, but what he didn't know was that I wanted to beat the both of their asses instead.

"No, I don't get down like that," I answered in sorrow for the next man.

"You're a square ass nigga!" Barse said with a disappointed look on his face. The beating lasted about two hours, and then my name was called. I had never been in jail in my life. I always made bond before it made it this far. Now I'm getting a taste of what jail is really like.

I thought I was going to a better part of the jail, but little did I know, the worst was yet to come.

"The jail is so crowded that we are putting inmates in the gym on the floor," an officer told me while taking me to the gym.

I was given a mat to sleep on. Just when I was about to lie it down…

"Lowe, what in the hell are you doing in jail?" Todd asked while helping me place my mat on the floor.

"I don't know." I responded.

We began conversing about the good ole days when we were musicians. We talked until we ran out of words and were tired from the hassle of going through intake, so we laid down and fell asleep.

"Lorenzo! Lorenzo!" An officer, who was one of my homeboys, was calling my name to be moved.

"Over here!" I yelled back to the officer.

"What's up, what are you doing in here? This don't fit you."

"Man, what am I doing in here? I done fucked up." I responded.

The officer's name was Corporal Lee.

"I saw your name on my list, and I know you don't want to be on this floor. I'm taking you to the lower level. You will have a cell."

From there, I was in a cell by myself. Once I made my bed, I laid back and began to think to myself, 'this is it. This is the end of my music career.' I tried to put something together to tell the judge. However, one thing I realized was, if I started telling one lie, I would have to tell more. So, all I did was face it as it came.

From the way an officer laid my charges out to me when I first came in, I was guilty on 75 percent of everything that I was being accused of. However, the way courts had things set up, I had no choice but to plead guilty to all the charges.

I lay back on my bed and fell into a deep dream. I could see Ann standing at the door. I told her to come to be with me, but she just stood there nude, not responding. I could see a man standing behind her, talking into her ear. She walked out with him and closed the door behind them. When I stood up out of the bed, on the other side, I was dressed in a suit. My mother appeared, putting a Bible in my hands. I took the Bible, put it under the bed, walked over to the door, and began running after Ann. I could see my mother's hands. They looked like they were coming out of the clouds holding the Bible. At the same time, she was saying, "Son, remember to read this. God has a calling on your life. It will help you through your ups-and-downs." I took the Bible from her hands, turned around, and put it back under the bed.

"Chow time! Chow time!" I was awakened by a loud voice, while my cell door was rolling open.

It was Sunday's breakfast. A tray was given to me. On it were two thin pancakes, two prunes, and a sausage patty with a cup of coffee. It was about 5 a.m. in the morning, and we weren't going to be eating again until 12 o'clock that noon. This is the kind of meal that goes in you and runs out of you.

When I was done eating, I stood at my cell door watching the inmates lie on their cell floors looking out of the bottom of their doors up and down the hall, which was called the rock.

They were trying to see if there was any food left on the trays, hoping and wishing for more. After that, it got very quiet.

I yelled out, "You better not fart or shit! If you do, you're going to be hungry as hell! Everybody better lay it down and be real still!"

Most of the inmates laughed at it, but somewhere offended, and I just didn't care. In the cell across from me was an inmate that looked to be about 4 feet tall. He was built like a little muscle man. All I could see was the upper half of his face when he was standing at his cell door. Everyone called him Shorty.

In the cell next to him was a man with no legs. He was called No-Legs. He slept on the floor most of the time, because he had a problem getting in his bed. These were two of the funniest guys you would have loved to see in action. They were the only two in the jail that had totes in their cells. The totes were given to them so that they can bathe in them.

Shorty kept his filled with water, so that every time a lady officer walked by, he would get in it as if he were taking a bath, washing his manhood with a towel and no clothes on.

Officers would laugh at him because of how funny he looked, calling him a freak show. They went back and told a sergeant. Her name was Sgt. Bradcher. The only time Shorty would do this is when he would hear the voice of a woman.

Sgt. Bradcher walked back through the pod only to see if Shorty was going to try her. As soon as she walked past Shorty's cell, he came up out of the bucket of water, washing. Everyone began laughing because everyone knew that this lady did not play.

"Awe hell no! You little short ugly mother fucker! No, nah, don't try to hide it now, you little gremlin! You son of a bitch! I'm going to hide you so far back in this jail, the flies won't be able to find your ass!" she yelled out while spraying pepper gas not only in his face, but on his manhood as well.

She then moved him, and he was never seen again.

The next morning, my name was called for court. On my way to court, going down the stairway leading to the court tunnel, there was all kind of things going on. Inmates were standing, sitting around and smoking, and picking on their curls.

As I slowed my walk to see if I knew anyone from the town, I saw a so-called player that was always in the ladies' faces. He called himself a pretty boy. He had the homosexual, Nay-Nay, on his knees, giving him a blowjob. He never even looked around to see who was looking. He just didn't care. The pot that they were smoking smelled better than the pot on the streets.

We were put into a holding tank to wait for court. "Johnny! Little Johnny!" A white man yelled out of the door at another white boy. Because of the white boy yelling out into the hallway, an officer closed the door shut.

"Oh! Oh, I'm sorry!" the white man yelled, while he was getting beaten by two black convicts for getting the door closed.

"I know you're a sorry son of a bitch!" one of the convicts yelled, while beating the white man. After he was beat down to the floor, they then stopped. At this time, 95 percent of the jail was loaded with black inmates. A white man didn't stand a chance. This was another time I wanted to help someone out, but all I could do was hold my peace.

When my name was called, the officer told me that I had gotten set off to another day, and I could go back to my pod.

"How in the hell can they set me off, and I never went into the courtroom!" I yelled at the officer as if he had something to do with it. If I was on the outside and missed court, they would put a warrant out for my arrest, but I here, they take care of your business without you even being in the courtroom. It was just not right.

When I returned to my pod, they had moved inmates into our cells. The man that was in my cell was asleep on the top bunk as if he were drunk. The little man with no legs was being pushed back in a wheelchair by a doctor and an officer. The man that was in No-Legs' cell had put his mat on the bottom bunk where No-Legs was supposed to be, and he was off to sleep. No-Legs would put his mat on the floor during the day, and on the bunk during the night.

"Hey, big man!" That's my bed! Get out of my bed!" No-Legs yelled at the big man that was sleeping in his bed.

"Fuck you, you no legged freak! You better lay your ass on that floor! Lay it down and be real still!" the big man responded aggressively, and then rolled over and fell asleep.

I stood on my cell door looking into their cell. I could hear the big man snoring aloud.

"Big man. Big man," No-Legs called quietly to see if he was in a deep sleep. No-Legs had some mighty arms from pushing the wheelchair. Some kind of way, using his arms, he hopped his way on top of the big man while he was sleeping. He put a hand around the big man's throat, took his other hand and beat the man until he awoke, and then put him back to sleep with some powerful licks.

"Hey y'all, look at this shit! No-Legs is beating the breaks off this big sorry motherfucker!" I yelled, while laughing.

"Officer! Officer! Help! Help me! Somebody get this crazy man off me!" the big man yelled in pain.

An officer rolled open his cell door and got No-Legs off the big man. "You got No-Legs fucked up!" No-Legs said while the officers were taking the big man to the second floor medical.

When dinner came around, it was fried chicken. I could see one of the convicts taking his chicken bone and filing it into a shank. Everyone must have gotten full, because later in the night it was quiet as a mouse. We had radios on the wall above our beds, and we could hear the music better when it was quiet. We could change that stations on the radios, but we couldn't cut them off. We were listening to the Quiet Storm, and they were playing all the love songs.

All of a sudden, "I can't take it anymore! I can't take it!" a man yelled from the back of the pod while listening to the radio and thinking about his wife being with another man. He then took his bed sheet, tied it around his neck, hooked it around some hangers on the wall beside the cell door, and hung himself until he died.

After that, there was silence for a day or two.

"Spencer! Spencer!" an officer called me to be moved to the floor. "Wait," the officer stopped me. I was so glad to be moved that I was heading out of the cell as if I was heading home, and I wasn't taking anything with me. "You have to get everything we issued you," the officer said. "Roll them in your blanket and follow me."

"I don't want to go up there! Please don't make me go! I can't; they will kill me!" an inmate yelled in fear while four officers were forcing him out to be moved to the fourth floor.

"Why he don't want to be moved?" I asked an inmate that was being moved with us.

"Being down here is like the dungeons of hell, the bottom of the pit. Have you ever been on the floors?" he asked me with a fearful look in his eyes.

"No, this is my first time in here," I answered.

"Well, you will find out when you get up there. It's like the top of the bottomless pit," he said. After witnessing a man hang himself, I thought that I had seen it all. However, when he told me that, it put butterflies in my stomach. The way he said it, I could tell that something wasn't right.

CHAPTER 3:
ENTER
"THE COLD GATES OF HELL"

We walked around the corner and up some escalators. There were convicts coming down on the other side of the escalators with mugs on their faces as if they were looking for their enemies. It was as if I was entering another world. Instead of going up to Heaven, it was as if I was going into hell. The higher I got, the colder it was getting. I assumed they kept the AC up to restraint the germs.

I saw a big black man coming down the stairs alone. The officers were speaking and respecting him as if he was the president of the jail. All he had to do was look at the officers that sat in the control booth a certain way, and they would open the doors for him to enter onto any floor. The rest of the convicts had to have a pass or be escorted. The big black convict's name was Big Ike. Not too many things went on or happened in jail unless he knew about it. One thing he hated was seeing inmates get jumped. He was pretty much the mayor the jail. As I entered the fourth floor, I entered a totally different world. This world was called, **THE COLD GATES OF HELL**.

I stood in the sally port waiting for the gates to open, which seemed like forever. I stood there waiting on an officer to come pat me down and look through my belongings for contraband. There was an officer, who everyone knew for his dirty ways, walking up and down the rock with his nose up in the air as if he was all of that and some more. His name was Officer Paylor, and he was one of the most lowdown officers in 201. He must have been waiting for me to say something to him that would have given a reason to violate me.

"You have any enemies on this floor?" Officer Paylor asked me.

"No," I responded.

"Good, because if you did, I would have to put you in the pod with them," he said to me before telling an officer in the control booth to open the gates and let me on the rock.

After patting me down, he walked me down the hall. While passing other pods, I could hardly breathe because of the thick marijuana smoke that was in the air. It felt like I had gotten a contact high from inhaling it.

Some of the pods were very quiet, but others were loud and noisy with men yelling as if someone was trying to holler for their life. As I walked passed the other pods, there were some nasty words being yelled at me.

"You think you're tough!" someone shouted at me because of the ruthless look I had on my face. This is when I realized that I was in another world.

I stood in the sally port that led to the other pod I was about to enter. When I turned around to look for the officer to let me inside, there was no one standing there but me. A convict walked up to the sally port with a string, bent over, and popped open the sally port bars to let me in.

"What in the hell is this?" I asked.

My focus was now on the men in the pod before me. About twenty of them ran up to me to look through my things. This was R-pod at the end of the hall.

"We are checking your shit for a pocket knife or a shank; that's what in the hell is going on!" an inmate said to me.

"It don't look like he got a shank, he look like he's jacking," another inmate said, while looking through my things.

Seeing all these inmates around me made me think that it was time to fight. I thought about what my brother, Cleveland, always told me, "Hit the biggest one and the rest will run."

But there is nowhere to run in here, we were surrounded by four walls.

"Is there a second life after death?" someone asked me sarcastically.

"Violate me and you'll find out with your smart ass!" I responded to his foolishness.

There were only three lights that lit the whole pod. There was a light in the sally port, one in the shower area, and the light from the TV. The phones, the TV, and commissary were the only things the inmates felt like they had. And if you were to violate that, you would be put in violation by the staff.

The staff was a clique of about 15 to 20 men. This included the pod-man, the assistant pod-man, the tv-man, and four phone-men, which were separated into two in the morning and two in the evening.

In addition, the shower-man, two two-for-one-men, and about four G-I-men to make sure everyone cleaned up but the staff.

The tv played only two channels - the news, and the Jukebox Video. I couldn't make out anyone's face, because of the dimmed lights.

Mostly everyone was sitting or lying down. There was only one bed in a cell, but there were about eight bunks on one side of the wall. They were stacked three-high, and the inmates that slept on them were called O-B's, that stood for outside-beds.

Some of the cells had mats on their floors that inmates could sleep on. At times when the jail would get over crowded, there would be inmates sleeping in the back of the pods on the floors and on the benches.

The two pod-men and the TV-man sat under the TV on a steel picnic-like bench.

While I was making my bed, two inmates walked up to me and gave me the rundown on the rules.

"Look man, it take all of you to go through my property?" I asked.

"We do everyone that comes through the bars like that," one of the staff inmates said to me. "That's just the way it's organized in here. We could tell you didn't like it, and the pod-man liked that. He said you got heart, and he wants you on the staff."

"No, no, man I'm not going to be no one's boy. I'm not going to be on the staff," I said to him.

"Hey man, you got some weed?" the other do-boy asked me.

"No," I told him, and they walked off.

When I was done making my bed, I laid back and checked everything out. This was my first time in this type of environment, and I admit, I was green to those facts. However, I came in as an inmate and ended up a convict.

I got out of bed, took a shower, and fell asleep hungry. I began to dream about my mother's cooking. I was sitting at her table waiting for her food. She had prepared a full course meal and a buttered roll for dessert. She had fixed me a plate, but just as I was about to bite…

"Chow time! Chow time!" someone yelled, awakening me.

"Line up to eat!", another one of the so-called staff members shouted.

Some of them thought I was weak, because like the other inmates, I was complying with the pod rules. I could tell that some of them began to take my kindness for weakness. I was the last one behind, walking slow.

"Look man, you ain't no better than anyone else. You better catch that line before you miss out," the assistant pod-man said, while I walked out slowly.

Once the staff had everybody lined up in the hall, the officer came out to the front of the line and walked everyone to the chow hall.

Then, I could see everyone's faces really good. We were now in the light, and no one had the homemade shower caps on their heads. Most of them had jerry curls, and they were wearing their pants off their butts. Most of the staff had gold teeth, but those who were not on the staff had no gold teeth, and their curls were dried up.

When I looked deeply into some of the inmate's eyes, I could see fear. I could see that they wanted to tell me something, but they couldn't.

While walking through the serving line, I saw the same big black convict that the officers respected working on the line. When he looked at me, he gave me two what was called, murder-burgers.

"What's up, cuz?" he asked.

"What's up?" I responded before walking away. "Why did that man call me cuz?" I asked myself. I was hungry, but at the same time, I'm in jail, and you have to be careful when someone puts extra food on your tray.

The murder-burgers were made with some kind of soybean and ground beef. But as hungry as I was, they were good.

"Can I have some of your burgers?" an inmate that was sitting beside me asked.

I never said yes or no. I just looked at him as if I was the devil himself. He got the message behind that.

Some of the inmates on the serving line must've said something to the big black convict for giving me extra food, because suddenly, and argument broke out.

While the big black convict was arguing, I asked one of the inmates who was sitting at the table with me who he was.

"You have the same last name," he said to me, "they call him Big Ike."

From there, I knew why he called me cuz.

"I tell you bitches what," Big Ike was yelling, "you got me fucked up!" He grabbed a broom from out of the corner, broke it in two, and began going up and down the serving line beating inmate with it while yelling, "You hoes got me fucked up!" He put knots over the heads and backs of the entire serving-line crew.

The officers had us to return to our pod while they got big Ike under control.

While back in the pod, an inmate yelled, "Line up, phone call!"

Everyone that was not on the staff had to get in line, if they wanted to use the phone. The inmates were being rushed off the phone in one or two minutes.

At this time, the phone-man asked an inmate in front of me to get off the phone, but he just kept talking as if he didn't hear him.

I could see the remaining phone-men walking up on the inmate that was on the phone.

"You heard me the first time!" the phone-man exclaimed. One of the phone-men hung up the phone on the inmate's party, while the remaining phone-men was beating the inmate down to the floor. Afterwards, the staff picked him up, put him in the shower, turned it on, and made him stay in it for about 30 minutes.

It was now my turn to use the phone, but what I had just saw made me almost change my mind. After the bloody beat down, I made a call to someone I knew had money, a car, and owed me. It was my baby sister, Trina.

"Lowe! Lowe, you're next on the phone!" the phone-man yelled. He had to call me twice to get my attention, because after what I had just seen, I was in a daze.

"Hello," Trina said, when she picked up the phone.

"Hello. Trina, I'm in jail and I don't have time to tell you why. All I need is for you to bring me 20 dollars and put it on my book."

"Bye," she said and hung up the phone.

By making my phone conversation short as possible, I didn't give any of the phone-men a chance to say anything to me.

Afterwards, I lay back on my bed and reflected on my day and how things were going on in my surroundings.

All of a sudden, a dispute broke out between two Muslims. They were called into a cell where the head Muslim was. He told them to settle their differences by fighting it out. They all came out of the cell, and the head Muslim spoke saying, "No one gets into this fight! This is between no one but my Muslim brothers!"

Believe me when I say that this was the funniest fight I had ever seen in my life. I could tell that one of the inmates couldn't fight from the way he shook his arms and fists. It was as if this red funny-fighting inmate was about to do his opponent in. He was backing his opponent up while shaking his fists. He walked towards him real slow going down the rock. When they made it back to the back of the pod behind the steel benches, all I could see was rumbling.

When they came up off the floor, Red began to back up shaking his funny fists and arms with knots on his face and two black eyes. When the head Muslim saw that Red was bruised up, he stopped the fight.

Later that night, the TV was turned up loud on Juke-box Video. Half of the staff was sliding around doing a dance that had just came out called *The Memphis Gangster Walk*. The song that was playing was "I'm Too Short" by Too Short. The smell of cigarettes and marijuana was very thick in the air.

The pod-man walked up to me and passed me a joint, and it only took two pulls to get me high. After that, there was no more bloodshed. They walked around the pod all night Gangster Walking, until we all fell asleep.

"G-I!" one of the cleanup men was yelling the next morning waking everyone up.

I got out of bed a little slow, because I didn't want another inmate telling me what to do, and they could tell from the look on my face. *But do you think they cared?* No. Not one bit.

Everyone had to get up and clean around their beds and other areas. I made my bed and joined in.

There were two inmates still laid in their beds.

"Get up!" the pod-man began yelling. "Get your funky asses up!"

Two of the staff members posted up behind him waiting on him to give the word, and to let them know when to take action and start stabbing them with shanks.

They got up and made their bed without another sound, but that wasn't good enough for the pod-man.

"Give them toothbrushes," the pod-man said. The clean-up men gave them toothbrushes.

"Get on your knees and scrub the floors!" one of the clean-up men yelled.

"And this goes for anyone else who thinks they can fucking lay in bed while everyone else cleans up!" the pod-man yelled.

He was very cocky and arrogant; no one could tell him anything. Being a pod-man in Memphis' 201 Poplar jail was probably the biggest thing that he had ever done in his life. He was the kind of man that care to jail and, as the army always says, "Be all you can be." He was a very irrational man, and if you don't know what that means, he stunted, fronted, lied and was negative about everything.

"Look, for those that don't know me, you can call me Stan," the pod-man yelled, "and if I tell you to do something and you don't, you will be dealt with. You can count on that, and you can stand on it, that's why they call me Stan."

While I was wiping off the table and TV, I wanted to snap, but it was too many cowards for one man to fight, plus I'm not Superman, so I kept my cool.

"Man, I know who you are," one of the inmates whispered to me. "I have seen you fight. You need to go ahead and whip some of these tricks."

"Every dog has his day," I said to him.

"Chow time! Chow time!" the officer yelled into the pod, and one of the staff embers repeated after him.

While in the chow hall, I didn't see Big Ike, but all the service crew was busted up. We had gravy, stew, oatmeal, two slices of bread, and two prunes. This tray was called, shit on a shank.

Whenever our pod came into the chow hall, we would sit on one side of the room to eat, and a pod from the other side of the fourth floor would sit on the opposite side. While we were sitting, the inmates from the other side were in line for their trays, and a fight broke out on their side.

Two inmates began yelling at each other. "You are going to pay me, or there is going to be blood on my shank or shit on my dick!" one of the inmates said, whose name was Mike.

"Man, I don't have any money on my books, and I'm going to eat my food," an inmate, who was much smaller, said in fear.

"Okay, that's what you want, eat your food! And when we get back to the pod, I'm going in ya like a jalapeño!" the convict Mike yelled with no morals or shame.

The whole time this was going on, Mike was standing close up on the inmate. The little inmate pushed Mike back off him. Mike picked him up over his head, body slammed him in the floor, and got on top of him.

"Boy I'll fuck you right here!" Mike said.

The officers pulled him off the inmate and took him out. From the hard slam to the floor, the little inmate had to be taken to the second floor medical to get what the doctors always issued out, Tylenol, no matter how serious the injury may be.

"Shower call! Shower call!" the shower-man shouted.

I was already on my way to the shower when the call was made. Once I was out of the shower, I heard someone yell from the other shower.

"Awe Hell no, someone shitted in the shower!"

On the way to my bed, all I could see was a line of naked men with only towels wrapped around them.

"They are standing too close up on each other," I said to myself.

Someone stuck out like a sore thumb, and it was the only white boy in the pod.

"Who was in the shower before you went in?" the shower-man asked with a nasty look on his face as if he smelled doo-doo.

"The white boy came out before I went in," the inmate replied.

"Mike, come here!" the pod-man yelled while the remainder of the staff was gathering. "Did you shit in the shower?" he asked.

"Yes, I didn't know where to use it or who to ask, and I couldn't hold it." White Boy Mike said, as if he was about to urinate himself.

"You little shitty motherfucker. Pod meeting after shower call," the pod-man said.

I could tell that something was about to go down. A pod meeting was when the pod came together to resolve something that needed to be resolved or when someone had a matter against another.

During the pod meeting, White Boy Mike tried to deny it after he admitted to doing it, and it only made matters worse on his behalf.

"This is an example for the next man that want to piss or shit in the shower. That's the only place we have to keep our asses clean is in the shower. STAFF, TAKE CARE OF YOUR BUSINESS!" the pod-man commanded.

Before the staff could put a hand on him, Officer Paylor walked into the sally port asking, "What's going on here?"

"We're having a pod meeting," the pod-man answered back as if he was the shot caller.

"Okay, that's good. I want to hear some rumbling," Officer Paylor said and closed the sally port door. He knew that whenever a pod meeting was going on, there was going to be a bloody beatdown or someone was going to get something broken on them.

When Officer Paylor walked up, I just knew he wasn't going to let this happen. But when he closed the door, the staff wasted no time before grabbing the white boy.

They began to beat him down to the floor as if he was a spike and they were hammers, nailing him to the ground.

I had to turn away. I couldn't look on it. It made me feel like a coward just by looking and not helping. When they were done, it seemed to be no life left in him. They picked him up and threw him in the shower as though he was a bloody rag.

When he awoke, they beat him some more, holding his head into the mess he had made in the shower, and forcing him to eat some of it.

After it was all over, Officer Paylor came back into the pod and looked things over. "Someone drag this piece of shit out of here and put it on the rock," he said looking out of the top of his glasses with a smirk on his face.

Afterwards, the staff began dancing around as if nothing ever happened.

A few days later, "phone time rolling!" the phone-man yelled to the top of his voice.

"If you are sleep or don't get in line now, you won't be using the phone later. You will get only two minutes to tell your family, 'if you love me plenty, send me twenty,' the other phone-man yelled while the inmates rushed in line to use the phone.

"Hello," Vamp's mother said, answering the phone.

"Hello, how are you doing?" the convict named Vamp responded as though he really cared.

"I'm not feeling so well," Vamp's mother replied.

"What do you mean?" Vamp raised his voice, disrespecting his mother.

"Son, your mother is old, and I'm hurting all over," she said sickly.

"I don't want to hear that bullshit, bitch! You low-life female dog! I will vamp on your ass! You better get down here and put some money on my books, hoe! I don't care if you have to ride a bicycle down here, hoe! I better have some money down here today! You low-life, shit-eating, dick-sucking, booty-blowing, nut-licking, snot-dripping, pussy-sucking, cum-drinking ass bitch!" Vamp yelled over the phone to his mother as if she wasn't human. He then slammed the phone down in his mother's face. Because it was quiet in the pod while everyone used the phone, Vamp thought everyone was afraid of him. If you could find weakness in someone in jail, and if they let you then take advantage of them fine, but don't take advantage of your own mother.

"Yeah, that goes for any weak ass bitch in here. I'll vamp down on one of you hoes in here. Somebody better hope the judge let me go home, because if he don't, I'm going to vamp on one of you hoes," Vamp said.

The same inmate that whispered to me once before trying to get me to whip some of those tricks said to me,

"That boy there thinks he's tough anyway. I hope someone gets him."

I said, "I hope the judge don't let him go. He will be my first victim. I'm going to beat his ass until he gets back to hell, just for talking to his mother that way," I said to DJ with flames of fire in my eyes.

DJ wanted to see me beat someone down, but I knew that it would not be a one-on-one, and I did not care. If was the devil I wanted, and I found him. I once heard someone say the devil walks around like a roaring lion, and I thought that Vamp had to be him, and he was probably the one that got me in here. I was raised around several of my sisters, and my mother taught me not to put a hand on a woman or disrespect your mother like that. I would get a chance to put a boxing show on soon.

Thinking to myself, not knowing any better, I really believed that this was Satan himself, and God knows that's the truth. I just knew I was about to beat Satan himself down. That's just how stupid I was. This man kept using the word *vamp*.

At one time I stood and waited for him to take off flying like a bat and bite someone. This was my first time in jail, and I didn't know what was in here. It was my time up next on the phone and before getting on, I could tell something was flaring up from the movement of the convicts in and out of the cells. I could barely wait to hear what my sister had to say about putting money on my books.

"Hello," Trina answered.

"Hello, did you bring the money down here?" I responded.

"No, I forgot," she said.

"What? I owe someone, I have to pay," I eased out.

"Well I don't have it now!" she said unruly and hung up the phone in my face. I then called my baby boy's mother. When the phone-man saw me dial back, he asked, "What are you doing?"

"No," the Muslim interjected, "let him call back. He owes me. Give him all the time he needs." I wasn't going to give up the phone anyway. Even King Kong couldn't have made me give it up. That phone-man was going to get whipped.

"Hello," she answered sweetly.

"Hello, how is the baby?" I asked.

Knowing that she asked me to marry her a week ago, it had to be something that I was doing right.

"Could you get someone to bring you down here and put some money on my books?" I asked. "I'm in jail, and I need something to eat."

Click! She hung up the phone in my face. I acted as if I was still on the phone talking to someone. I felt so embarrassed.

"Okay, thanks a lot baby," I said playing it off cool, and then I hung up the phone.

I then lied to the Muslim, whom I owed, as if she was just now on her way to put money on my books. I've never been in this kind of situation before. If my sister had never told me that she was coming to put money on my books, I would've never gotten the food. Now, I knew there was no money on my books, and I believed that it was time to fight.

All I could ask myself was, "What has she gotten me into?"

Thinking about my baby's mother, my heart dropped, because she really was the lady I was in love with. Since she and I were on bad terms, I fell weak for Ann, but I loved my baby's mother, Denise.

As I laid on my OB-bed, there was a convict pushing a mop bucket mopping the rock and singing simultaneously. I grew up on music, and when I tell you that it sounded good or that someone could sing, then he or she could really sing.

This convict's name was Little Otis, which I guess was because he had the voice of Otis Redding. He was pushing that mop bucket, mopping the floor, and singing so good that it sounded like he had music behind him. He was singing a song called 'A Change is Going to Come.' While he was singing, it was so quiet that you could hear a pen drop. I could see a group of officers following behind him while he sang. At times, they would slip him some money just to hear him sing.

A few days later, the news was on. The TV-man always changed the channel from the Jukebox Video to the news only to see some of the inmates and convicts that were in the pod with us on TV, and to see what their charges were.

When someone had a rape charge or a charge against a child, they would get beat down on the spot, and raped afterwards. When an inmate or convict got out of jail as a homosexual, it's not always the case that someone turned him into one while he was in jail. Nine times out of ten he was one before he came to jail.

After the news went off, there was an inmate name Mike, who would walk around the pod saying something so wrong, which was, "Boys do what they are told, and men do what they want to." The right way is, "Boys do what they want to, because they don't know any better. A real man does what he's supposed to do."

There was an inmate named Parcy trying to be a convict. He was kind of a slick coward, or should I say his game was predictable. He would walk around trying to prey on those who he thought were weak.

Because I was quiet and stayed to myself, he thought I was weak, but he had another thing coming. He walked up to my bed and asked me, "Are you hungry?"

"No," I lied.

"How would you like to make a deal on your tray?" Parcy asked.

"What are you talking about?"

"I will give you my lunch sandwich for your main course on your tray." Parcy made me a deal, and I fell for it, knowing that I was hungry.

"Deal," I responded.

He quickly gave me a sandwich. I wasn't thinking, all I could see was me eating the sandwich. Once I accepted and ate it, I knew that I had made another mistake and another enemy. But I was so hungry the night before that I was about to eat some toothpaste. I would get so hungry over night that it felt like someone was beating me in my stomach. We would eat all three meals in about ten hours' times, from 5 am to 10am, and from 10am to 4pm. When I ate the sandwich, it tasted like steak, but I was still hungry when I fell asleep.

The next day, Vamp returned from court. The judge didn't let him go. He was quiet and didn't backup all his talk, and the staff didn't like it.

"Pod meeting!" the pod-man yelled out.

Quickly, I put on my shoes thinking it was time for me to fight, knowing that I owed someone. Everyone gathered around, and the pod-man began to speak.

"Man look, some of us are not going home, and we are not in here bluffing. So, none of that wolfing and disrespecting is going down like that in here. Staff, take care of your business!"

Because of the way Vamp talked about his mother and said he was going to do if the judge didn't let him go, but he didn't do anything, the staff saved me a job. I was asleep when he came up in from court.

While the staff beat him, the pod-man would use the same words that he used on his mother. I didn't like to see anyone get a beat-down, but I shook my head in a way that said, 'that's good for him.'

When the so-called staff was done giving Vamp a beatdown, they threw him into the shower so hard that the sound reminded me of a high school base drum. They turned the shower on to rinse off the blood. This was done on the ten o'clock shift, so they waited the next day because they knew Officer Paylor would be on.

Overnight, they made him sleep behind the bench in the back on the floor under a blanket, so that the officers that came in to count couldn't tell that he was busted up.

"Lay down bitch ass boy and be real still! Don't move or the next beating will be harder!" the pod-man said before walking into his cell.

"If a mother-fucking man get beat any fucking worse, then his dick-sucking ass would be dead," I said to DJ and Donnell.

"Lowe, could I ask you a question?" Donnell asked me. Donnell was an older inmate that talked a with a lot of knowledge and had respect.

"Yeah, what's That?" I responded.

"Why is it that every time you talk, every two or three words you use is a curse word?"

"Man look, how the fuck do I know? That's just the motherfucking way I talk," I answered not meaning to disrespect.

Later that night, I could hear some of the staff talking about how they beat Vamp, because of the way he talked to his mother.

The next day, Officer Paylor came in to count. "You got one going outside for medical for stealing," they told him.

I could see a smirk on Officer Paylor's face. He would get rock hard when he saw someone blooded up, beaten badly, or when he saw any kind of wrongdoing.

But as I always say, "Every dog has his day."

Whenever someone was beaten badly, the staff would lie as if they had stolen something. "Damn, this boy is fucked up bad. Who is that?" Officer Paylor asked. He couldn't even make out Vamp's face, someone he talked to everyday.

"That's Vamp," one of the staff members said.

"Is he dead?" Office Paylor asked.

"No," the pod-man responded.

"Then hurry up and throw that piece of shit out on the rock," Officer Paylor said, before walking out smiling.

I could see Vamp look up at Officer Paylor with a look in his eyes that said, 'I'm going to pay you back, if it's the last thing I do.'

A few days later, the Muslim that I had gotten commissary from noticed that my name wasn't called to go downstairs, and he was upset with me. But for some reason, he had patience with me. Had it been any one else in my position, that person would have gotten a beat-down and lost their tray to the person that they owed or certain food off their tray of that person's choice.

"Man, you need to pay me my shit! If you couldn't pay, you shouldn't have gotten it," the Muslim said, and before I could say a word, he walked away.

Later that night, when everyone was done picking up their commissary, the ones that made store-call would put an item into the bag. Everyone that didn't make a store-call could walk up front and put their hand into the bag and get one item to eat. This bag was called the Do Right Bag.

The word got around quickly to the staff and other inmates that I owed someone, and I wasn't allowed to get anything out of the Do Right Bag. That was why every time I used the phone, some of them were in and out of the cells trying to hear my conversation. That's what was flaring up.

"You can't go up there," the pod-man told me just as I was about to go and get in line to get something out of the bag.

I walked back to my bed hungry and embarrassed with my head down thinking about my family.

The Muslim that I owed later called me to the side and said, "Let me get your hotdogs off your dinner tray tomorrow."

"Cool," I said, thinking that this was going to be a way to pay him back for what I owed. I don't try or like doing anyone wrong, but the inmate Parcy would have to wait. I would pay him later for the lunch sandwich; to me he was just a small fry anyway. He was a part of the staff, but he was more laid back.

After everyone was full of sugar and needed to lose some energy, the pod-man yelled to the top of his voice, "Thunder Dome! Thunder Dome!"

There were mats laid out on the floor to cushion the hard falls, but that was only a front the get others to participate as if they weren't going to get hurt. There were inmates hurt so bad that they would have to go to the hospital. I saw men get their arms and legs broken or knocked out of place. I saw inmates being slammed on the steel tables and getting their heads busted. This was a wrestling match, the staff against the O-B's. They were trying to get me to participate, but I refused and told them, "I'm not a wrestler, I'm a boxer."

"I told you he looked like he can fight when he first came in," one of the staff members said.

"Mmmm, he don't look like shit to me," Parcy said thinking that I didn't hear him, but I overlooked him.

When I got a good look around the pod at all the inmates, big and small, I told DJ, "I will go toe-to-toe with any motherfucker in here."

"There you go with the bad words, man. Don't you know that one day you have to answer to God for your every word?" Donnell said considerately.

"Man, fuck that. I'm in jail; I don't want to hear that shit," I responded.

The next day, I tried to call almost all my family members and not one of them answered the phone. I knew unquestionably that the ones who weren't out at the casino spending money, were out shopping. All I could do was ask myself, *what have I done for my family not to help me when I needed them?* I never did anything to any of them but help them. I know some of them were looking at their answering machines noticing the jail phone number, and knowing that it was me, they refused to answer it. This was another painful and embarrassing moment of my life.

That same night, I was so hungry that after I was done brushing my teeth, I took the tube of toothpaste to bed with me, covered my head, and began eating the toothpaste. When I was finished, I quietly cried like a baby and fell asleep. While I was asleep, I had another dream of my mother cooking a big meal. The dessert was butter-rolls. My entire family was sitting around the dinner table eating.

As soon as I was about to take a bite, "Chow time!" someone yelled loud awakening me. I was so hungry and angry, because I just knew that I was about to taste some of my mother's delicious foods.

I left home at an early age trying to take responsibility as a man. My mother tried to tell me in a mother's loving way that it wasn't time for me to leave, or that the woman I married wasn't the wife for me, but I found out the hard way. I called myself running from God, and I realized that my wife wasn't the woman I thought she was, *furthermore she couldn't cook at all.*

One thing I learned was that you never miss your water until your well runs dry. The grass isn't always greener on the other side. Everything that shines isn't gold.

Being incarcerated was as though I had sold my soul to the devil, and the things that he gave me were a way of sitting me up high, only so I could fall. Moreover, people were waiting to see if I was going to do some time so that they could get the things that he gave me. They were like vultures.

The devil will paint you a pretty picture having you think something is there when it's not, and when you fall, great is your fall.

Sometimes it's good to go through the fire in life in order to become a man.

Being a fully-grown man in age doesn't necessarily make you a man. A man must go through trials, so that he can come out like gold. Sometimes self-experience is the best experience. Sometimes we must find out the hard way because we just won't listen. And we all know that the same person you see going up, you will see him when you come back down.

The next day, I could tell that it was going to get a little heated from watching Mike walk back and forward through the pod saying his favorite quote, "Men do what they want to, and boys do what they are told."

For some reason, Donnell would watch me from the corner of his eyes, and I could tell. He would pretty much stay to himself and didn't bother anyone. He tried to put me on the right track, and I just would not hear it. I could tell that Mike was looking for trouble by bothering others, and he barked up the wrong tree.

Donnell was a lot older than Mike. Donnell was coming out of his cell on his way to watch TV when Mike bumped into him.

"Old man you need to watch where you're going!" Mike said aggressively.

"My bad," Donnell apologized.

"Yeah, you're really going to be looking bad the next time you bump into me!" Mike said.

"Look Mike, it wasn't like I tried to bump into you," Donnell responded.

"So, what's up with all that talk?" Mike asked Donnell.

Behind those words, Mike threw a closed fist to Donnell's face. This let me know off top that no matter how old you are or how much you try to respect someone in Memphis' 201 Poplar jail, you will have to fight.

Most of the inmates thought of respect as being a part of weakness. If you were talking trash on the streets and you had those guns in your hands, it made a difference.

However, there are no guns in jail. So, if you are talking smack in jail, you may soon realize it was the guns that prevented you from getting your butt beat. Now, you had to fight, and it was too late to learn.

I could tell Donnell was an old convict and could take care of himself. The lick from Mike stung Donnell, but that was all it did, besides make him angry.

"Oh shit!" Mike yelled as Donnell began to open a can of old fashion whip-ass on Mike.

As Mike began to back up from the blows that kept coming, he stood no chance of getting another lick in. There was a panic button on the upper panel of the wall over one of the outer cell doors. The button could be used to call the control booth if needed.

Mike tried his best to push the button, but Donnell just wouldn't allow him. The only reason the fight stopped was that Donnell threw one of his blows so hard that he threw his shoulder out of place. That was the only thing that saved Mike from getting knocked out and going to the outside Med.

The whole time that the fight was going on, I could see Officer Paylor standing in the sally port smiling. That showed me that when having a one-on-one fight or getting double-teamed, don't look for an officer to help you. You are inside of our walls, and you can't run. You'd better put your back against the wall and fight, and may the best man win.

When Donnell grabbed his shoulder, Mike ran to his cell, grabbed his blanket off the bed, wrapped himself up in it, and got under the bed on the floor. Everyone laughed at him.

Mike stayed in his cell all that day. When he did come out, he was given a new name because of the black rings around his eyes. He was called Raccoon.

When it was diner time, and time for me to give up my food, I was so hungry that I had made up my mind to eat my food. No matter whom I owed or who asked me for anything off my tray, they weren't getting it.

I still felt bad that I was the only one who didn't go to the store and couldn't get anything out of the Do Right Bag. The whole time we were on our way to the chow hall, I was giving the Muslim an evil look, as if he was the devil and I was going to take his head off. I knew he could tell I was up to something from the way I was looking.

"What's up, Lowe. Are you alright?" DJ asked me, seeing the killer instinct look in my eyes.

The Muslim must've known that I was going to eat my food, because he didn't say a word. He also saw it in my eyes that I just wasn't going.

Once I got my tray, I sat down and bit off the hotdog sandwich so fast that your head would have twirled.

"Let me get the rest of that," Parcy asked me, while reaching for my food as if he was going to take it off my tray.

I pushed his hand out of the way with one hand and almost hit him with the other. I pulled back and caught myself, and an idea sparked I my head.

Depending on my sister's word had gotten me into trouble, and I had to get myself out of it.

While returning to the pod, I rushed back, stood by the phone, and waited on Parcy to come into the sally port. I know I can't beat an army, but one man was going to catch hell. This was a way to get out of the pod, so I thought.

"Shit, ooh! Man, what you hit me with?" Parcy asked me while his knees buckled as if he were going down to the floor. So, I let up just enough to keep him awake.

"What in the hell was that?" someone asked aloud from the other end of the hall hearing the first lick that sounded like thunder.

The sound was as though someone took a two-by-four and slapped it on the top of some water. My plan was not to knock Parcy out, although I knew that I could have when I gave him his first blow. But I was trying to get the officer to move me.

When a fight went down, they would move one inmate and leave the other in the pod. Parcy kept looking at my hands trying to see what it was I was hitting him with, but it was only my closed fist.

"It's a fight!" someone yelled out, and the officers and inmates ran to get a glimpse.

I had Parcy jammed into the phone corner, where he couldn't get out. I made it look as if it was really a fight. At the same time, I was yelling, "Officer! Officer!" while hitting Parcy. That made it sound as if someone needed help.

The officers pulled me away from Parcy. "Pack your things!" the officer told me. He was about to move me to another pod.

"Man don't move him, he owe me," the Muslim said to the officer.

"I told y'all that motherfucker could fight!" one of the staff members said.

The officers moved Parcy and left me in the pod.

"Man, why did you whip him like that?" the pod-man asked me.

"Because he tried to put his hand on my food," I responded.

"His ass won't put his hands on no one else's food," DJ said with a smile on his face.

Later that night, an officer yelled into the pod. "Ikey, pack your things, you're going home!"

Ikey was the Muslim that I owed. But he told one of his friends that wasn't a Muslim to collect his pay from me.

Once Vamp was beaten and taken out of the pod, I thought someone else was Satan. I began to look around the pod to see if I could spot him by his reaction. My mother and others told me that Satan walks around like a roaring lion, so I really thought that I could walk around and find him. I had it made up in my mind that Satan was in this jail, and I felt that since he turned my family against me, I was going to get him. I didn't know any better. Vamp couldn't have been Satan from the way he went out, I thought to myself.

There was another inmate that I thought could have been Satan as well, which was the Muslim that I owed. He never came to me and asked me for the commissary that I owed him. I really could see fear in his eyes. That next week my mother put money on my books, and I paid my debt.

It was a convict from Chicago that we called Chi. He told me, "You shouldn't have paid Tommy anything. I have seen you fight. You can whip them with one hand."

The only thing that was on my mind was getting out of debt. I wanted to beat someone for doing wrong, not because I owed them. Besides, while that inmate was talking to someone else, he looked me straight in the eyes saying, "I won't fight him. I would have to shoot him, and it sure in the hell are no guns in here." After that, I knew that he wasn't the devil, and I began to look elsewhere.

CHAPTER 4:
LOWDOWN CONVICTS

'That's the sound of a man, working on a chain, gang!' Little Otis sang while mopping up and down the rock. Everyone just loved to hear this man sing. The inmates would turn off the TV's as Little Otis walked pass the pods singing. After Otis was done singing, Officer Coozy, who all inmates knew, would follow Little Otis around just to hear him sing. He would every now and then come in the pod to try and up lift the convict's spirits.

Officer Coozy pushed a button that was on the outside on the front entrance of the sally port; this was to alarm the officer in the control booth to open up the front gates so he could come inside the pod. It still felt like we were in gates inside of a gate, as if we are locked inside of two boxes, where there was no way out but through the courts system.

Officer Coozy was holding a cup in his hand when he was walked pass me; I could smell the booze on ice. He walked to the back of the pod and kicked the back bench about five times.

Officer Coozy said, "Man I can't stand to see this shit, they have all my homies locked up in here. But they are doing just as much crime as you do. There's got to be a better way. This is a new modern-day way to slave men, and you are falling into their traps. Man, if we could come together there would be a lot that we can change. We can close this jail down. I be looking for my homies on the town, but they are all in here locked up! You all are hurting each other worse than they are, and they know it. There is a law library outside the window, and there is never anyone in there. It doesn't cost you anything to learn. You should be in there every day learning the law. You can find a way to hurt each other; you need to find a way to help one another." Officer Coozy said his good byes and walked out as if he was the coolest officer in the jail, drinking on his cup of booze.

After Officer Coozy walked out, I began to look out of the back cat walk window. I could see the Mayor, Sheriff Jack Owens, and the city leaders having what they call "THE BIG DIG," getting ready to build the Pyramid.

It was as if they were bringing in evil spirits into our city. When this was done, it was as if everyone started going to jail. Egypt had a city with pyramids that was called Memphis, Egypt. Pharaoh had everyone locked up and now it is no different here in Memphis, Tennessee.

On my next court day, I appeared before Judge Joe Brown. While I was sitting there, Joe Brown ordered this man to write a thousand-word essay. He told him to have it done when he returned to court, and he could go home.

When it was my time to stand before the judge, I didn't have to say a word. My lawyer took care of all the business for me. He asked Joe Brown, could he give me another court date in his court room, because he was going to try and get all my charges ran in together.

Judge Joe Brown looked at me and asked me, "Is this what you want?

"Yes sir." I responded, because my lawyer had already told me what to say.

"No one is putting you up to say this?"

"No sir."

The Judge agreed.

Then I was taken into Div. 8 Judge McCarty. I was put into a holding tank; I stepped on a convict foot, he looked like a nerd.

"My bad, I apologize," but he gave me no response and that made me frown.

He was a little fat and had eyeglasses on. He folded his lips as if he was mad. At this point, I didn't care because he didn't respond. I was still looking for the devil, and he could have been him. I believe he would have tried me if he wasn't up to something.

"Come on, look out Gangster Tedd." Fred said to one of the convicts that was in the tank.

While Gangster Tedd looked out of the window for an officer, Fred was lifted up to the ceiling by two other inmates. Freed then opened up the light that was in the top of the ceiling and pulled the lining out of it. He had a steel piece of metal rod to make a shank with it. He then put it under his clothes.

"Spencer!" An officer called me to go into the court-room.

While I was sitting on the bench waiting to see the Judge with some more inmates, someone was about to be sentenced by Judge McCarty. He put his hand into his pocket, then pulled out some change and stated to the convict. "Look, I'm going to throw this change your way, and you better catch it, because whatever hit the floor that's how much time you will be getting."

I thought it was a joke, but he really threw it. I don't know how much hit the floor, but the bailer took 57 cents out of the convict's hand and gave it to the judge. When the judge was done counting, he made this statement, while looking out the top of his glasses. "Since you want to go out there and commit some stupid crimes, I did something stupid right along with you, and now you have some stupid time."

There was a nice-looking lady and one more male inmate in front of me. When the lady inmate was done they took her out of the courtroom. When the male inmate was called, he began looking around and up into the ceiling as if he was spaced out. While his lawyer was speaking to the judge for him, the inmate pulled some toilet paper out of his top pocket and asked an officer for some paper as if he was going to blow his nose. He then put all of the paper together, pulled down his pants, bent over and wiped his butt as if he was wiping fecal matter. But before coming into the courtroom, he put some peanut butter in his crack. He did this trying to get time knocked off his sentence, but it didn't help. The judge gave him more time for that.

Judge McCarty yelled out in anger looking as if he bit a bitter lemon. From hearing rumors about Judge McCarty and now I see him in action; with all the charges I have I thought I wasn't going to see the streets for a long time. When my name was called my lawyer told the judge the same thing that he told Judge Joe Brown, and I was sat off and taking out of the courtroom, but I didn't like the way the judge was looking at me out of the top of his glasses.

For some reason my mind began to reflect back on the lady inmate that was on the bench beside me. When she walked in front of me my manhood got hard and long as a pipe. The officer put her in the same tank that they kept the men in, because he saw no one in there, and he took everyone else back.

By me being last coming out of the courtroom, the officer escorted me, while putting me back into the holding tank he didn't look in the toilet area. The lady inmate was using the toilet when he locked me in. When I sat down I could see out of the corner of my eyes that someone was back there, and I could see the color orange and that meant it wasn't a man.

"Oh my God," I said with a glow in my eyes. When she walked from behind the stall. It was as if we were about to attack each other off the top.

"What's up." I said up to no good, and ready to please her in every way she wanted.

"You," she responded to me with a sexual look in her eyes as if she had been locked up for years without touching a man.

I took another look out of the window to see was there an officer around, it wasn't one in sight. Before I could turn around and make my move by asking her, she had her arms around me while standing behind me. It was if she had everything under control with my manhood in her hand stroking while licking her lips.

My manhood was so hard until it was as if the top of it was about to burst open. Turning me around with one of her hands, she dropped down to her knees and swallowed hard of it slowly while stroking it with her mouth.

The warm moist feeling made me close my eyes. "Mmm,mmm." I let out; while looking down at one of man's loveliest sights I wanted to see at that time.

While picking up her speed trying to taste her sweet milk, she could sense that I was looking down at her. She looked up at me and began to blink her eyelashes. I grabbed her ahead with both of my hands and began to pump faster.

When I was about to pull back from releasing in her mouth she pulled me closer with my entire manhood in her mouth, she swallowed all my sweet milk.

After, that I couldn't take the rush; we both pulled down her clothes and we didn't care, if we were in jail or not, we were going to reach out highest climaxes. My pants were down to the floor, and she was totally naked. She sat up on the face bowl while I was between her legs. Before she could take a second breath I had half my manhood into her womanhood, and it was very tight that I could feel the inside walls gripping.

The wetter it got, the deeper it allowed me to go into her body. I put her legs in each of my arms while she had her arms wrapped around me holding her body up. I then began pounding her with everything that I had. She kept slipping off the face bowl; I then walked to the other side of the room while we were still locked together.

Without her feet ever touching the floor I put her back up against the wall and pounded her to the highest climax, until she quietly moaned to the top of her voice.

When I let her down off the wall, she went down to the floor as if she melted holding her hands between her legs, and then put them over her mouth as if she was in shock looking at me as if she fell in love at the same time.

"Get up, get up. Here comes an officer. Put your clothes on. You go out first; it's the officer for you." I told her as she walked to the door fixing up her clothes as if she was using the bathroom.

When the officer opened the door, I hid behind the stall hoping that he wouldn't come back there; they left and I wasn't seen. When the officer came to open the door to let me out, he looked at me as if he knew something had happened.

"Damn, it's stinky in here, it smells like pussy!"

He then took me back to the courtroom.

My lawyer and Judge McCarty must have been talking about my case before I came in, because the judge began to look at me out of the top of his glasses as if I had killed someone.

"Listen here, you think I'm going to run all of his charges together, and he has an assault on the officer also, well you have another thing coming, not in my courtroom and no time in the future!" The judge yelled out looking at me while talking to my lawyer while his jaws shook as if I just had killed the president. That was so much for that, I was denied, and now I have charges in two different courtrooms running wide.

On my way back to the pod, I had a relief besides what the judge said, as if I was free as a bird. While back in the pod, I wanted to tell DJ or anybody about the sex I just had, but they wouldn't believe me even if they saw it with their own two eyes. I walked to the front of the pod, leaned on the sally port bars and talked with DJ.

While we were standing there talking, Donnell was on his way out to be moved down stairs to the second-floor medical pod because of his dislocated shoulder.

"See you later," I said good bye to Donnell.

"Lowe, I haven't known you long, but God has given me this to tell you. There is a man named Paul that went down the road to Damascus and if you don't change your life and do whatever work it is that God has called for you to do, you will go down the road of destruction." Donnell told me on his way out.

"Have already done construction work before," I responded for a lack of knowledge, not understanding the wisdom that he was feeding me at all.

After that was said, I walked back over to my bunk, laid down and slept through the noise. For almost two days, behind that good sex, I couldn't hear a sound. All of a sudden, I was awakened with a loud yell. A fight broke out, or other words, a beat down.

"Look, he is sitting on the staff table," one of the staff members said to another, as they walked into the pod man's cell to tell him.

"Deal with him. Don't stick him. Put that soap and sock on him!"

The pod man gave commands. "Oh wow!"

The inmate that was sitting on the staff table cried out, after he was hit in the back of the head with some soap in a sock.

You could see a patch of his hair, flying out of his head with some meat on it. It stuck to the top of the wall. It came out of his head as if someone threw it up there. He ran down through the pod like a chicken with his head cut off. He was trapped in a back corner where he was beaten down to the floor. But some kind of way he came out from being beaten by five staff members and ran to the panic button, trying to push it but they didn't allow him to get it. He kept reaching for it while he was being beaten back down to the floor. When it was as if he had no more movement in his body, they picked him up, and threw him into the shower as if he was a dirty piece of paper.

As soon as it was all over, Officer Paylor showed up and walked into the sally port gates.

"We have one going to the Med. He got caught stealing," a lying staff member told Officer Paylor. The staff got the other inmate to get him out of the shower and gag him up front.

"Damn, when you all get ready to beat someone down like this, call me before it goes down, I would have liked to see that killing," Officer Paylor said with a disappointed look on his face.

After what was called a blood bath, the inmates threw him out into the hall, and he was a bloody mess. This is what was called, a bloody bath.

"Get up, get your good stealing ass up. You won't steal nobody else's shit," Officer Paylor said and didn't make things any better.

He grabbed the badly wounded man by his arm and began dragging him while stinging him with his stun gun.

"Someone call medical; one got caught stealing," Officer Paylor said.

"Oh, please, no, I didn't steal anything," the inmate cried out.

Later on that week, I had gotten so hungry I took my shoes to a staff member name Dogg and traded them for some commissary. I didn't get $5.00 for a new pair of $65.00 sneakers, and the next day I was hungry all over again. I looked at Dogg wearing my shoes, and I almost cried. Before I knew it, the word had gotten back to my family that I had no shoes on my feet. I had to wear jail house shower shoes. I got a visit, one time after that. I didn't see one family member in years; I never did anything to hurt or harm them. In fact, some of them owed me and still owe me for the rest of their lives. But I will never hold it against them or charge them, because I love them more than money. There were people locked up that did their family so wrong, and they still put money on their books and came to see them. I heard some of their conversation over the phone, and I knew it was no way in this would I could talk to my family like that.

Later on that night I fell into a deep sleep, and this is what I saw. It was as if I was standing on a flat land all alone. It was as if I heard God, as if he was telling Moses to take off your shoes, you are standing on Holy ground. I looked down at my feet and had on no shoes. But when I looked up, I never saw anyone. I then turned to see who voice that was talking to me, and there still wasn't anyone. When I turned back around again, I saw my mother's hands giving me the Bible. The hands looked as if they were coming out of some clouds.

"Mother, where are you?" I asked looking up into the clouds.

"Here, son, take this. Read it; live by it, and don't worry," she said, and everything vanished away.

The Bible was in my hands, but I turn around and there was a bed. I guess I was still being hard headed. I took the Bible and put it under the bed and walked out of a room over to a cage, and it was if I was in the cage, it had gates on the front gates, and I couldn't get out.

"Mama, Mama," I cried looking for my mother.

"Lowe, Lowe," someone awakened me, and I was in a cold sweat, and it was cold in the jail. "Lowe, you want a Bible? They are giving them out on the bars." DJ told me.

I got out of my bed, walked up to the bars, got one of the Bibles that were being passed out. I then walk back to my bed laid back down and tried to read it glancing through it, closed it back, and put it under my mat. Deep in my heart I wanted to read it, but I couldn't. I just didn't know how.

I laid back on my bed and watched the days go by. I looked up at the sally port gates, and there was a 6'6 or 6'8 convict coming in the pod. The same one that slammed Ron to the floor in the chow hall; his name was Mike. He was known for taking the weak, back-hole. When he walked in the pod, I didn't see everyone run up to him like they did me.

Mike dropped his things and walked around looking for someone's cell to take. It was so quiet that you could hear a pin drop.

To me, it looked like he was looking for someone that he thought wouldn't give him a fight. It was one of those weaker staff members. He walked into his cell and threw all of his things out. This is one of those things that makes a difference between a convict and an inmate.

A convict will do things on the down low, in order to keep the police out of their business. And at the same time, he wants to keep his macho title name. It's not what you do; it's how you do it.

An inmate will draw the police to them, they will tell it on themselves. They are always in the officer's face running off at the mouth and bringing heat on themselves.

A convict is laid back and will stay as far from the police as they can.

An inmate will say the first thing that comes out of their mouth. They never think, they just do, and keep up loud noise.

The staff member looks for another staff to help him, but they all tucked their tails like cowards they were.

"From now on, I'm going into the pods the same way, hard," I thought to myself. Mike picked out his victim that had his own cell and did what he wanted to do.

"Boy, get your shit and get the fuck up out of here," Mike told the weak staff member, while faking at him as if he was going to hit him.

"What are you talking about?" the staff member said, while getting his things and almost running out of the cell.

"Just what I said, hoe ass boy. Get on, before I fuck you in the ass," Mike told him, while slapping him upside of his head and kicking him in the butt.

Once Mike got him and all his things thrown out, he said out loud, "Anyone has a problem with it, anyone want to get'em up?"

"This is y'all fucking staff," I said, and O-B's laugh at it.

Behind that, things were kind of at ease throughout that night. All I could hear were the radios that were on the cell walls. I could hear some of the inmates crying out from thinking about these girls having sex with big boy Jodie.

I was also thinking same thing, wishing I could be there with Ann. By this time, I had given up on Denise. I didn't let her go, she let me go, and it seemed there was no hope for our relationship. But thinking about my sons and not being there, my heart began to cry out for them. But after a while, my mind would go back on Denise, thinking how good of a girl she was. I could hear the song that was playing by Booby Womack, "I Wish He Did Trust Me."

All I could ask myself was, who was making love to her now?

The song that came on next must have put Mike in a mood. Mike and one of the convicts were in Mike's cell smoking a joint. The convict that was with Mike, his name was Dirty Red. It was only two white boys in the pod with us, and probably on the whole floor.

Ice was one of the white inmates who acted as if he was black. He had something you didn't see to many white guys with, and that was a gold tooth in the front of his mouth. Ice smelled the smell of pot in the air and couldn't resist from finding it and asking for some. He walked past Mike's cell about two times.

"Damn man, what's up my brother, let me get a hit of that shit? It smells good," Ice asked, not knowing what he was about to get himself into.

"Come in. Here, you can smoke all of that," Mike said as he passed the rest of the joint to Ice.

"Red, let me holla at him for a minute," Mike said and Red stepped out.

Mike then begins to hang a blanket up to the face of the cell door. The blanket only covered the mold part of the door, and you could see the upper parts and the lower parts of their bodies.

"What's your name?" Mike asked.

"Ice, damn bro, that's some good marijuana. I'm high as hell." Ice said, while laid back on the bed as if he was cool.

"You like that?" Mike asked.

"Yeah man, that's cool," Ice responded.

"You know that shit cost."

Ice was listening to the radio and to what Mike was saying. While Mike was talking to Ice, at the same time he was reaching for some petroleum jelly that was up on his shelf.

"You know a joint of marijuana cost about $25.00 in jail, and you are going to pay for it, you know there's nothing free in jail." Mike said, while he was blocking the door, and at the same time begins to pull out his manhood and greasing it up.

"I don't have any money or commissary," Ice said standing up off the bed as if he was going to leave.

"That's ok, you got something else." Mike said, while Ice was trying to get around Mike and out the door.

Mike hit Ice so hard in the side of his face that it put fear in him as well as his voice. He sounded like a crying girl. Mike forced Ice to bend over and pulled his pants down at the same time. He then put the jelly on Ice's back-hole.

"Ohm, ohm mm, ohm," Ice yelled and screamed out while Mike began to enter into his back-hole back and forward. Mike reached for a nude playboy picture he had, then took a sheet and cover Ice's whole body, and laid the picture on Ice's back while pumping him until he released.

"Hum, ohm," Mike said, while looking at the playboy picture.

When Mike was done he slapped Ice upside of his head and kicked him in his butt out of his cell.

"Get out of here, you done smoke all of my blow, you fuckin motherfucker!"

Most of the staff began to laugh out loud at Ice. Ice was getting ready to get into the shower.

"Hell nah, you're not getting in that shower, in fact, Officer! We got one that can't hold his shit, he needed to go to the second-floor med!" The pod man told the officer.

"Come on out of there," the officer told Ice.

"And get all of your shit, I bet that was the *firess* dope you ever had," one of the staff members said.

"It's the best you ever had, once you go black you will never go back," another staff member said, and everyone laughed.

When Officer Paylor opened the gates to let Ice out, he was holding his stomach, and reaching for his backside.

"Come on out of here, what up you really have thrown a rod," Officer Paylor said with a lowdown look on his face.

Mike then sat on the so-called staff table looking at the video's like he was cool. The so-called staff wasn't dancing around like they were at first. I stood in the back of the pod talking to DJ about how I needed to beat all their asses at one time for going through my things when I first came in. While the song played on the TV, I made up my own words and sung them out loud.

"Your staff ain't any men, you're bitches, some hoes!" I repeated out loud.

Half of the staff laughed, while the remaining had their puppies on their face. I pulled off my socks and stood on the back of my shower shoes, ready to fight, bear-footed and flat-foot jacking.

Nothing was said, and I began to focus on Mike. I heard about David and Goliath, and from the thoughts that ran through my head it looked as if I would have that kind of fight on my hands. I told everyone that I had to fight coming up fighting against some big guys.

The way Mike came in, quiet but violent, this had to be the devil himself. I had finally found him, I thought to myself.

Mike stood every bit of 6'8 tall. Mike and the pod men stood up off the table and stood on the outside of Mike's cell talking.

I walked to the shower and got one of the GI towels and act as if I was wiping the walls. I wiped my way up beside Mike and wiped up high to see if my fist could reach his face, and it could. I kind of hit right beside Mike's face with my closed fist.

"Bro, is you alright?" Mike asked me.

"Hell yeah, I'm all right." I responded with my mug on my face. That was enough for him to try me.

A few days passed by, and I thought things were at ease. I heard and saw a white boy hang himself, but I never seen a black man hang himself until I came to jail.

A love song was playing on the radio in the cells. It was one cell that all the O-B's used when they had to go to the bathroom; it was called the O-B's toilet. A black inmate called Duck put his blanket up to cover the facing of the door as if he was going to use the toilet. He was in there making a rope out of his bed sheets. I could hear little Otis singing *A Change Is Gone Come* while he was mopping the rock. One of the O-B's was walking to the O-B's cell to use the toilet.

"Hey, how long will it be? I got to use it." An O-B said as he knocked at the door, but he got no response.

He then pulled the blanket back only to see the inmate hanging from the clothes hook by the neck.

"Ahhhh, Ohhh, Shit, he's dead!" the O-B inmate yelled out in fear.

A staff member ran to the cell and snatched the blanket off the door, and we all could see a dead man hanging with no life in him at all.

"Woe." I said, as I felt a cold light wind blowing through the pod.

It had to be the spirit of death himself passing through. The officers and doctors came in and took the dead body out of the pod. The officers asked a few questions and after that, things continued on as if nothing had ever happened.

FIGHT #1

The next few days, there was an inmate trying to act as if he was hard because he was put on staff. He would always walk around yelling to the top of his voice, as if he was demanding inmates to hold down the noise.

On that very same day, DJ and I were standing in the back talking while looking out of the window. There was a group of inmates standing not too far from us talking very loudly. This inmate just knew he was tough and thought the staff had his back. All they used him for was a send out. His AKA name was Head. You have all kinds of heads in 201 jails, there's Hick head, little head, big head, Jar head, flat head, bean head, box head, dick head, potato head, long head, short head, bucket head, and head. This inmate head was so big, he was just called head. He would look at you as if he was the toughest man in the world. He put fear in a lot of inmates and so-called convicts, but God knows, I wasn't the one.

"Hold that noise, you hear me!" Head said with a real puppy look on his face, and we had eye-to-eye contact.

"Bro, look, the police aren't going to stop me from talking, and I know you are not; besides we were talking low anyway, and we are not that loud," I responded in anger, knowing I had been falsely accused.

"Mother fucker, I don't give a fuck who it is. I say hold that noise!" Head yelled out while walking my way. He was now close in my face, and I didn't have time to think about the staff jumping on me, when it was a man facing me. I'm not a coward and I have nuts like he does.

"Damn," everyone yelled out. Before Head could say another word, his nose was busted and bloody. He must have staggered backward five feet.

I could see his legs buckle as if they were giving out. But big as his head was, he remained conscious. I knew then I had a fight on my hands. This man outweighed me by 30lbs, and I could tell. I stood off him and jabbed his face and his big head for a good little while. He couldn't take too many of my blows, so he tried to wrestle me, but I wouldn't let him. I came out of it throwing lick after lick.

"Ohhh, wild," the crowd yelled out, while looking at one of my quick six packs being dropped on his head.

I glanced slightly at the staff, watching my back for Head, just knowing he was about to go down to the floor. Not realizing how close I was up on him, he landed a heavy right to my nose.

Behind that I had to backup to recoup, but oh boy, when I came back on him, I didn't let up. It sounded like fireworks in the pod; I drowned him like a hot potato. The entire pod yelled out loud, and I could see Officer Paylor looking happy as a log.

"Now, that's what I'm talking about," Paylor said.

When the smoke cleared, you couldn't hear a word from the staff or Mike. They saw how Head was busted up and made plans to jump me. I sat on the table to get some rest, before I could look up the weak staff began to rush me.

One of the littlest inmates on staff hit me in the jaw so soft I thought he was playing. Pulling me off the table, they tried to wrestle me to the floor, but when I busted loose they all ran into their cells.

I thought they were going to get their shanks, but they were running because they didn't want to be hit by the licks that they saw Head was hit with.

I didn't get a chance to throw not one lick.

Another officer was at the bars, he asked. "What's going on in here?"

"This weak ass so-called staff trying to jump me," I responded.

When the officer opened the gates to let me out, the pod-man ran up to the bars.

"Man, you don't have to go, that boy you wiped is going out of here, and you have the wrong man," the pod man tried to explain.

"You want to move?" the officer asked me.

"Yeah, get me out of this weak-ass pod, before I catch a case."

"That's the wrong man y'all tried to jump!" The pod man yelled out to the staff.

He told them to jump Head after I had already beaten him down. From there, the officer moved me to the other side.

CHAPTER 5:
MY HEART WAXED COLD

Now that it seems that I have been through a small example of hell, I know Satan is not out to get me, but I must get him first. Knowing that I'm going to be here for a while, I know what I must do and what it takes to make it in jail here at 201. When I first came in I wasn't a convict, I was just a man looking for justice for my wrong doing. But now, I don't only feel, but I know I have been forced to become a convict.

Just from looking at some of the events and conversations that has gone on, I know everyone on here on earth isn't from here. They have got to be aliens in a human form. Man built a billion-dollar jail, but there was just one thing they forgot to do, and that was classify everyone where they are supposed to be. They will throw you anywhere, as long as you are behind bars.

The city was in debt, and they needed money, and the sheriff promised that he would fill up the jail.

"You don't suppose to be on this floor, or you don't suppose to have a red dot on your arm band, they fucking up," the officer that was moving me said.

"Man, I call jail anywhere," I responded.

"Why you didn't stay in there?" the officer asked me.

"Man, I can't fight an army," I responded.

"Yeah, you have to ride or get rode on in 201," the officer said.

As a black man, we hurt ourselves more than anybody. Before the officer put me in the pod I thought to myself, maybe I'm looking for the wrong somebody, or in the wrong way. *Sometimes, we war against ourselves that is within you and can be our worst enemy and don't realize it.* Truly, there is a percentage of blacks that are locked up for committing a crime, but for the ones that didn't do anything, they only stuck like chuck.

I know the County Government owes me, if they only admit that they were wrong. I was taken out of society for the first time, and put into a cage with robbers and murderers, carjackers, kidnappers, rapists and any other convict you could imagine that committed a crime.

I heard all kinds of plots, schemes and scandals that a white-collar crime convict wanted to do. Not only that, but the neglect I received from my family all together gave me a whole new outlook on life, in a bad way.

To me it is now, a dog-eat-dog world, and I'm about to be hard as a rock, and 'My Heart Has Waxed Cold.'

"Stand there until we find a pod to put you in," I was told by the officer.

I could see the reflections on myself through the glass from the control booth. My hair had grown wild and dried up, because I had no money on my books to keep it up. All I could do was rub it backward using my hair for a comb. I could see the flakes fall from my head and skin on my face was very dry. I had put on some weight and looked kind of wild.

"Spencer!" an officer called my name from the other end of the hall.

"Yes, sir," I responded, while walking his way with my things rolled up in my blanket thrown across my back.

"You're going in G-pod," he told me.

From remembering the way Mike came into the pod, I had a convict's idea on how I would enter this new pod. When the officer walked off, and I walked in the box of the sally port, I begin to kick the bars and yell.

"Where is the damn pod man? Let me in this mother fucker!"

Not giving the staff a chance to rush me, although I saw them getting ready to when the gate came open.

"Where's the damn pod man? What? He's scared?" I said, as if I wanted to kill him, getting everyone's attention.

'Cut that shit out, little wild ass man," a big convict said while walking my way with a smile on his face. He was coming out of the back cell. But at the same time, I could tell he had heart.

"You must be the pod man," I said.

"Yeah, what up?" he responded.

"I have got to have one of these cells the easy way, or the hard way!" I yelled to the top of my voice, and believe me, there wasn't a bit of fear in my heart at all. Know it was whatever with me, and I'm not getting rolled on or rolling anyone. They could see it in my eyes, I was out for blood.

"Man, don't touch my shit!" I told one their staff member that was reaching for my things, while I flinched at him.

"My name is Lowe, and I'm going to get a cell. I'm not with that O-B ass shit!" I yelled to the top of my voice.

"Look, everyone go back to what you were going, I got this," the pod man said in command to another weak staff.

"Big Joe is my name, what's yours?" The pod man asked.

"My name is Lowe," I said, as we began to walk around looking for whose cell I was going to take.

"Hey, you're Lowe from the Mound," Big Joe asked.

"Yes," I responded.

"Look, to keep down the trouble in here, this is what I'm going to do. I'm going to put Lowe in the cell of the last man that came in. Tony, you have to move out," Big Joe said.

"Man, man," one of the staff members said, but before he could say another word.

"Man, Man my ass. What's up? What you want to do, boy? Get your shit up out of that cell," I boldly said in Tony's face dropping my things on the outside of the cell door to free my hands.

He began to back up into the cell with fear in his eyes, and at the same time getting his things out of the cell.

While putting up my things and making the bed, Big Joe and another inmate that was from Orange Mound stood at the face of my cell door.

"Are you some kin to Big Ike?" Big Joe asked me.

"Yeah," I responded. After I said that, it opened more doors of respect.

"All shit, you're from the Mound. Dig that homey; it's all good," the other staff member said to me with a greet.

Later on that night, everyone ran out of matches to light their cigarettes. I remember once I was working as a maintenance man, cleaning carpets, floors and appliances. I had a headphone radio on while bent over a bucket that I had in it my cleaning supplies. I had some SOS pads mixed with some tissue lying on top of everything. The batteries fell out of my radio into the SOS pads and tissue paper and sparked a fire. The tissue caught on fire, this happened in 1981. I wanted a cigarette worse that anyone I saw. I saw some SOS pad over behind the toilet in my cell; I grabbed it and a piece of tissue and walked out of the cell.

"Anyone have some batteries that I can use?" I asked out loud.

My brother always told me, negative and positive don't mix. Once I was given some batteries, I pulled the SOS pads apart, twisted up some small pieces and put them on each end of the batteries, then put some tissue paper on the SOS and flamed it up in fire.

When the fire ball hit my table, someone ran into my cell with a cigarette, lit it and began to smoke.

From there every time someone wanted a smoke, they would have to come to me, and that's how I got my smoke on.

Another convict asked me how to make a fire. That's how I was given the name Wick. I then made them what I called a bomb from some rolled up tissue paper. He had some coffee in a peanut butter jar. I then made a rope out of some stripped up bed sheets, and tied it around the top of the jar, and lit the bomb while it was sitting on top of the table, and it heated up the coffee.

After that I took a rubber band that came out of the jail pants, put it on a around a piece of garbage bag. I then folded the tip end down together. I had a shower cap, to keep our hair from getting wet while in the shower, and it kept the jerry-curl juice from getting our bed sheets wet.

I then took a fire bomb, laid some meat on the top of the table, and held the fire bomb under the table and cooked the meat.

The next day, when it was time to go downstairs to the commissary, the pod man and some other staff members began to get bags and put shanks in their pants and stood at the front entrance of the gates.

"Lowe, you want to go, you need something to eat right," Big Joe said.

"Yeah, hell yeah," I responded.

"We going to the commissary. Come go with us," one of the staff members said.

"Big Joe, you told me I could go this time," another staff member said.

"It's enough, stay back," Big Joe gave orders, while bent down putting a rope between the bottoms of the sally port bars.

He pulled up on the rope at the same time pulled back on the gate door, and it popped open.

"Let's go; let's roll!" Big Joe said, and we made our move downstairs.

When we made it to the second floor where everyone would return with their commissary in the breeze way. An officer was in the far end of the control booth but paying us no attention. It was about four of us standing in the lobby, not far was the Chaplin.

"Here they come, everyone pick out their man, and take his sack," Big Joe said.

I watched for a while as if I was chicken. Big Joe and the staff were pulling out shanks with one hand and hitting inmates with the other hand in the eye. When the next man was coming, I didn't have a bag. Big Joe nodded his head at me and then at the inmate at the same time for me to make my move. I just wasn't with taking something from someone, especially a weaker man. When I tried to grab his bag, he pulled back trying to get around me. With a killer look on his face, that took my mind off the point, I was taking something. I stepped quickly in front of him, landing a punch in the center of his nose with everything that I had. He went back out of the door and landed on the floor in front of the escalators.

"Jesus, what did he hit him with?" Someone yelled out, as the sound almost scared me.

I bagged up his commissary, and we headed back up the escalators. I had to step over the inmate that I knocked out, laying as if he was dead. The other convicts had smiles on their faces, but I just didn't feel right. I glanced back to see the outcome. The officer who was in the control booth never looked down. If she had, she would have seen an inmate laid out for the count.

While back in the pod, the convicts were bragging on my one-hitter knock out. I wanted to pay them no mind. I just didn't feel right I walked into my cell, got most of the commissary and began giving it out to the inmates that didn't go to the store. All I could think about was what if that was me, and someone could have done me like that.

As weeks passed by, Big Joe and the staff would go out and rob for commissary. I never went back, it just wasn't my style. After a while, I walked back into my cell and picked up a Bible that was lying on the table. I laid back on my bed, opened it to Second Kings, and tried to read it.

It was as if something was telling me to get the key, and the key was to pray first before I read it. But I shook my head, not trying to hear it, but I tried to read and couldn't understand it or read it. I then closed it up, put it on the floor under my bed and fell to sleep.

I dreamed as if my son's mother and I were getting married. When I was about to put the ring on her finger, it was as if I turned to look back only to see she was getting married to another man. As I stood there looking at her getting married, tears began to roll down my face, and I couldn't do anything about it. It was as if I woke up, but I was asleep. I then saw the Bible again, but it was as if it was coming through the walls, while I was still in my jail cell. I looked at my arms and saw no hands on them. I then looked on the wall of the cell, and seen my hands pushing the Bible back through the wall, as if I was rejecting it. I didn't want to believe that they were my hands, but when I looked closely I could see three of the fingers were cut off on the left hand and that let me know that it was my hands. The tips of my fingers are cut off, and I woke up looking at my hand and started to cry.

"FIGHT #2"

"Pod meeting," someone yelled out to the top of their voice.

When I made it to the back of the pod, I put my back against the wall. Something I learned during pod meetings or just around in jail, always keep your back against the wall and watch your surroundings at all times. Never get caught slipping, especially when there is animosity in the air. When everyone else was in place and ready, Big Joe spoke out saying, "Listen here men, it's the same old shit, we are going to eat in a little bit. And remember to hold down the noise and walk in a straight line."

"Most of y'all have just started coming to jail, so you know how this shit go."

Some of the staff made a few speeches and Big Joe began to talk again.

"Look, Lowe is my homeboy from Orange Mound, and I will be leaving soon going home or going to do my time. Before I go, I'm going to make Lowe the assistant pod man."

"Man, as long as I've been in here, I haven't been shit but a damn shower man, you're going to let that mother fucker in the front of me, fuck that damn boy," Rome said, with his doggy look on his face, as if he was scaring someone.

But if looks could whoop someone then I wouldn't have to fight, because I could look way uglier than he could.

"Look, man, I'm not going to be all of these mother fuckers, and shit by the way, I didn't ask to be a pod man," I said, as I begin to man up for myself.

Before I knew it, Romeo was in my face, in striking distance, and I had already sized him up. He was about three inches taller than me and outweighed me by 20 pounds.

Off the top, I knew to stay up close on him and go for the knockout. He walked a little too close and met a quick left to the upper top of his forehead, and behind that, I didn't let up. I landed every lick hitting my target until he went down quickly to the floor.

"Oh shit, damn man, that son of a bitch can fight!" Someone yelled out.

"I mean he can go some!" Another inmate said out loud.

Different ones yelled out in the crowd while someone dashed him with a cup of water to wake him up. When he stood up, he spun around looking for me, and I was in his face.

"Take him all the way out!" One of my home boys said, that was from Orange Mound, his name was Lawrence.

I really thought this man was losing his mind. I thought he was going crazy. After the beat down I put on him, he was afraid to walk my way. He went into two or three cells, getting bars of soap and began to throw them at me.

"This isn't a soap fight; this is a fist fight!" Someone yelled out.

The whole scene was funny. Everyone laughed. Everyone stood in the face of the cell doors; it was only him and I that had the floor. I caught two bars of soap and threw them back at him. One hit the wall and the other hit him in the side as he turned. That really had him hot. He went to one of his friends asking him, "Will you help me wipe this punk ass boy?"

"Let's make a shank," his friend told him.

They went into the back cell, while they were in there, Lawrence walked up to me and said, "Lowe you shouldn't have let up on him, you should have taken him all the way out. Lowe, they are back there making a shank, and he is coming back. So, watch your back."

When he came back out he was swinging a small shank at me with the rope around the end of it. The shank came out of the rope, it slid under someone's bed and couldn't be found. I then began to chase him around the pod and got a few more licks in and an officer saw us and moved Romeo next door.

The very next day I was called out by Sergeant Sanders, which later on I found out that he was Romeo's cousin. While I was standing talking with Sergeant Sanders, Romeo walked out of the door that the officer or Sanders left open for him. While my back was turned, he swung and hit me on the side of my head.

After that he didn't land one lick, but Sergeant Sanders grabbed me from the back, and they wrestled me to the floor. While the officer was holding me, Romeo gave me a few weak blows to the midsection, and I broke away and walked back into my pod.

"Man, they set you up, they got you that time. I told you to take him all the way out, you just stood over him when they dashed him with that water you shouldn't have let up," Lawrence said, as if he was a brother to me.

"All, they didn't do nothing I didn't get a scratch." After that I took a shower and went to sleep like a baby.

The next day a crazy white man came into the pod that we saw on TV, for cutting up a six-month-old baby, and then he put the baby into a pot and boiled it. The inmates called him the silence of the lamb. There were two other inmates that were on the news that came in for killing someone and buried them under some dead people's coffins.

Later on, my name was called for court, and while I was waiting to be seen by the judge McCarty, I sat on the court bench laughing my heart out. The convict that was being seen before me had come to jail four times with about four different a.k.a. names. The name was, Superman One, Superman Two, Clark Kent and Eddie Cadillac Seville.

"You have got to be the stupidest or dumbest son of a bitch in the world."

When the judge was talking about this man, everyone in the court room was laughing. When my charges were read out to the judge, it was so many charges until I was set off again and given another court date. Before I could leave out of the courtroom, convict Superman came back in the door saying, "Judge, will you give me some community service?"

At the same time the officer was trying to pull him back out of the door by the arm.

"So, you want out of jail, well let me see if you can fly out, superman. Take him back out and lock him up!" the judge said out of anger.

The people in the court room laughed again. Sometimes it takes judges like this because of the crimes some of the convicts commit. But because of the years of time that Judge McCarthy is giving out, convicts had a hit on him, and want to kill him. He would ride to work in a helicopter.

When I was taken back to the pod, the convict that the judge threw the pocket change to for him to catch was in the pod sitting on the table watching TV. I sat down beside him, and he began to talk to me.

"Lowe, I'm glad you beat that boy's ass out there, he would always pick on folks, Man, and did you see how the judge did me?"

"Hell yeah that was wrong. It has to be some kind of law against that, they probably keeping it hid from us. They say a judge can do anything that he wants to in his court room, but that's a lot. Everyone has rules and laws that they have to abide by under the law," I said, feeling sympathy for the brother.

"Yeah Lowe, you have a point, and I'm going to look into that, and I will find out one day, and when I do, I will be getting out, one day, yeah, one day," he said out of sadness.

After that, from that day forward, we called him One Day. Later on that week, One Day left going to Fort pillow to serve his time.

As I sat or just laid around watching other inmates and convicts, they were always in the female officers' faces whenever they would come in to count or just conduct a search. Inmates would act and talk as if they were the biggest player or had everything in life that it takes to take care of a woman. And believe it or not, sometimes some of the officers will go for it, and I can't hate. I would just stay out of the way and listen to the game. A man always tries and give the next man his air time, but when it don't work, most of the time he will hate on the man that it works for. But when it doesn't work for you, don't hate on the next man when he accomplishes it. Or don't try to put yourself up; by downing the next man, it only makes you look bad. Again, one thing inmates can do really well when they come to jail, and that's be all that they can be. A lie isn't nothing to tell, it's just waiting on someone to tell it. And if you can hear, these are not convicts they are inmates.

They would also call themselves pretty boys not by words but looks. They are always in the mirror looking at themselves or picking with their hair. Not only was I told, but I learned, a woman doesn't want a man that is prettier than she is. And for the so-called pretty boys that are in jail, most of them are chosen by punks.

A real man is going to put that punk in his place. If you put 75% of the pretty boys behind closed doors with a gay man you'll find out they are gay too. I saw inmates fight over the phone to talk to the ladies, and as soon as they were off the phone, they were in the gays' faces.

While sitting on the table watching TV, we looked up and it was the gay boy called Shay Shay, standing in the sally port on his way in. After a few days gone by, I could see a change between the inmates and convicts.

Inmates that weren't in the mirror were in it and putting on the best state clothes that they had. I can't believe it, I began to say to myself.

We all know that one lies down, and two gets up. Some of them were gay all the time. It just took another gay man to bring it out of them. When Shay Shay first came in, one told him to get in the shower or the staff didn't pat him. Not only that he walked straight to the staff table and began watching TV, and no one said a word to him.

"Hey, what's your name," a staff member asked Shay Shay.

"My name is Shay Shay," he said, trying to talk like a woman.

"The pod man wants you, he's in the back cell."

Shay Shay got up and walked back there.

Big Joe was going home, and a new pod man was an inmate called Slick. When I would see Shay Shay sitting on the front table, I would stand up in the back of the pod and talk with Lawrence. When Shay Shay walked into Slick's cell, Slick would put up a blanket that we called putting up a violation. We couldn't see what was going on but from the sounds we could tell there were gay activities going on.

But there is one thing about a gay man, he will lie good or tell everything that he has done with the next man to make himself feel like a woman and likes to gossip.

Whatever went on in there, Shay Shay came out with a smile on his face. Slick came out sweating and out of breath, headed to the shower. Later on that night you could see Shay going in and out of the cells and when inmates were done, they would get on the phone, talk to their ladies as if nothing ever happened, and if it was cool.

There was a staff member that called himself Nal Nal. He always admitted he was a pretty boy, and before Shay Shay came in, he was always on the phone and was a phone man. He was always in Shay Shay's face, and they could hardly get him to run the phone or talk on it. He wasn't the only one, but he started doing things to impress a Shay

Shay. He started to eat food around Shay Shay and give
him food when he wouldn't give anyone else any.

You could see him falling out with some real brothers
just because of Shay Shay. Even some lady officers would
tell Nal Nal how handsome he was. The staff gave Shay
Shay a cell and Nal Nal walked in and put up the violation
and that was all Nal Nal wanted.

He acted as if he had been chosen by a real woman.
The sheet that was up at the door was kind of thin, and
you could see clean through. They were too busy trying to
get their rocks off and paid it no attention. With the light
on in the cell, you could see them good, and Lawrence
made it no better. He walked around the pod telling
everyone to come and see. We could see Shay Shay pulling
down Nal Nal pants and giving him oral sex. You could see
Shay Shay on his knees taking care of business. After a
while Shay got up, pulled his pants down.

"Put it in me," he told Nal Nal, forgetting to change his
voice and sounde like a man. But at the same time, it was
as if Shay was forcing Nal Nal to do it. He was a lot taller
and outweighed Nal Nal. He couldn't do nothing with
Shay but give him what he wanted.

Shay Shay took over and forced Nal's manhood up his
back hole. We began to laugh, but you could hear the real
man coming out of Shay, his manhood must have gotten
him hard.

"Hey, it's my turn," Shay Shay said and bent Nal Nal
over on the bed and entered into Nal Nal's back hole. We
could hear Nal Nal yelling out as if he had been stuck with
a shank.

Everyone stopped looking on, and it was hard for
someone to believe, but oh boy it was true. When Nal Nal
came out of his cell, he took a shower and went back in

and stayed in unless he was going to court or was going to eat. He had been turned out, his manhood had been taken and he was no longer the same.

FIGHT #3

Another inmate here wanted to be a convict, tried to act tough and went by the name Red. He was just a little bigger than I was. I was sitting on the top of the staff's table watching the Jukebox Video, when he sat down beside me. I got up and moved to the back because he sat just a little out close to me, and I never been the kind of man that likes another man close to me, only if it's my woman, especially when we been tippin into another man's cell that is gay. I saw him come out of Shay Shay cell, and after he came out he took a shower. Then sat close to me like it's cool.

"Boy, I'm not contagious!" Red said to me while I was standing in the back.

"Lord, not another fight," I said lowly to myself.

Red was the one who asked Big Joe to let him go and take some commissary. But Big Joe told him that it was enough and stay back! He put his dog on me. He had some of the inmates thinking that he was tough, and some was afraid of him. But now things are looking and sounding bad. The only thing that was on my mind was running into a long shank. I wasn't on the staff, and I didn't want to be on it. I'm not with that raiding someone or getting rolled on. About five or ten of them were gay and didn't know it. Least a homosexual knows what he is and is proud of it and will tell the world. Everybody have a choice to be what they want to be.

"Look Red, you had animosity against me from day one, it's not just because I got up!" I said.

"Man, fuck you!" Red said, cutting me off.

"Nah, fuck with me, that's what you do, you red piece of shit!" I yelled in a bold way letting him know I wasn't barring none.

Red walked my way to the back and this was just what I wanted. I was told he liked to use shanks, so I gave him no chance to go for one. I knew I had to take him out quickly. It was now a little too much talk, and I was about to go back down, because I almost allowed Red's muscles to intimidate me.

"I'm going to tell you one time to get out of my face!" I yelled, trying to get Red to calm down, but it only gotten worse.

"FUCK YOU bitch ass boy!" Red yelled again, walking in my face. I backed up a little trying to avoid this fight. But I began to think, this just might be the devil and I'm still looking for him. My first mistake was I let Red too close up on me that allowed him the first lick in. It rocked me off balance, and it was a good one. I got one back in on him, but it wasn't that effective. Behind that Red gave me two blows to the face, what seemed like everything he had. But I could dish them, and I could take them. When I backed up to recoup, I felt the bee stings that he put on me and shook them off.

I always remember never to let a man that outweighs you grab you, and never let a man that's taller than you stand off of you while fighting. Stay up on him no matter what.

I came out of my shower shoes to get a better grip on the floor. Now bare footed and no shoes on, I'm flat footed and jacking.

"Ohhh, ohh," Red said as I hit him with some of my death blows to the face and then to the ribs. Causing him to grab me trying to throw me to the floor, and at the same time stepping on my toes. A convict by the name Rat, a school mate of my baby brother was pulling us loose.

"Stop, hold up, here Lowe, put on these shoes," Rat said, giving me a pair of sneakers. While I was tying up the shoes as if something was talking to me saying, 'Yawl, this is the Devil, you're looking for him; now you find him.' I heard in my head while keeping my eyes on Red.

"Oh yeah, it's on, yeah old ass boy, you're going down," I said to Red while bouncing his way and looking him in his eyes. While I began to pull in on him, he landed a few blows on me but they were not solid or effective, they were wild flat and soft. I had to take his blows in order to get up on him. I got all the way in throwing a hard right to his ribs, he then bent over, and that broke him down to my size. How kill the head and he body will die, I thought to myself. He was tall and long like a snake. With top of nothing but bare knuckles, I gave him a quick 8 pack that cause him to go down like a hot melted candle.

"Damn this mother fucker is jacking, that mother fucker is flat foot jacking out the frame," Rat said, and the pod went wild while I was picking Red up off the floor. I then walked to the shower with him in my arms and threw him into the shower and turned it on. Everyone laugh out loud that wanted to see Red go down. But there was few that were hating on me, because that was they boy.

A few days later, not only because of me beating down Red, but I would every now and then let out loud words about them messing with Shay Shay saying, "One lay down and two get up."

So, they came up with a scheme to jump me. The word got over the jail quickly. They knew once owed someone in the pod I came out of, they talked an inmate into getting me to get something from the two for one man, I was hungry, and so I did it. By then, my sister Brenda had bought me a pair of black sneakers and we were allowed to get them in. She was also able to leave me $20 and from that day I have always loved her even the more. Sometimes it's more than just telling someone *I love you*, it's showing it. After that I never went to the store again the whole time I was in 201. The information that the staff leaked out on jumping me was heard by Big Ike, and he was out of the hole. This I didn't see it coming, even though I would always watch my surroundings. Someone turned the TV up very high, so if there was some yelling the officers couldn't hear it. I walked out and stood in the face of my cell door. All of a sudden, the staff was coming my way.

"Lowe, I need to holler at you," the pod man Slick said, standing in the front of them, with nothing in his hand. "Look, you are in here getting these folks shit and you can't pay it back, what's up with you!" he said and at the same time tried to slap me in the face, but my alertness and quickness allowed me to block it, and the lick hit the back of my hand, while my reflexes almost hit him with the other hand but catching myself and saying, "Man let me explain to you about my family and the problems I'm having with them."

"Man, let me tell you something, damn you and your family, you're going to pay my boy his shit, or else we are going to get in your shit, around here getting these folks shit and can't pay," Slick said, while looking back at his staff, as if he was waiting on them to make their move.

I had all the chances in the world to take Slick out, but it was as if something was holding my hands. Because, my back was up against the wall, and so none of the staff couldn't steal on me. Watching my back that made a big

difference. After the fights, seeing me downing my oppo-
nents the first to make his move was going to get it.

"Ok, Lowe we know you got some fight in you, but we
will be getting back with you a little later," Slick said, giving
his staff a cue to pull back.

The inmate that they were giving cookies to and telling
me we were going to pay half and half, they already went to
him and was sending him out. They all could see blood in
my eyes, and they all knew that I wanted to sleep so bad
that I could taste him. I just didn't want to get rolled on or
stuck on.

A week later, nothing happened, and I still hadn't been
to the store. The inmate that would go in half with me on
the cookies, his name was Morris. He gave me the word,
they would give me a week to get the cookies.

"They said if your family loves you, they better put
some money on your books." After Morris told me that, I
called my family, most of them didn't answer the phone,
and the rest just wouldn't help me. My heart dropped and
waxed even colder.

Later on that night, "Pod meeting, pod meeting," one
of the staff members, as my heart got weak and my knees
buckled, I've never been in a pod meeting where someone
didn't get beat, stuck, jumped or it was a fist fight, and I
just knew it was my time.

"Man, let me tell you something," Slick said out loud,
talking with his hands moving to every word. Slick is
known for sticking on his victims, and with the staff
behind in, believe me, he will.

"You boys around here getting these folks shit, you are
going to pay up one way or another, look I said you are
going to pay up or catch up. This funky motherfucker has
owed for two months, and this is an example of what we

do for those that owe!" Slick ended his saying with a knife pointed at an inmate that was named Fred.

"No, please no, ohhh, ohh!" Fred cried out in pain for his life. The whole staff jumped, stuck and beat him up until he didn't live. When I saw this, I said to myself, "all of them must be Satan. I wanted to take the Devil on one-on-one, not his whole army." Just seeing the fight took all the fight out of me. I never thought that I would see the day, a man got beat to the point of death for a row of cookies. I owed for a whole pack, but missing store, it ran up to three packs. If Fred got beat down like that for a row, I knew what I had coming for a pack.

"What's up, what in the hell going on in here?"

Everyone looked back toward the sally port, to see the voice of Big Ike, standing in the fates. Everyone that popped open the bars had to use a rope to get them open. But Ike grabbed the bars with both of his hands and snatched back on the bars so hard until they came open. It sounded as if the whole pod shook.

"Let me see the pod man, the assistant pod man, the phone man, the shower man, the cleanup man. I want the whole damn staff!" Big Ike insisted.

When all of them walked from the back to the front of the pod, "Lowe, come here!" Big Ike called my name and said to me.

"Now, let's beat some asses!" Big Ike and I began giving them the beat down that they gave everyone else.

It was so easy to hit them, because they were too busy trying to get away from us, and at the same time they were running into each other. One of them ran so fast, not only did he drop his shank, he ran into the back wall while trying to run into one of the cells. That was the least of the problems we had to worry about, he knocked himself out cold.

"I'm sorry, I'm sorry!" One of the men I was beating cried out as he apologized.

"I know you a sorry, sad, son of a bitch!" I responded back with no sorrow.

But if you ask me, it really was all Big Ike's doing. He beat almost the whole staff by himself. I stood at the front of the pod and watched his back, while I was rubbing on my fist allowing them to cool down.

"You bitches want to jump on someone in here over some cookies, here cook this!" Big Ike yelled out while beating on the last man.

I got who I really wanted, and that was the pod man, Slick.

"Let me tell you all something, here Lowe, take this, and if these hoes try and pull out one of their homemade shanks, stick it so far up their asses til you can't pull it out!" Big Ike said as he gave me a real six-inch knife.

"Yeah, that's all I have been waiting on, and that's one good mother fucker to help me bust y'all asses up. Now let me hear of you son of bitches ever fucking with a *Spencer* or anyone in here, I'll make it rain down body pieces in this mother fucker!" I yelled out and meant it with blood in my eyes. With that, Big Ike could tell I had things under control. He walked out, slammed the bars closed and left.

"Everybody let's clean up!" I yelled out.

After that, there wasn't much said about cookies. The pod man and his staff began doing like everyone else, and that was asking to use the phone and cleaning up as well.

Shay Shay would not give up on what he was doing. Everyone else would put up a blanket at their door for violation, but Shay Shay would hang up a bedsheet, so everyone could see what he was doing. There was an inmate that called himself pretty Tony. He would do the same thing that Nal Nal was doing. He was dancing around the pod from the back to the front, all up in Shay Shay's face. Then when a lady officer would come in the sally port, he was in their face trying to come up with one.

On this particular day, Tony was dancing while the Jukebox Video was playing on the TV. He was doing the Memphis Gangster Walk; he slid his way into Shay Shay's cell while Shay Shay had his see-through sheets hanging up. Half of the pod was looking on, and we could see Shay Shay on his knees giving Tony oral sex.

"It's so good, I'm going to do you." Tony said, and Shay stood up while Tony's got on his knees and gave Shay oral sex.

"That's fucked up. It feels so good til he's going to suck the boy dick, now that's whose ass y'all need to beat," I said and walked up to the front and leaned on the sally port bars.

The rock man Little Otis was mopping the hall and singing 100 and 10th Street by Bobby Womack. When Shay came out of his cell, he went into the shower and one of the staff members went in with him. After seeing that, I said to myself, "It's time for me to go. I have seen enough."

A week later, I came up with a plan to move out of the pod. After I saw a convict pop open the bars and left his homeboy out, that gave me an idea. While I was in my cell packing my things and twisting up me a rope out of a piece of bedsheet, half of the pod was gathering around my door trying to talk me into staying.

"We want you to be the pod man," one of the staff members said to me.

"Yeah man, if you become the pod man, we won't have that many problems in here, then you can get rid of some of the mess that's going on in here." Another one said.

"Yeah, I know you can fight, I used to see you fight in the Boxing Arena," Lawrence said, trying to talk me into staying.

My mind was on moving and going home at this time, and nothing or nobody was going to stop me. With my things packed and at the door, I was pulling back on the bars with the rope, popping them.

"I will see you brothers down the road." I said, after I closed the bars behind me and walked off.

Little Otis and Big Ike were out in the hallway holding a conversation.

"Is everything ok?" Big Ike asked me with that killer instinct look on his face, as if he ready to go back into the pod and start another beat down.

"Yeah, everything is damn good. I'm just moving to another pod." I responded, and that stopped him from going back into that pod.

"Stay here with Little Otis. I know what pod I will put you in, I'll be back in a minute." Little Otis and I stood and talked for a while, and before we could get done with our conversation, Big Ike was on his way back.

"Come on, Lowe, I have a cell for you in 4G and if you need me for anything. I'm in 4M," Big Ike said as I followed his lead.

CHAPTER 6:
GANGSTER STYLE

When I entered into G-pod, it was so dark until I could only see about ten feet in front of me. The worst thing to do is move into a pod with one of your homeboys that was up to no good, and that is just what I did. I also moved into the worse pod in the jail, a pod no one wanted to move in. But only because of Big Ike, I was ok.

"Lowe, what's up?" Kelvin greeted me on my way in.

"What's up Kelvin? I spoke back.

"Nothing much homey, it's all good. The pod man is asleep, and we have to keep it quiet in here while he's asleep. His name is OG. Big Ike has already talked to him about you moving in here. That's the pod man cell in the back where you see the two body guards at the door. This is your cell, I will holler at you later." Kelvin said and walked off.

Night and day, OG has a staff member standing on each side of his door at all times while he slept. Once I was done putting my things up, I walked around the pod looking things over. All the cell lights were covered with different colored papers to darken them. Inmates began mugging me as if I had done something to them. But like I said once before, I can make even an uglier mug, so I mug them back. I guess they had looked that way for so long, until they disfigured their faces.

The inmates that were standing in the back of the pod were so quiet, until you could hear a pin drop. As I looked into the eyes of some of them, I could read the word fear, and please help us. Some of the officers knew the things that were going on in these pods, but they just didn't care.

There was one Officer Good. He would always talk to the other officers about how tough he was when it came down to fighting. Some of the officers were telling him about how good Big Ike could fight.

But officer Good was convinced that he could whip any officer or convict in the jail. But you must always remember, there is always someone tougher than you.

"Tell y'all what, set up a date for Big Ike to meet me in the gym, and we will fight," Officer Good said, as the other officers began to place their bets.

Some bet on Officer Good, but the majority bet on Big Ike. Before they could set up the fight or talk to Big Ike, they were passing money. While back at the pod, I didn't sit at the front table, I stood up in the back, so that I could see the staff and my full surroundings.

When the pod man turned his light on, his body guards walked off. When he walked out of his cell, I recognized his face. It was the same nerd-looking convict that had on glasses the day that I was in the holding tank waiting for court, and I almost stepped on his foot.

I got a better look at the convicts that were sitting on the front bench, and one was his charge partner, Tedd. And I remember the long shanks that they pulled out of the light fixture in the holding tank. And knowing their reputation on the streets and from in here, they would try something. This pod was more laid back and enforced their rules more brutal than the other pods.

"Oh no, no, men please don't put me in there!" An inmate pleaded out for his life as Officer Paylor was still up to his same old lowdown tricks. This inmate had enemies in this pod, and they were out to get him.

"You'll deal with him; he's a smart ass," Officer Paylor said, while he forced the inmate into the pod.

The staff didn't waste any time on making their attack. Not only did they go through all his things, but they made him go into the shower and pull off all his clothes to be sure that he didn't have a shank.

For a while, he tried to resist at first, but he realized that he was outnumbered, and all of the staff had shanks and would use them. He gave in and let them have their way. That pod man sat at the front table and gave hand signals that cued them on what to do. The staff was acting on OG's shot calling.

OG kept looking at me as if he was trying to prove a point to me, that he was the man. The other inmates acted as if they were afraid to look on.

"What's up Lowe, I'm pod man, and they call me OG. Come on let's go in my cell and talk." While in his cell, he tried to get me to become an OG. And I gave him direct words of refusal l, and I meant no.

"I will be my own man." I told him and walked out.

He followed behind me saying, "They have told me how good you can fight."

I said to myself, that's probably why he wants to put me down.

"Yeah, I can handle myself pretty damn good," I told him and took a set on the front table.

"You know you have something to bring to the table, but a lot of them don't," OG said to me as if he wasn't giving up, but I didn't respond.

The next day, Officer Paylor stepping into the sally port and said, "Is he still in here?"

"Who," OG asked?

"That smart mouth punk I put in here yesterday."

"Yeah, he's still in here. What's up with him?" OG asked as he walked up to the bars and talked with Officer Paylor.

Officer Paylor put something in OG's hand and said, "Here, I need for you to take care of my lightweight."

Officer Paylor walked off, and OG cued about four of his staff members to come into his cell with him. From the marijuana smell, they smoked the pod out. The smoke was so thick in the pod, until I had gotten a contact high. From the look of it, it had to be an ounce of pot that Officer Paylor gave OG.

"Oh boy, it's a hit out on that boy's head, and we got to have him," Tedd said to OG, as they gave each other a gangster hand shake while they all walked out of the cell, while the marijuana began to motivate them.

"Hey, Officer Good and Big Ike has agreed to tangle up in the gym!" Little Otis yelled out into the pod and ran off.

From what we heard, officers from all over the jail began to place bets on the fights.

A few days later, 1989 rolled out and 1990 brought on a new look throughout the jail.

Inmates and convicts began to cut off their curls and wear fades. It was almost as if everybody was trying to see who could be the *wickedest*. It was as if 201 turned into the pits of hell. It was like the Wild, Wild West, almost every man for himself.

The second floor and the outside Med had more patients coming from the jail that they could handle. They were beat up, cut up, and more busted heads that I have ever seen.

The food that was being fed to the inmates and convicts wasn't good enough for a dog to eat. The city of Memphis was in debt over their heads and was looking for a way out.

Overloading the jail must had been a part of helping the city to get money. The sheriff and mayor must have come up with all kinds of laws to fill up the jail.

I had never in my life heard something call, "jump and grab."

The Big Fight was on. Officer Good vs. Big Ike and at the same time the inmate that Officer Paylor put a hit out on, was getting ready for his bloody and brutal beat down.

Now, there were more white inmates in the jail than it had ever been. It was a crazy white boy who was on the staff, his name was Birdman. He would do anything and did anything just to get on the staff.

"Bliii, blleeiii," This was the funny sound that the Birdman made before he called Little Moe.

"Lit, lit, litlitlit, Moe, Moe, MoeMoeMoe, Moe, Moe, Blillilliibip," Birdman yelled out some of the most unusual and awkward sounds that ever came out of a human being's mouth.

While the entire staff was getting shanked up and ready to have a blood bath, the pod man, OG, sat on the staff front table before everything started. He then looked back at me, while I was standing on the back wall.

"Lowe, come check this out," he said as I sat down beside him to look on. He turned the TV all the way up.

While in the gym, it was a nice little crowd, as the lady officers and lady counselors looked on.

Officer Good came out of the weight room with Officer pants on and a black T-shirt, bouncing around as if he were in a ring.

Big Ike came through the gym door with a shirt on and small patches of hair grease that he had rubbed all over his head, face and body. This was a thing that the convicts would do when they get ready for a fight. So, if your enemy would grab you, you could slip out of his hold, and his licks would slip off as well.

They both stepped into the middle of the gym floor, bouncing around in a circle gearing up for one to throw the first blow.

"Oh, it's like that," Good said to Ike because of the grease all over his body.

"Yeah, it's like that, what you think I came to do, play?" Ike responded with a slap to the face of Officer Good.

Good looked as if he had never been slapped before and balled his lips as if he was so mad, looking as if he was about to cry.

"Yeah boy, I can slap you all night like a bitch." Big Ike said as he felt in his comfort zone.

While back in the pod, Little Moe backed up slowly in the middle of this floor, as if he had some war to run. Birdman walked towards Moe, with that crazy look in his face with a shank in his hand. Moe was so focused on Birdman until he didn't see the staff members standing in the cell doors waiting to attack. All of a sudden, the staff began to make their move along with Birdman sticking and beating on Moe. This was the worst beating I have ever seen.

All I could say was, "I wish I was Superman." I looked on for a while, and then looked up side of OG's head in a way to let him know, it wasn't cool, and then I walked off into my cell.

"Don't take it personal," Big Ike said.

"NO, you don't take it personal," Officer Good responded to Ike, as they walked around as they sized each other up. Big Ike rushed into Good, in order to get the first knockout blow in, but when he swung he missed.

"Ooohwwooo," the crowd yelled out, as they felt the pressure in the air from the powerful blow that big Ike threw, but fast on his feet with good defense, Good ducked the throw and Ike missed his target.

Most of the officers knew Good was an ex-boxer, but it has been a while since he stepped into a ring. Good gave Ike two shots to the face stinging him, and that put big Ike on his toes at the same time making him hot. Ike rushed in on a good and gave him a body shot to the ribs. Good came out from bending over with a left hook to Ike's jaw. Ike came back with some straight shot blows to Good's face to get the upper hand. All of a sudden, Good came up with some hell of a blows. Big Ike began to bleed front the mouth and nose. After that, Good felt that he had the fight won. But out of nowhere, Ike power kicked in like a bull giving Good about ten blows to the face, one after another.

"Come on, come on I'm going to put it on you," Good told Big Ike, as he began to wipe he blood from his face and eye so that he could see. The both of them stepped in at the same time, landing blows to each other's faces.

Big Ike had too much power for Good, and Good couldn't take anymore licks.

"Shit, that's enough." Good said, while giving up and walking out of the gym.

"Damn, man, I had all of my money on you," one of the officers said, and the others agreed.

Everyone paid up, and Big Ike made some money also.

While back in the pod, Officer Paylor stood in the sally port with a smile on his face looking at the ten-against-one bloody stick and beat down. Every time Officer Paylor would see some sticks or blows that would almost take little Moe out, he would smile.

From the floor, Moe looked up over his head and saw the panic button, and with the last strength that was in his body some kind of way, while he was still being beat, he pulled himself up off the floor. He then pushed the button, when Officer Paylor saw it he stopped laughing walked down to the control room and stopped the oncoming officers that were about to respond to the cell.

"It's okay, it's alright, and it's just one of them fools playing with the button!" Officer Paylor lied, while turning the officers around to head back to their duties.

I stood in my cell door looking on. It looked like one of Little Moe's eyes was poorly hanging out of his head. Officer Paylor opened the sally port gates and pulled Little Moe by one of his legs into the hall.

"One been stealing. He's going to the Med," Officer Paylor said as he lied again.

About two days after that, two of the staff were about to fight, and they asked Officer Paylor to look out for them because Sgt. Fuller was on the floor, and he didn't play. It was two of the same that helped beat Little Moe. When they began to fight it went from one end of the pod to the other. They ended up on the floor in the front of the sally port. While Officer Paylor stood in the frame of the door and looking at one of the weakest fight I had seen, he looked down the hall to see Sgt. Fuller was coming and put that smirk on his face. He then walked to meet Sgt. Fuller.

"They're fighting and I'm tired of this shit!" Officer Paylor lied to Sgt. Fuller, as they rushed into the pod. While the two inmates were on the floor fighting, Paylor stood behind Sgt. Fuller with a smile on his face.

Sgt. Fuller wore a size 14 in shoes, and he had on some pointed-toe boots. He was kicking the both of the inmates with the top of his boots in the crack of their butts. Sgt. Fuller was kicking one of the inmates so hard, until he kicked one of his butt bones loose. I was standing at the back of the pod at the time, and the sound of his kick was like a base drum beat.

When the two inmates were separated, the one that ended up with the broken bone had a situation accusation with. Sgt. Fuller, and held his butt at the same time.

"I told you all one time to stop fighting and to get up, you didn't, so that is what got!" Sgt. Fuller said while pulling one of the inmates out into the hall.

One was moved, and the other was taken to the outside Med. There were a lot of things I was told that Sgt. Fuller did that I didn't see. But after seeing this with my own two eyes, I believed all of it.

Things were slow for a few days, but after that, there were new inmates that came into the pod, and two of them had gold teeth in their mouth.

Later on that night, "Pod meeting, pod meeting!" One of the staff members yelled out, and everyone walked to the back of the pod.

"Look, there is just something I don't tolerate in here, and that's a weak-ass boy with some gold teeth in his mouth. A full gold grill, staff, deal with him!" OG said, and behind that the staff rushed to the back of the pod where the two inmates were standing and began beating them down to the floor.

They were hit and beat in the mouth until all their gold was knocked out. Behind that, their mouth was a bloody mess. The staff then took the gold teeth and put them into a sock and gave them to OG.

"What size shoe do you wear?" OG asked another inmate who had just came in wearing a nice pair of British Knights.

"A twelve," he answered.

"That's my size, take them off!" OG said, as the staff began to muscle the inmate out of his sneakers.

"Pod meeting is over!" OG yelled out as about six of them walked into the back cell to look over their goodies.

The staff did not know that Little Moe had a family member that worked in 201 jail. When he saw how badly Moe was beaten, the next day, he sat things up for one of Moe's gang members to be moved into the pod where he was beaten. He gave him a .22 handgun. The convict with the gun was named Boo.

Classification classified Moe into the wrong pod, and he couldn't get to the staff but tried to get moved. When he noticed that he wasn't going to be moved, he tried to pop the bars, but he didn't know how. He then saw Officer Paylor walking pass the pod and fired shots at him, only missing him by inches. The sound of the gun blast was like a 12-gauge been fired. When Boo ran out of shots, he threw the gun out into the hall, where the captain confiscated it.

Boo was then taken out of the pod into Administrative Segregation lockdown. He was then charged for shooting at Officer Paylor and for the gun. We never heard from him again. From what we heard from inside the jail, Little Moe's family told some of his gang members on the street about Officer Paylor getting off work and killed him. When we saw it from in the jail in the news, we could see sadness on the officers' faces. But some of Officer Paylor's co-workers were happy that he was gone.

Over 75% of the inmates and convicts yelled out in cheers while watching it on tv. I had never seen so many men so happy over someone's death.

At the same time, Jack Owens was the sheriff of Memphis. He was loading the jail down with inmates, and about 97% of them were blacks. It was so crowded until there were inmates not only lying on the gym floor, but they were up and down the halls. The food had gotten even worse than before. The violence in the jail had gotten so bad until the med stayed full.

The pod made a small change, and the other homosexual moved into the pod. He looked half-woman and half-man. But everyone treated him like a man and didn't give him any gay play. The staff was waiting on him to make his move on someone, and the plan was to beat him down, as soon as he did. At that time, he was standing in the back of the pod close to another inmate. Some of the staff had already told him that they didn't want him nowhere around the front table.

"Hay, what's up? My name is Nay Nay," he said to the inmate that he was standing beside.

"What's up," the inmate spoke back.

"Do you want some of this fire cap?" Nay Nay asked the inmate.

"Hell no. Get the fuck back off me," the inmate yelled out, and walked off with an angry look on his face.

One of the staff members were close by and heard it. He told the pod man, and he called for a meeting.

"Pod meeting." OG had a look on his face as if someone had done something bad to him. "This is another thing that we just don't get away with in here, and that's the gay shit. Staff take care of your business!" OG commanded the staff.

They beat Nay Nay with a bar of soap in a sock and kicked him until he didn't move. After that, they called for an officer to move him for stealing. It was another bloody mess that the inmates had to clean up.

CHAPTER 7:
THE 1991 RIOTS

When the '1991 Riots' took place, the convicts began to pass kites all over the jail from pod to pod. It was letters on them that said, "Tell your entire pod that if they don't riot with us, they will be rolled on, because we are tired of the way we are being treated." P.S., Head Honcho

Some of us thought that it was a joke, until doing shift change that night. The riot was on with a rude awakening from the loud and crazy sounds of the voice of Birdman.

"Bbbblipppp." Behind that it was a heavy and loud noise like thunder. Almost everyone put their hands over their ears. The Birdman has an iron pipe that he started everything off by smashing out the windows at the end of the hall. When he hit it, it was like the whole floor shook.

"Oh my god," I yelled out, while hearing the loud thunder-like noise of repeated pounding and glass breaking. When I came out of my cell I saw about 50 convicts running around in and out of the pods with all kinds of weapons in their hands. Some of them had pipes as long as my leg. They all had masks on that were cut out from the bed sheets so that the officers couldn't identify who was who.

When I looked at the back of the pod, I saw that the catwalk window was knocked out. When almost everyone was out on the catwalk hanging out of the windows, and convicts from the pod ran out of the sally port door, I sat down on the front table and began to watch TV.

Suddenly, it was breaking news on TV, and I could see the outside of our catwalk. I then looked at the sally port gates to see about 20 convicts coming into the pod, and they all had on masks. One of the leaders of the pack had to know me, because he called me by my name saying, "Lowe, what's up with you?"

"Nothing much," I responded.

"Man, look, all I can say is riot or get rolled on, so what's it going to be?" he said to me with 20 rioting convicts standing behind him waiting to hear and see what my decision was going to be.

"Let me see that pipe," I commanded the pipe out of one of the convict's hand.

I then drew back and smashed out the TV screen, and it popped like a gunshot.

"Now, what does that tell you," I yelled out.

"Let's roll!" One of them yelled out, and the remainder of the convicts yelled out while we all ran out.

I was given a mask, and I put it on, but I still lagged behind the crowd. I walked up and down the hall seeing all kinds of violence going on, and some that made me sick to my stomach. When I walked to the other side of the floor, it was a long line down the hall starting at the counselor's office. I walked up to the door to see what was going on.

They had the lady counselor lying down on the top of her desk nude and tied down. With each of her legs tied to one end of the desk legs, and her arms were tied to the other end of the desk. She was hogtied with her legs wide open. They had a sock stuck in her mouth with a rag tied around it.

While she was surrounded by such a dark cloud of convicts, I made eye contact with her. As she turned her head and looked at me, tears were running down her face.

I could read her eyes saying, "Please, please, help me." But there was nothing I could have done but almost shed tears myself. It was if I could see one of my sisters needing help. It was about 50 convicts in line, and maybe 100 had already been in. I couldn't look at that anymore. I walked off the floor.

However, it was only to see things looking worse. There were officers on the 3rd floor, and they were the ones that went for bad, and were always talking rough to inmates. I could hear sounds of homosexual inmates being raped, and I walked up on two female officers getting raped. There were convicts that were fighting with officers, but they didn't stand a chance. They were beaten down to the floor. Commissary was flooding in the water. That was one day I didn't have to worry about being hungry.

The convicts had broken into the commissary room. As I ate and walked up and down the halls looking at the violent events, I got so full until I had to sit down. Although the jail was cold, I had eaten so much and was so full, I was sweating.

I walked into a pod with some other convicts and watched TV. It was breaking news with live coverage of the jail.

"This is Eyewitness News, Live Downtown Memphis, at the Shelby County Jail at 201 Poplar. I am Trina Spencer, and as you can see the inmates are yelling out of the windows of the jail as if they are angry about something and trying to tell the world. I'm sure time will tell what this is all about. As I speak, you can turn the cameras to the upper floors of the jail, and you can see there is a fire. I can see balls of fire falling from the catwalk windows. It looks like bed mats that are on fire. If you look all around the building you can see inmates hanging out of broken windows as if they are really trying to give a message. We will keep you updated on what's going on, as for now we have to take a break. This is Trina Spencer, and we will be back."

While back inside the jail, the Birdman and his wrecking crew were bringing down the jail, while other convicts were doing their thing.

Big King and Birdman took the cake. They walked around knocking out inmates and officers as if there was a war going on. They were throwing blows as if everyone was their enemy.

I could see a trail of inmates lying out on the floor like dead flies, behind the crew. But most of the convicts began to come together and prepared to talk to the city leaders, hoping that they could work something out.

I was now walking with Big Ike and some others.

"Birdman, Big King, stop that! Enough! It's time to come together and talk business with these folks!" Big Ike gave his command.

The Muslim brothers played a big part in helping to get things organized. While everyone was gathering and talking, there was an inmate lying out cold on the floor in the water. He was about to get up when Birdman made his sound, then looked at Big King, and pointed at the laid-out inmate, giving King a signal to knock him back out. King hit the man, put him back to sleep, and stood up like nothing happened.

"Bird, King, I said stop!" Big Ike yelled out to them again.

"This is the World News, and we are live in New York, on a follow up with Trina Spencer, and I'm Peter Henderson. Trina, from our view it is a nasty sight. Could you tell us the cause of this riot or tell us if the Memphis Mayor is trying to do anything to stop the riot? Is he trying to work something out with the inmates?"

"Peter, as far as we know, the mayor, sheriff, and the city counselors of Memphis are on their way down here to see if they can talk things over with the inmates and bring this riot to an end," Trina Spencer explained.

"Trina, could you tell us who are the people that we see behind you?"

"Yes, they are the families of the inmates that are here in the jail," Trina answered.

"If anything happened to the inmates, do you think something will jump off out there?" Peter asked.

"Not really, I believe that the National Guard and the MP's will take over and close the city down before that happens," Trina said.

"Trina, I still haven't gotten an answer on what started the riots. Could you tell us what triggered this?" Peter asked.

"Well, the rumor is the inmates haven't been getting fed properly, and they would have to get up at 3 or 4 am to go to court. They didn't have to be in court until 9 am. They would have to sit on steel benches, some of them for over five hours, before they would go into the court rooms. They also said that there isn't any justice in the courts or out of the courts," Trina answered.

"Do you think the mayor will get things worked out and end this peacefully?" Peter Henderson asked.

"Like I said, as of now, I don't know, but I feel this will bring on some kind of change. This is Trina Spencer, and this is Eyewitness News. We will give you further updates later on the 201 Poplar riots."

The inmate on the inside of the jail came up with a spokesman to talk for everyone to see if some justice would be done. The law says you are innocent until you are proven guilty. But by the way Shelby County Justice Center was set up, you are guilty until you are proven guiltiest.

I tried to make my way back to my cell. I could hear a lot off hollering and yelling. I could tell someone was in pain or yelling for their life. I knew there were some officers that were knocked out, because there were convicts walking around in officers' uniforms, and they had the officers' stun guns. It was so much water coming down the escalators until I had to go down to the second floor.

While on the second floor, it was about to be a stand-off with the officers against the convicts. Although I still had on my mask, I was noticed. So, I played a part to fit in.

"Let's do this shit. Fuck the police!" I yelled out, and behind that, everyone exploded.

Not far in the front of me, I could see a new team that the jail officers had to control the inmates called the D.R.T. Sergeant Hightower was a black man that was first degree black belt. Whenever an inmate would go for tough, or a fight got out of hand, they would call on him.

We were facing the D.R.T. team face-to-face, and it looked like it was going to be a standoff. But when they saw that we were not turning back, and they were outnumbered, they took off running and locked themselves in the control booth of 186 first floors and closed the sally port doors.

By the D.R.T. doing that, we couldn't leave the floors.

The convicts tried to come up with an idea to get into the main control-186 but couldn't. If they would have, they could have taken over the jail, and their next move would have been the streets, where they would have been free.

When the Birdman saw that we could not get through the sally port doors or through the thick glass, he licked his tongue on the glass at one of the lady officers and made his bird sound, while we all walked back up the escalators.

When I made it back to a pod that had a TV, the news was showing how officers were teaming up to come in and try to get the jail under control. There were one set of officers who were called the cowboys. They were well-experienced in this kind of work, and it looked like all of them were exactly the same size in height. They were tall and big men to fight against. They convinced the MP's and the Memphis Police Department that if they could go in first, they would get things under control. But they were told by the Sheriff and Memphis Mayor, they could not go in until they get approval from someone that had higher authority.

The riots and violence rolled all night until the next day. There were ambulances and firemen backed up waiting to carry all injured inmates to the Med. Some of the injured officers some kind of way got out of the jail alive and were able to tell what was showing on inside of the jail. From there, they were taken to the Med. By them breaking free and telling what the convicts were doing on the inside, that gave the Cowboys and MP's a better outlook on how they were going in.

"This is Eyewitness News, and I'm Trina Spencer. We're live here at 201 Poplar with the Memphis mayor, where the jail riots are out of control. The inmates' families are looking for answers. Mayor, could you please tell us what the inmates are asking for, and why they are rioting?"

"I have been on the inside talking to the spokesman of the riots. The convicts have some points, but they are going about it the wrong way in getting justice and solving the problems."

"Mayor, could you give us more detail on what the inmates want?"

"Yes, Trina, they are asking for better food; they would like to go to court at a proper time, as well as being respected by the chaplains, the officers and all of the jail staff. It's several things that they are asking for. But if they don't stop the riots, I don't know if all their requests can be met."

"Do you think all of the officers that you have could hold up against all of the inmates inside of the jail?" Trina asked the mayor.

"With all of the enforcement, ammunition and K9's that we have, I think we will bring things under control, but only time will tell."

"Thanks a lot, that was words from Memphis Mayor, and he's getting ready to have his officers to move in and make their attack. They are now having everyone to vacate the area, so we have to go. This is Eyewitness News live, and I'm Trina Spencer."

When the officers came in, we were watching it over the TV. The convicts that thought they could hold up and stand their ground. They tried to fight against the officers, but it only lasted for a while. The officers began using rubber bullets and dummy 12-gauge flask that made loud sounds and lot of smoke. Eventually, the inmates began backing off and returning to their cells.

"Damn, they're coming in!" I yelled out, as the inmates that were watching on with me all ran to their cell.

I got up and rushed up the escalators, headed to my cell, knowing I was out of place.

By the time I made it to the top of the escalator, on the 4th floor, I looked back and could see officers on the 3rd floor at the bottom of the escalators beating convicts with slap sticks.

While some of the officers were sticking stun guns to convicts, others were letting dogs bite them, and at the same time kicking them as if they weren't human.

Before I made it to my cell, I looked back while taking off my mask and I could see officers were on my trail. I tried to pick up speed, running in the water, but I couldn't. It was like a dream; I was running but wasn't getting anywhere. The officers were gaining on me, but I made it to my pod. I ran and got under the bed to hide from four of them.

"Come from under there!" an Officer yelled out to me, while the others were pulling me from under the bed.

"I haven't done anything!" I yelled out to the officers, pleading in fear.

"You should have done something; we're going to beat your ass anyway. Come from under there, I said!" Another Officer hollered at me while they pulled me from under the bed.

"Ooooh, ooh," I yelled out in pain, while one of the officers slapped me. The other two officers were kicking me so hard until it sounded like someone was kicking on some empty boxes. The kicks really hurt, but the way I was curled up, I was able to block some of the slaps. I wanted to get up and fight back, but I knew it was only going to make matters worse. So, I folded and took it like a man.

Once they were done bruising me up, and I was locked in my cell, I saw officers beating inmates so badly that it didn't look real.

Just hearing the gun blasts, men hollering, and the dogs were enough to make any convict bow down.

As I stood in my cell door, watching them bring in inmates that were was beaten so badly until they couldn't walk, I could hear convicts fighting up and down the hall. I was glad I was locked in my cell, because they were fighting a losing battle.

It was not an easy job for the officers to get everyone back in place, but they did. Some of us had sense to fall in place on our own. I never heard of anyone was charged for the rape of the officers and counselors. All the officers or staff members that worked for the jail were taken to the Med. They were taking care of first, then some of the inmates were taken out and treated for their bad bruises and wounds.

"I want my mama, Iiiii!" A grown man growls out in pain from the bad beating he had taken.

The more inmates and convicts that officers brought back into the pod, the more broken arms and legs I saw. Some of the convicts were running back to the pod so fast, until it looked as if they were running on water.

Once we all were locked into our cells, there was a convict that called Silence of the Lamb who showed out. He was one of the strangest looking men I had ever seen. He was locked up for cutting up a little baby, then putting it into a pot of hot boiling water and boiling it until it was cooked. He must have beaten an officer down really bad, because he ran into the back of the pod and jumped on the table with an officer's shield and slap stick. The shield and slap stick had blood all over them.

About ten officers ran in behind him with eight of them surrounding the table. Two of them looked to be captains, because they were telling the other officers what to do. But both of them had been badly beaten. As long as he had been in the pod, we never knew that he could fight like he was a 4th degree black belt. He began kicking the officers and smacking them with the slap stick like in a movie. Every time one of the officers would try to come up on him, they would catch a lick upside the head or across their arms.

"This is Eyewitness News, and I'm Trina Spencer, live at the Shelby County Justice Center with the mayor of Memphis. Mayor could you give us an update on what's going on in the jail, now that it has been two days of riots?"

"Trina, I have gotten a report from some of my officers who are on the inside, and they have gotten all the inmates back in place and have a full count for all but one inmate. As we speak, they are trying to restrain him now."

"Could you tell us how many officers and inmates were injured?" Miss Spencer asked him with a concerned look on her face.

"At this time, I'm not for sure."

"Well, could you tell us if anyone died?"

"I wouldn't know at this time, but there were officers and inmates hurt badly and taken to the hospital," the Mayor answered.

"Is the jail in too bad of condition to be used?" Miss Spencer asked.

"Yes, I will admit that we will have to move some inmates out to S. C. C. C., until we can get the jail back in working order."

"Ok. Thanks a lot Mayor. This is Eyewitness News. I'm Trina Spencer, and we will give you more detail tonight. Thank you for watching."

Back inside the jail, the Lamb had kicked two of the officers out cold. The other six were getting busted up trying to run in on him. The scenery was really serious but at the same time funny because of the funny laugh that the Lamb was letting out every time he hit one of the officers.

The captain called for another force, and when they came in, some of them had K9's. Some of them had 12-gauge guns with the rubber bullets. They were giving commands to open fire on the Lamb.

"Fire again!" The captain yelled out, while the bullets were hitting the Lamb. The dogs were barking, and the Lamb was going down and laughing at the same time. After the Lamb was crippled by the rubber bullets, the cowboys rushed in and finished him off by beating him to a pulp.

That next day we were put on a bus and taken to a different correctional facility.

CHAPTER 8:
PENAL FARM

While at the Shelby County Correctional Center (S.C.C.C.), which were called the Penal Farm, we were there until they got the jail back in order. Only a few weeks had passed since I'd been in the S.C.C.C., and it was time for me to fight again. I was still looking for the Devil to be walking around in human form - thinking I had to get him before he got me.

At times, it seemed like trouble was looking for me even if I was minding my own business. I would always try to stay to myself and away from others. We couldn't mix with the inmates that were already there doing their time. We were called pretrials. The inmates that helped the officers to stop the riot were placed on PC (Protective Custody), because if the convicts would have gotten their hands on them, they would have beaten them down.

When we would go to eat or pass the other inmates, there was one inmate that was with us who always tried to act hard or show out. On this day, he was talking trash while walking behind me. I overlooked him and stepped out of line and let him walks past me.

For some reason, I could hear that voice in my head saying, 'the Devil walls around like roaring lion.' This inmate was called Big Dee. For some reason, he just didn't like me, or you can say that he hated on me. Why? I just didn't know. I could tell that he was slick picking at me and pretended as if I didn't see him.

One day, there were some pretty ladies in plain street clothes getting a tour of the compound by the captain. We were looking out of the window as they passed by. When Big Dee noticed that I made eye contact with one of the ladies, he tried to muscle me out of view from the window.

I stood my ground against the 300-pound man. When he saw that he couldn't move me, he put his mouth to work trying to down me.

"Man, get your ass out of the way. They don't want to see you, ugly mother fucker!" Big Dee said to me while trying to push me out of the way.

Behind that, everyone laughed at me. I was told that words don't hurt, but that's a lie. They hurt spiritually not physically, especially when you are carnal-minded. To make things worse, I responded in a defensive way.

"FIGHT #4"

"You Big out of shape ass cow, they don't want you either, looking like the Kool-Aid man!"

By me saying that, everyone laughed. It uplifted my spirit a bit. While everyone was looking at Big Dee behind my joke, he began looking at me with fire in his eyes.

When the ladies walked off, I got a good look at Big Dee's eyes. I could see the word *fight* in them. He could dish it out, but he couldn't take it back. He kind of caught me off guard. He pushed me so damn hard until I really thought I was hit.

When this happened, we were in the front of the day room, near the door that separated the two dorms. My back hit the glass window so hard until it took me a second to get my breath back. I was kind of bent over, but when I stood up Big Dee caught an unexpected upper cut to his chin.

Behind that I have him a loud sounding blow to the jaw. When I tried to throw another blow, the big man that I thought could have been the devil grabbed me. He began squeezing the air out of me.

I could see his eyes saying, "Hell nah, this man is hitting me too damn hard."

I bowed and wrestled with him until I got loose. By me shaking back off him, he landed some wild blows upside of my head. *This big man is not playing with me*, I thought to myself. As he rushed back in on me, I threw two more licks to his face. One of his blows caught me in the mouth. I rubbed it only to realize it was bleeding.

Rubbing my mouth, the second time while backing up, it was so numb until I thought my teeth were loose. I backed off him a little more to recoup. That gave me time to think.

A fight is not fair, and I had got to do whatever it took to win, because I realized I was fighting for my life.

When Big Dee rushed in on me with his 300 lbs., I gave him a solid lick to the stomach.

"Ohh, shit!" Big Dee yelled out in pain as he bent over gasping for air, but I didn't let him get it.

In close on a big man is the best place to be when fighting him, and that's where I was.

Lick-after-lick, I didn't let up or stop putting it on him. He threw up one of his hands, trying to tell me that it was enough, but I was not going to stop. This man was too big to be given a second chance.

When I dropped my last and fast six pack on him to the face, he went down with a hard fall. Behind that, everyone began to yell out in cheers.

"Damn, that was a good fight; I haven't seen one like that in a long time!" someone yelled out.

"From now on, I'm not going to call him Lowe, I'm going to call him a little man with a big heart!" another convict said, while I was walking to my bed in pain.

Later in the week, I was taken to court. Judge McCarty fairly gave me time for all my charges but one. That was the one charge that I had in Judge Joe Brown's court room. As far as the charge that I had from fighting the police, some kind of way, it was dropped. I guess that happened, because they were in the wrong. Once I was done getting my time, I was sent to the main frame. That is the old building at S.C.C.C.

This was a whole different world, or you can say a world within a world. Before we could be housed with the other convicts, we had to take a shower with water hoses. About twenty of us had to go into a big shower room and take a shower at one time. It was twenty water hoses running out of the wall that we used to shower. The whole time, I kept my back against the wall watching my surroundings.

While turning my head one way, I couldn't help but see something God knows I didn't want to see. It was a man in one of the showers across from us who didn't look real. His anatomy looked like something that a horse got between his legs. It made my flesh crawl so badly until I almost had to close my eyes.

When we were done going through intake, we were housed in the new gym where there were beds stacked three-high. There was an inmate 7-feet tall that got up on the top bunk and fell asleep. He kept rolling from side-to-side of the bed. He was so lanky until his legs were hanging over the end at the top of the bed. As I laid on my bed watching him and shaking my head, he finally rolled off the bed and hit the floor.

He hit the floor so hard that it sounded like a building was falling. Everyone yelled out loud and some of the convicts laughed at him.

When the officers came rushing in after hearing the loud racket, they thought someone had knocked the seven-foot man out. The officers called in the doctors, and they popped open an ammonia bag and place it under his nose to wake him.

"What is going on? Are you alright?" One of the doctors asked him.

He pointed at one of the white officers and said, "He knocked me out!"

Behind that event, everyone laughed at him. He had a knot on his forehead the size of a soft ball. Some of the inmates told the doctor what actually happened and from there, he was taken to the Med.

"FIGHT #5"

The shoes that my sister Brenda had bought for me had begun to come a loose. From walking back and forward in the rain to eat, fighting, and playing basketball, the sneakers had seen its day. I was moved to the horse-shoe in C building.

I called my brother, Calvin, to bring me some shoes. When he did, that let me know that there was someone out there who still loved me. That also showed me there is more than saying you love someone; it's about showing them as well.

When I called Calvin on the phone to let him know that I had received the shoes, and to thank him, his wife Addie answered the phone. She told me that Calvin was still at work, and she had some news to tell me.

"Your grandmother and nephew, Sarell, have both passed away. Also, your mother is in the hospital."

My heart dropped. I could not say anything, because I didn't know how to accept it. All I could do was cry.

"Lorenzo, are you okay? It's going to be alright. They are in a better place, where they don't have to suffer, and your mama is strong. She always pulls through."

This is one of the reasons why Addie was my favorite sister-in-law. She had a way with words that would comfort you as if God was there Himself.

When I was done talking with Addie, I called my mother while she was in the hospital. It was a line of convicts waiting on the phone, but no one was going to stop me from talking to my mother.

"Lorenzo, how are you doing son?" she asked.

"I'm ok, Mama. How are you doing? Is everything going to be alright?" I asked in response with tears in my eyes.

"Yes, you know Mama is going to be alright. The doctors told me that they will be giving me a bypass heart surgery. After that, Mama will be alright. I will feel much better. Little Cornelius is sitting beside my bed," she said.

"Tell him I said hello, and I love you Mama with all my heart. I have to let you go. There are guys waiting to use the phone."

"Lorenzo, I love you son, and don't forget to read the Bible and do what God wants you to do. I love you too and bye," Mama said and hung up the phone.

While I was on the phone, a convict named Louie was trying to interrupt me by telling me that I needed to get off the phone. I turned my back and paid him no attention. While I was standing at my bed worrying about my family, he walked up to me with a knife.

"You have one more time to hold up that phone like that, if you do I'm going to stick this in you," Louie told me while showing me his pocket knife.

If he was going to stick me, he would not have been talking. He would have stuck me when I turned my back while I was on the phone. I was already hurting on the inside and felt I had nothing to lose.

"Man fuck you. That's not your phone, and you can't tell me when to get off it!" I said while balling my lips and blood in my eyes.

Louie walked to the other side of the dorm.

"Lowe, he is putting on his shoes, and he got a knife. Here take this." One of my homeboys gave me a lock in a sock. I stuck it in my back pocket where it wouldn't be seen. When Louie walked my way in a rush, I posted up sideways, where he couldn't see what I had.

"Yeah, what's up, bitch ass boy?" I yelled out.

I wrapped the end of the sock around my hand so that I could get a solid lick. When he took his knife out of his waistband, I knew just what I was facing. I knew how I was going to make my attack.

"Did I tell you, Ooooh?" Louie yelled out in pain with blood gushing out of his forehead.

He then began to back up off me, something that he should have done at first. His head was open so wide until I could see the white fat. Louie took one more step and passed out.

I walked over his body to put the lock and the sock in the trash can, but before I could about five officers were running in the door up to me. An inmate was pointing his finger at me.

Someone had pushed the button, because they grabbed me so fast until I didn't have time to get rid of the lock in the sock. I was taken to the hole and written up. That was a weapon fight and one of the quickest fights I had ever been in. From hearing some of the officers' talk, they didn't like Louie, and they were glad that I had busted him up.

While I was in the hole there was a convict in the cell next to me on an upper role. He was yelling at another inmate in a cell next to him.

"When the doors roll in the morning, we roll. Don't reach for your tray, reach for me!" The convict yelled out. Then he asked me, "Hey brother that just came in, do you have some grease that I could use?"

"Yeah, take you some out and give it back." I told him, and he did.

I really don't like giving anyone I don't know my things, especially when they are in jail. I thought maybe he wanted it for his hair, but when he passed it back he had gotten too much.

"Thanks a lot," he said.

"Man, you got too much of my damn grease!"

"Look bro, do you smoke?"

"Yeah," I responded.

"Here you some cigarettes," the convict said, while passing them to me.

All that night all I could hear was the convict doing pushups and talking to himself. I couldn't sleep, so I began to do some pushups myself.

That next morning, an empty petroleum jelly jar was thrown out of the big man's cell and hit the other side of the wall. I thought to myself, *what is this man doing with this grease?* I then thought he was going to try to attack me when the cell doors came open.

I pulled off my shirt and began to do more push-ups, knowing that we were about to eat, and the gates were going to come open. This was a big and tall man. I had to make the first attack and try to take him out first.

At this time, all I could hear in my head was my boxing trainer telling me, "kill the head and then the body will die."

But I remember getting a good look at this man when I first came in, not only was he big and tall as hell, but he had muscles in his head as big as my fist. I thought to myself, *why do I have to fight all of these men?* Can God just show me Satan, and I will kick his ass for what he has done to me?

"Chow time!" A rock man yelled out and the doors came open.

The hole, at this time, was in the old building, and the cells were only on one side of the pod. It was a small hall between our cells and a brick wall. When I stepped to the outer facing of my cell door, I leaned over to my right in a post-up position as if it was about to go down. When I was just about to make my move on a man that was two times my size, he turned the other way.

It was going down, but I wasn't involved.

When I looked at the big man, he had grease all over his face, head and body walking toward the other cell. The man that he was into it with before I came in was reaching for his tray, while the big convict was reacting for him. When I got a good look at the other man, it was Big King from 201. He didn't have anyone to help him this time. He was on his own.

"You got drama with Bow? You got Bow fucked up!" The big convict yelled out letting his name be known, while he was making his attack. The rock man that was serving food dropped the trays and ran.

"All of that shit you talked yesterday on the bars, now look at you, you piece of shit!" Bow said, while beating the brakes off King.

Every time King would try to grab Bow or hit him, his licks would slide off because of the grease.

The officer that opened the doors for us to eat just stood there and looked on.

Don't get me wrong, King was a big man, but Bow was bigger and uglier. I know size doesn't make a difference when it comes down to fighting. But King didn't have the heart or the fight in him.

Whenever you are talking trash, and you are locked behind bars in a cell be careful.

When the gates come open, watch your surrounding cause it might be hell.

King tried to run to the end of the rock looking up to the officers for help, but that only made things worse. King had his back turned.

"Oh shit, officer!" King yelled out for help while Bow was beating him in the back of the head.

All I could say was as officers looked on was, "what goes around comes around."

Every time King would try to run, Bow would beat King in the back of his head so hard until it sounded like a base drum.

"Yeah, you bitch ass boy, this is for the brothers that you jumped downtown!" Bow said, as he gave King a lick that sent him to the floor, out cold. King tried to raise up but only to lay back down.

"Get up, you pussy, get up, and I'll fuck you up some more!" Bow said, while standing over King waiting for him to get up, but he never did.

Bow spit on King, walked into his cell and laid down as if nothing had ever happened. While I stood in the face of my cell door the whole time, I got a close look at someone who had done wrong and wrong had come back on them.

When the officer called medical to come and take King out, the sergeant that gave me my all of my time came with them also.

"Hi sergeant, are you married? I asked flirting with her.

"None of your damn business."

"I love it when you talk greasy to me," I responded.

I just love a jet-black woman, especially when she has smooth skin, and real hair short or long with a nice attitude.

"I just knew it was you in here fighting. I don't want any more trouble out of you," the female sergeant told me, then made her rounds and walked out.

King was taken to the Med, and Bow was given more hole time. Afterwards, things were calm all of that night.

The 30 days that I was in the hole, all I did was push-ups. When I was released out of the hole, I was still wearing my red jumper that convicts wear only when they are in deadlock.

"Spencer, you are going to 7-block," an officer told me.

While walking down the rock in the old building convicts were standing on the gates. It's the thing to do whenever a new arrival shows up.

Some of them were looking as if they were tough. Some were trying to act as if they were so hard. And I had just seen someone who thought they were hard, get beat down to the floor.

It's always someone harder and tougher than you, and that was the man that I was looking for.

When I walked into the block, it was like I got respect for wearing the red jumper. That let everyone know that I didn't take no mess.

When the gates open for me to go into 7-block, I felt a burden release off my shoulders. I couldn't fill animosity in the air. The marijuana and cigarette smoke were three times louder and thicker than the smoke at 201.

While I was making my bed, a convict asked me, "You want a hit of this?"

"No," I responded, and the convict walked off.

When I laughed at the way he looked that let me know that I was already high from inhaling the smoke.

As I sat down on my bed checking out the scene, an inmate walked up to me and said, "What's up? If you need some clothes washed, let me know. I will do it for you. My name is May-tag."

"No, I'm straight," I responded and started laughing. This man would go around washing inmates' clothes for cigarettes or something to eat. He was really like a washing-machine, that's how he got the name May-tag.

Almost everyone had their areas blocked off in sections. The areas were sectioned off by neighborhoods. The main hoods were Orange Mound, South Memphis, North Memphis and Binghamton. They were the hoods with the biggest clicks, and the little hoods didn't stand a chance.

When I was walked into the bathroom, convicts were standing around getting high. The dope was so plentiful in this block until someone had to be a major pusher. It was the prime time of the day and everyone was getting high.

"Would you like to hit this?" a convict asked me.

"Yes."

A joint was passed to me, and I hit it real hard. Because of my system was clean, when I hit the joint I was too high. All of a sudden, a convict burst out free-styling with a hip-hop rap. He sounded so good until I couldn't hold back.

I busted out with a rap I had just written in the hole called "Lowe Down."

When I was done, they all gave me an applause and shook my hand. Behind that, I had to go sit on my bed, because I was so high. I began to reminisce about my family, friends and the outside world. I thought about the things that meant so much to me. How I gave them up by making the wrong decisions and choosing to do wrong. I was thinking that I was going to get away every time. I realized no one put a gun to my head and made me do anything. I was the one who made this choice to go down this road. I made my bed, and I had to lay in it.

Behind that thought, I laid down in my bed and fell asleep.

When I woke, the officers were doing a shift-change count. When they were done, I had to use the bathroom, but I had no tissue paper. I had to ask someone for some paper. This was another thing that I gave up, if there is no tissue then I can't use the bathroom. When I was using the restroom, I had to sit on a toilet next to another man.

The toilets were so close together you could smell the next man drops.

"Man, shut up talking to me!" I had to tell the inmate that was on the toilet next to me.

When I was done, I took a shower in an old shower that smelled bad.

If your family didn't bring you towels, shower shoes, and soap, you would have nothing to bath with. That's why I thank God for my brother, Calvin.

When I was done bathing and dressing, the officers turned the lights on in the block, and I saw two familiar faces that I knew. Little Joe from the old school and Herb from Orange Mound. When I saw Herb, the answer to my question about all the marijuana smoking on the block was answered. He was one of Orange Mound's biggest dope pushers. Little Joe was a gambler from way back. We sat around talking about the good old days until it was time for the officers come and count heads.

After that, Herb fired up joint-after-joint, until we couldn't get any higher.

"Lowe, you want to play some cards with me?" Little Joe asked me.

"Yes, but if you are gambling I don't have anything to put up," I responded.

"Don't worry about nothing.   I got you," Little Joe said.

After I argued to play, Joe walked off and came back with another one of our homeboys that was from the old school. His name was Johnny, and he was a top-notch gambler.

"Lowe, where is that beautiful sister of yours?" One of the side lines who was looking on said as he was getting ready to play. His name was Neal, and he was also from one of our old-school hoods.

"Which one are you talking about?" I asked him, knowing that all of them were spoken for.

"Brenda, man, I had a crush on her all of my life," Neal said.

"Neal, her kid's daddy is on his way out here. I saw him on the news robbing the bank. He is from Detroit, and he's 6'4". If he walked up in a bank and robed it, you know what he will do to you if you mess with his woman," Johnny said with a serious look on his face.

Behind that conversation, everything got quiet, and the game began. Little Joe put commissary up and just seeing it made me hunger. My hunger bug was telling me, *you better not lose*. I know that I was playing for my beans and bread and won five games before we lost one. That made Johnny a little hot.

He walked over to his bed and got one of his locker boxes that was full of commissary and sat it down beside the table. Seeing all of that, my eyes were gleaming, and my stomach was talking.

"You did yourself a favor. Now, you don't have to walk back and forth, all you have to do is reach in the box and pay me." I told Johnny, and he moaned behind that, because he didn't like losing. After that, we played all of that day until night without eating lunch or dinner. Not only was Johnny a big-time gambler, but he was the two-for-one man that supplied about four of the blocks their commissary.

After everyone saw Johnny taking his empty locker-box over to his bed and getting another one that was full also, they crowded around the table. Johnny wasn't a small man, and he like eating. Before we could break him for everything that he had, he stopped playing.

"I have got to keep me something to eat. Lowe, you are the first someone to break me. Good game you all," Johnny said and walked off.

Behind that, I ate the commissary for two weeks along with the food that we were being fed in the chow-hall. I stayed full. I began to work out and by doing so, I got bigger.

One day, while in the chow hall things were going smoothly and quiet. All of a sudden, "Lowe, Lowe what's up!" someone yelled out my name who was glad to see me.

"What's up?" I responded.

"Hey, get your ass down through this line!" an officer that was named Tate yelled out rudely at me.

I caught up with the line and over looked him. But Little Joe frowned at the officer as if he was talking to him. I made it back in the front of Little Joe and got my tray and sat at the front.

"What in the hell you are looking at me like that for, you little punk!" Officer Tate said in a disrespectful way to Little Joe.

I was always told, if your fist could reach a man's face then he could be knocked out. Little Joe was a little man, and Officer Tate was a very big man. But he was so hot at the officer for the way that he yelled at me, he talked bad to him.

"Oh shit!" Officer Tate yelled out while going down to the floor from the lick that Little Joe put on him.

The big man wasn't knocked out, but he was in a daze lying on the floor while holding his jaw. The officers restrained Joe and took him to Segregation Administration lock down.

Officer Tate's jaw was broken and had to be wired shut, so we didn't see him for a while. I got a chance to hear the same sound that everyone was talking about when I hit a man. When Little Joe hit Officer Tate, it sounded like someone was having a blowout on a car.

While back in the block, Herb called me in his cut where he had the name of our hood painted on the wall. The name of the hood is called Orange Mound, and he was a known-drug dealer in the hood. We must have smoked pot and watched TV until our eyes were tight like Chinese.

Herb wore gold necklaces around his neck and lots of rings on his fingers. He had a long Jerry-curl and his eyes were light brown. At that time, almost everyone on the compound had curls. My hair was still looking dry and had grown longer. Looking at everyone and how they kept themselves dressed neat and their hair fixed made me want the same.

"Hello," I called my sister, Brenda, and she answered the phone.

"Hi, how are you doing?" I asked.

"I'm doing ok, and I'm glad you called. I wanted to tell you that Brad is on his way out there. Will you look out for him, because he has never been locked up before?"

"Yes, I will, Brenda. Will you put some money on my books so that I can get me something to eat and get my hair done?"

"Yes, I will do it when I come out to put some money on Brad's books."

The hold time that I was talking to my sister, Herb was asking me to let him talk to her. Sometimes it makes a convict feel better just to hear someone's voice from the free world.

"Brenda, will you say hello to my home boy? His name is Herb."

"Yes." She responded.

She only talked to him for a little while and brushed him off in a respectful way. He then gave me the phone back. After that, Brenda and I said our goodbyes and hung up the phone.

At this time, it was very hot in the block. Herb and I walked to the end of the block and sat in the window and smoked about two joints. Herb spoke to everyone that walked by, but every time that they get out of sight he would make fun of them. I was laughing so hard until tears were running from my eyes. After a while, it was time to eat chow and believe me, we were hungry.

"Brother, lets lay and wait for everyone to go out first," Herb told me.

He always wanted to be the last one out so that if his money and dope stash came up missing, he would know who was involved. From that day on, Herb started calling me brother-in-law.

When we were done eating and back in the block, later on that night some inmates were playing dominos. It was a wooden chess board sitting on the table that no one was using at the time. An older inmate named Pat was beating some of the other inmates so bad while talking bad to them at the same time that two of them got mad and jumped him.

Pat was beating one of the inmates real good while the other one was hitting Pat from the back. The inmate that was hitting Pat from the back couldn't fight or his lick wasn't hard. But he knew he had to get Pat off his friend. He picked up the wooden chess board and hit Pat so hard across the head until it broke in half. It looked so funny and unreal that it made us laugh.

When Pat got up off the inmate, the inmate ran over to his bed and came back with a shank and stuck Pat.

From there everything stopped, and it was all over. Pat went to the Med, but it wasn't a bad wound.

 Pat was placed back in the block. The other inmates and Pat would walk around mugging each other but nothing else ever happened between them.

It was the 4th of July. Herb and I sat in the window smoking on a joint waiting to eat a meal that inmates look forward to every year.

"Lowe, it is going to be a fucked up 4th," Herb said to me in a sad way.

"Why do you say that?" I asked.

"Because I'm almost out of marijuana, and I don't have anything to drink." Herb responded.

"If you get me everything that I need, I can make some wine," I said.

"Just let me know what you need, and I will have it in here today," Herb said.

When I was done telling him the things that I needed, it was chow time. S.C.C.C. served ice-cream, watermelon, coleslaw, baked beans, Kool-Aid and a big slab of bar-b-que ribs for lunch. The ribs came from the farm where they bred cows and buffalos. The S.C.C.C. gave the meat the name buffalo. These were some of the biggest ribs that a man could eat.

On the way to chow hall, we walked fast, however, on the way back, we were so full until it was like everything was in slow motion. We walked slowly. Once we returned to the block, we smoked so much pot until I couldn't smoke anymore.

Herb sold pot all that day.

"Lowe, come here," Herb called me back into his cut and gave me all the ingredients that I needed to make the wine. He then turned his table down on the floor and showed me about a pound of marijuana taped to the bottom of the table.

At the same time, he had one of our homeboys standing on the front gates with a mirror looking out.

"This is where I keep my money stashed at." He also had about 8 or 9 hundred dollars taped to the bottom of the table as well.

"Damn, that dope looks like some fire!" I said, but the whole time I was wishing that I had some of that money. It explained why Herb was always the last one to come out of the block when we would go to eat. He was always surrounded by three or four homeboys that kept shanks on them.

The next day, there was an inmate on the phone, and he must had gotten some bad news. His name was Black Jerry. He always had beef with the convict that cut or fixed everyone's hair. We called him Arber-the-Barber.

Barber would always tell jokes and have everyone laughing while he was doing hair. He never bothered anyone, and no one could tell that he could fight.

This goes to show you that you can't underestimate any man. Don't judge the book by its cover.

Barber didn't look or talk like he could fight. His body looked like he was off the comer. When Jerry got off the phone, I looked into his eyes and could tell that he was looking for trouble. I was laid back on my bed and still looking for the Devil. All Jerry had to do was come my way, and he would be barking up the wrong tree. The two inmates must have had animosity against each other for a long time, because Jerry went directly to Barber.

"Yeah man, anyone that's who here thinks they can get down with this 175 pounds, all they have to do is try their luck. I'm downing my victim!" Jerry said, while looking at Barber.

"What's up with you, man? I'm tired of all that talking!" Barber said, calling out Black Jerry and fed up with his talk.

Before Barber was done talking Jerry pushed him in the chest. Jerry retaliated first with a closed right fist. It dazed Barber a little, but he shook it off. While the inmates looked on, Barber threw some haymakers that shocked everyone. After Jerry opened fire with his first lick, from there on he didn't stand a chance.

Arber the Barber was all over Jerry like white on rice and he didn't let up until it was all over. From that day on, Jerry was quiet as a church mouse.

Later that night, I got on the phone and called a young lady that I had sex with in the past. She told me that she had a baby, and it was mine. She then told me that she talked to my brother, Danny, and he was going to bring her to see me.

After we were done talking, I talked to Herb, and he told me how to have sex during visitation with a lady. The next day I called her back and told her what to do. I had her to wear a long dress with no underwear under it. I told her to keep the baby in her lap while she was sitting in my lap. I was going to pull her dress up from the back and run my manhood up in her while she was bouncing the baby up and down.

When she came, we did so, and it worked. When I got a good look at the baby, she didn't look like me nor anyone in my family. When I called her back I got her to tell me the truth. She told me she said that because she wanted to be with me. She then told me that it was some man's baby that stayed down the street from her. After that we stopped talking, and we never saw each other again.

Herb had been in and out of jail a few times, but it was my first time. I never told anyone but Herb. He then hipped me on a lot of things when it came down to the way a real convict did his time. He also told me what to do in order to stay out of the way of officers and ignorant inmates. That next weekend, I had Ann to come and visit me, and we had sex the same way that I did the first time. The only difference was Ann had someone else's baby.

With the chemistry that Ann and I had, things worked out fine, believe me it was good. But soon as we were done there was a couple that was doing the same thing. But the inmate couldn't maintain his posture. The sex was feeling so good to him until he told an inmate to hold the baby. He then turned his girl over on the floor in sight of everybody.

While he was on top of his lady releasing his pressure, the officer walked up to them and said, "When you are done, get your ass up, you are going to the hole!"

It was so funny to most of the visitors, but some were upset because their children had to see it.

"And for you, young lady, you can't ever come back here again!"

When I made it back to the block, I told the convicts and they did the same that most people did, and that was laugh.

A few days later I got a letter from Zelbron, the girl who tried to blame the baby on me. I thought the world of her for writing me.

"Herb, will you read this letter for me, I don't know how to read?" I asked.

"Yes," he responded and read it to me.

I was so impressed from the sweet words she said. Not only did that the letter make me feel like a man, but the words made me feel as if I was on top of the world. That's why deep in my heart I will always have love and respect for her. She was the first lady who wrote me and showed me that she cared. Not only that but it was $5.00 dollars in the letter.

Moments later, some inmates begin to sing on the bars while a lady officer was listening. Just looking into her eyes, I could tell that she was about to fall in love with one of the inmates who was singing. It was as if the song was hypnotizing her. At the same time, I was reminiscing about Ann. But when I got a closer look into the officer's eyes, she had the same face and eyes that my baby boy's mother had. My reminiscing changed from Ann to her.

I wanted her so bad until I could taste her. At this time, I was still in love with her and Ann or no one else could take her place.

I walked over to the phone and dialed her number, but only to get my heart broken.

"Hello," she answered.

"Hello, how are you doing?" I asked with a smile on my face, because I was glad to hear her voice.

"I'm fine. Have you heard the good news?" she asked me, sounding joyful.

"No!" I answered.

"I'm getting married soon," she said, waiting for me to congratulate her knowing that someone had stolen my love. I wanted to know who took my place.

"No, no one told me anything. Who is it? What's his name?" I asked with a change of face expression.

"I'm not telling you; it's none of your business," she said giving me a low blow.

Knowing that this lady asked me to marry her only weeks before, I came to jail, not only out of love but because she had my baby, I told her yes. She gave me something that no other woman ever did, and that was a son that looked just like me.

"Is he good to you?" I asked in a caring way.

"Yes, he treats me better than you did," she said only making matters worse.

Instead of hanging up the phone, she only stuck the spike deeper into my heart, just to find out that they had been making love.

"Does he make love to you better than me?"

She got quiet for a while; I guess it gave her time to think about the good love that I was giving her. At the same time, I could tell that she began to reflect back on us, knowing that I was the best.

"No, you are the best. You make love to me better than he do," she stated, and the truth came out.

"I still love you," I said in a hurtful way.

Click. She hung up the phone in my face.

I called back, but she never answered. I called back almost every day for a month, but she never picked up, so I gave up.

I then walked over to my bed got under the covers and cried like a baby. In so many ways, she was good as gold, and you never miss your water until the well runs dry.

After that thing, I was never the same. If you and your lover don't get along or break up, never hurt the children by holding them back from seeing their dad. It will hurt the both of them in the long run. I know that a child will grow up and be on his own, but you and your love ones will be as one. Until then don't let the love that you have for your lover stop the love that parents are supposed to give their child.

This happened to me not once but twice. Time passed on, and I called her again, and she picked up. She told me that her husband was locked up, and she took my son to see him. She then told me that she was pregnant by him.

I asked her would she bring my son to see me, and she yelled out no and hung up in my face.

The only way I got to see my son was through my sister, Brenda. She picked my son up and brought him to see me. I hadn't seen him since he was a baby, but he knew who his father was. He ran and jumped up in my arms saying, "HI daddy!"

"Hi son," I responded with tears running down my face, while looking at the other half of me. I was locked up but some kind of way I felt free in my spirit.

Hugging and kissing my son made it like music was playing. At the same time this also let me know how much my sister Brenda really loved me.

A week later, Herb was smoking too much pot and his awareness was down. He must have had the munchies from the marijuana and was in a hurry to eat. He rushed out by himself, and as soon as he made it on the main rock there were about five convicts waiting on him.

Before Herb could turn the corner that lead to the big chow hall, they grabbed him and pulled him into the bathroom that was by the back door. They took all of Herb's rings off his fingers and his necklaces off his neck. Herb kept about $200 dollars on him and it was taken also. They threw a sheet over Herb's head so that he couldn't tell who it was.

Some said that Herb knew who it was, but they threatened him not to tell anyone. We wanted to retaliate because of the pot that Herb had smoked with us. But when Herb didn't press the issue, I fell back.

A week later Herb had all new rings on his fingers and necklaces on his neck. From that day on, he started walking not only with me but with a pocket knife and about three of our homeboys.

"FIGHT# 6"

Herb and I were in his cut smoking on a joint when an inmate opened the curtain without knocking.

"Can I hit that?" he asked Herb.

"No man, next time knock!" Herb said to him.

But for some reason the guy put his mug on me. When we came out and on our way to chow hall he mugged me again, but I overlooked it.

This inmate began to hate on me for no reason at all. I had nothing to do with Herb saying no to him or telling him that he had to knock before entering. All I could say to myself was this man must have been kind of crazy. But not too crazy to know what was right from wrong. All it was from the jump; he wanted to get high but went about it the wrong way. It let me know that he was kind of smart. He must have felt that if he could get me out of the way, he could get close to Herb and help him smoke up some of his dope.

When we sat down and began eating, the inmate name was Tom sat down right in the front of me, still with his mug on his face. I guess because I was quiet, he felt that I was soft or weak.

"Mother fucker, I can't stand you!" Tom yelled out getting everyone's attention, and at the same time he threw a cup of water my way trying to douse me in the face.

This was one of my favorite and quickest fights.

Within a split second, I was in Tom's face throwing a quick left and right to his nose and face. It was only about four licks thrown. Tom was knocked out cold, bent over the table like a baby with his arms hanging in a limiting position.

The officers put a bag under his nose and bust it to get him awake. I was taken back to the block, and Tom was taken to the Med. We both were put back in the same block, and I always kept a close eye on him. But nothing else ever happen, so I guess he got the message.

Just by Herb talking to my sister that one time, he began to call me brother-in-law a little too much. I love my sister too much to see her life get messed off by some hood drug dealer. So, I began to fall back off him. Sometimes, he would offer me to get high with him, and I would just say no.

By Herb not retaliating against the convicts that robbed him, it only made things worse and it made him look weak. He should have responded when we wanted to. After things died down, he acted as if he didn't care. That made us not care also. That was one of the biggest mistakes of his life. That made them do it again and they got bolder with it.

Officers were already talking about how the marijuana in prison smelled better than the marijuana than they were smoking on the town. When our block lifted out to go and eat, this officer locked the door. So, the only way that the convicts could get back into the block is an officer had let them in. The same way that Herb showed me his mother stash, he had to have shown it to someone else. That someone was the wrong convict. The only reason that he showed it to me because some of our home boys told him how good I could fight. That made him feel like he had extra security.

Someone came in and stole his whole stash, money and all. It was told to Herb one of the convicts that was in the block with us got it. One of our home boys that was next door told Herb a convict that was in the block named Black got it. He was the same inmate that said he talked Herb into retaliating on Black. The both of them chased

Black around the block with their long shanks. It was as if Herb was really trying to stick Black.

But one of our home boys named Pat was pretending to stick Black. I could see through it like crystal glass. Black didn't know it; all he knew was to run around the block for his life. Black was hollering to the top of his voice, hoping that an officer could hear him.

Another one of our home boys came in to join us. He also had a two-foot-long shank in his hand. When I paid close attention, he wasn't trying to stick Black either. That let me know that they had stolen the loot themselves.

"Officer, help!" Black yelled out and an officer heard the hollering and open the door to let Black out.

"I didn't get your shit, Herb!" he yelled to Herb, telling the truth, and the officer moved him.

"You can't hide; I'm going to get you. You ass hoe boy, I know you got my shit!" Herb said with blood in his eyes while being deceived and betrayed by his own home boys.

All I could say was our two lying homeboys put on a good show. The two fake home boys walked back to their block, and we didn't hear anything else from them.

Two days later, Herb had a pound of marijuana and $300.00 dollars. He began to act really tight with his pot. He was still calling me brother-in-law and talking me into getting high with him.

Because of Herb being tight with his pot, someone dropped salt on him. A night later, the Captain came in the block with ten officers and had everyone to get on their beds.

They took Herb out of the block while they looked through his property searching through his things but couldn't find anything. The Captain sent for an officer that we called Boogie Dogg. He had a nose like a K9.

When he came into the block, he looked over Herb's things the same way the other officers did. But he didn't find anything. All of a sudden, he walked out into the hall and walked back into the block. He walked over to Herb's table where he kept his stash at and turned the table over.

"Captain, here is your loot!" Boogie Dogg yelled out to the Captain and walked out in a cool way.

"Bingo, I knew it was in there somewhere. Damn, that shit looks better than the pot on the town!" the Captain said with a smile on his face as if he was glad to see the loot.

"Send everyone in this area to my office one at a time," the Captain said, while walking out with the pot and money in his hands.

Myself and four other's were called into the Captain's office and were questioned about the loot. But no one knew anything. The Captain told others as well as myself, if we would claim the money, he would put it on our books. That was only to set us up to get the charge for the marijuana. If anyone would have claimed that money, they would have been dumb as a box of rocks.

Behind that, we all were sent back to our cell-block and nothing else was said. By them not finding the loot on anyone, they couldn't charge anyone.

After that, it was a draft in the block and main frame. You could only smell cigarette smoke.

A week later my sister kid's daddy, Brad made into the block. He was so glad to see me; he must have talked to me for about five hours. After that, an officer yelled into the pod.

"Gym Call."

Brad and I shot ball once before and took over the basketball court.

While in the gym, Brad and I were waiting for our down to play. We were up next and watching our competition that we were about to play. While waiting, one of my home boys saw me and realized who I was. Caught himself trying to impress me, by trying to start a fight with someone. He picked someone that tried to avoid him and didn't want to fight. My home boy name was Phil.

Phil picked up a ten-pound weight and followed the man all around the gym. While he was faking at the inmate with the weight, he was talking about him at the same time; it was another one of those funny scenes. Phil was so skinny till it looked like the weight was weighing him down.

Brad and I laugh until it was time for us to play.

"I will bust your motherfucking head to the fat meat, until I see the white!" Phil told the inmate while we were walking on the floor getting ready to play. It was so funny until everyone in the gym was laughing.

When Brad and I hit the court, it was just like I thought, we took over the court. I dropped in about five jumpers in a row.

"Lowe, let me shine some!" Brad said to me while we were setting up for defense.

Brad blocked someone's shot so hard across the court in my direction, I almost didn't get the ball from laughing at the sound from the blocked shot.

On our way back down the court, Brad was running up the other side of the court with me on a fast break. With his 6'5" tall height, he made it so easy for me to throw him an alley-oop. He caught it and slammed it so hard until everybody in the gym stood up and hollered. That closed everything out for the final shot that won the game.

"Let's go. It's time to go!" One of the officer's that was looking on yelled out to us to go back to our blocks.

From that day forward Brad was more than my brother-in-law, we became closer than brothers. We hugged and shook hands before walking off the court. While back in the block, after we took a shower, Brad began to talk to me about my sister, Brenda.

He opened up the conversation by telling me, "I'm sorry for slapping your sister when we were in Detroit at Williams Belford's party.

"Man, let me tell you something," I said, while having flashbacks on how my sister was in pain. "If you ever put your hands on her again, I will kill you, and I mean it!" I said while holding myself back from reaching out and touching Brad.

"Lowe, I promise you, I'll never do that again. You scared the hell out of me," Brad said, and at that same time he was trying to get me to stop Brenda from getting married. I told him that it wasn't too much I could say or do, because I was in a worse situation than he was. At least Brenda would bring his children to see him. My baby's mother wouldn't bring my son to see me, but she took him to see another man that was locked up.

Brad began to sing a song that made him think about Brenda. "It's going to be a bright sunshiny day!" His song while reminiscing on the good times that they had together.

Because of the condition of the old building, Administration moved us to one of the new building that was called 'The Horse Shoe'. It smelled a lot better and was a lot cleaner. We were housed in C-Building.

Brad got a bed the same way we were in the old building that was over the top of me. His mother and sister would send him all kind of things, like hygiene items. He would share them with me and by doing so my skin began to clear up. They would also send Brad money so that he could go to the store. He would feed me and talk to me about how much he loved Brenda. I would sometimes pretend as if I was listening just to eat. But some of the times, if I wanted to eat, I had to hear him out.

Other inmates began to get jealous of Brad and me. They were trying to turn us against each other, but it didn't work. Things began to get a little heated. I could tell that a fight was on the way, so I began to tone up by working out. I started doing 500 pushups a day. Not only did it tone me up, but it kept my mind off my family, Denise, my sons and the outside world. That was somewhere that I couldn't go.

As I thought how much I loved everyone, it was as if no one loved me. It seemed like no one cared about me. It was like no one cared if I was dead or alive. Sometimes, Brad would see me doing push-ups and start working out with me. But he couldn't keep up with me, so he would stop.

"Lowe, you are strong as hell; you need some pussy," Brad told me and walked off while I was still working out.

After working out and taking a shower, I would sleep much better. The next day after working out, I was in the bed on my way to sleep.

"Lowe, keep this for me, I'm going to visitation. Brenda is here to see me," Brad said while giving me some money and keys to his locker-box.

"Tell Brenda I love her." I told Brad while he was on his way out. But at the same time, I was very hurt because she or no one else would come to see me.

I stayed in the bed for a while with my head under the cover while my heart cried like a baby, wishing that I could hear someone voice saying, 'I love you.' Because of the love that I have for my family there is something that I will not say. But I would say to myself, *I'm your brother and I haven't ever hurt any of you, I only hurt myself. Why not come to see me?*

I got out of my bed and walked into the day room. As I stood in the window looking out I took a look at the trees I could tell time was rolling in and out of season. I could tell from the change of the trees. They had changed from green to brown from brown to naked and from naked back to green. I hadn't seen anyone in my family or talked to them in years. There had been three deaths in our family and no one came to see me or wrote me to encourage me in any kind of way. No one talked to me on the phone to let me know it was going to be alright.

As I stood there looking out of the window reminiscing about Ann, it kept my mind off of Denise. While I stood there, it began to rain, and I wrote and sang a song about Ann called, "Ann Tell Me."

"Damn, Lowe, that sounds good as hell. You should record that," Brad said, while a lot of other inmates were listening on, and they all clapped.

"Yeah, that's cool song!" another convict said that had just come into the dorm. He was from one of my old hoods when we lived in the projects. At the time we couldn't use anything to fight with. We would have to fight with our bare hands.

This home-boy name was Ren-Ren. Brad, Ren and I walked over to the TV area, sat on the table and began to watch TV. Brad and Ren were some red-skinned men. Look like they could have been brothers. The both of them were also tall with good hair. I introduced the both of them and we talked.

"Brad, when we were coming up, Lowe was a real fighter. He didn't know, but we use to bet on his fights and would never lose," Ren said, and at the same time I could tell that he was glad to see me.

"Yeah, I know he can go some. He almost got a hold of me when we were in Michigan. I disrespected his sister, and he came after me. I ran so fast that I almost shit on myself. If he would have caught me, I believe he would have probably killed me," Brad said with a smile on his face, while Ren and I laughed also.

As soon as Brad was done talking, an inmate walked up and change the station on the TV as if we weren't there.

"Hey man, what are you doing? I'm watching that!" I said with a change of facial expression.

The inmate looked back at me with a puppy-like look on his face.

"Hell naw, I know this can't be the Devil. Not this coward looking mother fucker!" I let out, while Brad and Ren was looking at me as if they were saying, 'what in the hell is he talking about.' Before I could say another word or do anything...

"Ooooh; I'm sorry!" The inmate yelled out in pain after taking an unexpected blow from Ren-Ren.

Neither one of us saw it coming.

"That's for Lowe. All of the money that you have made for me!" Ren-Ren said while looking at me in a way that was saying, *I'm showing you love home boy.*

After that, the inmate walked back into the sleeping area, got in his bed, laid it down and was real still. From that day forward, we didn't hear a sound out of him. He didn't watch TV anymore.

After that was over, Brad walked over to the phone and called Brenda. I'm her brother someone that will always be there for her, and I didn't have her phone number. It hurt me so bad to see Brad talk to my sister that he mistreated, and I hadn't talked to anyone in my family in two years or more.

"Lowe, you're gone?" Ren-Ren asked me.

"Yeah, I'm not feeling good; I'm going to lie down for a while," I said and walked out of the day room over to my bed.

I put my head under the covers while my heart was crying. It was as if my mind snapped. I felt I had nothing to live for. Not only that, but it was as if was always looking for my enemies, and at the same time I felt like I could kill Satan himself. If I kill the person that he was in, then I would be killing him. I felt that he was trying to take me out, so I had to get him before he got me. I tried to fall off to sleep but I couldn't.

Knowing that they were on the phone was like a spike was being driven throw my heart. I was saying to myself, I have been looking out for Brad and wouldn't let anyone put a hand on him. This is what I get in return. Sometimes he would be talking to his mother, and I would have to look out for him. He would be on the phone so long, until the convicts wanted to fight him, but they knew that they would have to come through me.

As soon as I was about to fall off to sleep, "Lowe, Detroit is in here talking bad to your sister, calling her all kind of bitches and hoes!" Someone yelled out to me.

They were already posted up and talking about how they were going to turn Brad against me. The inmates called Brad Detroit. I thought to myself, he is not putting his hands on her, and he can't get to her over the phone. When I began to listen in on more of the inmate's conversation, instead of going against Brad, I realized that I was going to become closer to him. However, I would let him know not to call my sister all of these names. So, I stood and waited on him.

"Weak ass boy; you let that boy talk like that to your sister!" Key-Key said while looking at me. He took his focus off me and started looking at someone else.

"FIGHT# 7"

"Look out!" One of Key-Key's friends said trying to get Key-Key to doge my first blow to his face. But it was too late.

"Oh shit!" Key-Key yelled out, as my mind snapped, it had me rush in on him with some of my most powerful blows, quickly laying him out on the floor.

He was down but not out and at the same time trying to use offense. He was only making it harder for himself. The good defense that I had allowed me to stop everything that he tried to throw. This guy was well cut and had muscles everywhere. But that was not what I was looking at or for. It was if could see a form of Satan flashing on and off his face. All I could say to myself was, I have finally found him. *Oh, I got your ass now, Lucifer, you tough mother fucker*, I said to myself.

I gave Key-Key about five or six more licks while he was on the floor back-peddling trying to get away. He stood up and ended up in the corner trapped. I began to come with everything that I had - left, right, left, then a upper-cut and I dropped a six-pack. I gave him all and some more at the same time. While throwing blows, I could feel my knuckles being dislocated. Every time that I connected with my target, I heard the bones in Key-Key's head crack. It was as if I was planting my fist into his head, jaw and eyes.

"Damn! Brenda, your brother is taking care of his business. He is beating the hell out of someone in here. I have got to go; I love you and the kid's bye!" Brad said and quickly hung up the phone.

By then Key-Key was coming up off the floor for the second time. From there, he took off running to the sleeping area busted up and bloody.

"Damn Lowe, you are a fighting mother fucker. What was that all about?" Brad asked me as he posted up on one side of me, while Ren posted up on the other side with a smile on his face.

"I will tell you later," I said cutting Brad's word short.

I begin looking over into the night-room at Key-Key and his friends. They were talking and planning a plot against me.

Man, I have got to kill the Devil and come out of here alive.

I know this had to be him. He took a damn good beating, and I didn't knock him out. But this time, *I will kill him with my bare hands*, I said in the back of my mind while rubbing my sore and busted up knuckles.

"Here they come, Lowe!" Ren, Ren said. Soon as Key-Key walked into the room, on his ass I went, but after few blows of six packs I dropped on him, he took off running again to the other side. He never got one lick in on me.

Not A One.

"What's up with you?" Key-Key's friend asked me as if he wanted to fight.

"You want some of this too weak ass boy?" I asked starting in on him. I had heard him talking around the dorm like he was tough.

They called him Nick. He called himself taking up for Key-Key, but he was going to get the worse beating he ever had.

"Kick that mother-fucker. He is flat foot jacking!" Someone told him, trying to warn him. "No Lowe, let me in on some of this; I got him!" Brad said while quickly coming between Nick and me.

"No Brad, I have got to kill the Devil." I told him, but he was insistent on fighting.

'That's alright, I don't want no trouble!" Nick let out in fear.

The tall coward this he is had a look on his face. Brad and Nick stood about 6'5" in height, but Brad was more hipped up. Nick looked deep into my eyes and saw nothing but blood. Key-Key was in the bathroom trying to stop the bleeding and patch himself up, and an officer walked in on him.

"Who did this to you, who jumped you like this?" The officer asked Key-Key.

"Lowe, he did this," Key-Key pointed at me while telling.

The officer walked up to me, cuffed me and began walking me out to the hole.

Brad and I exchanged words of brotherly love.

"I love you, Lowe," Brad said.

"I love you too." I then dropped my head saying to myself, *that must not been the devil, because he didn't die.*

"See you later, Lowe." Ren, Ren said, and we walked out.

It was about three weeks that I was in the hole. I could see myself getting bigger from doing a full work-out every day.

The Captain came to my cell and said, "I'm bringing some kids in here; I'm going to need for you to scare the straight."

"Ok, I will do so," I responded.

As soon as the Captain walked off, Brad knocked on my window.

"Lowe, I'm going home. I love you!"

"I love you too, brother-in-law," I replied in a sad way. But at the same time, I was glad for him.

Now that Brad was gone, I didn't have anyone to give me anything. I had to survive the best way that I knew how while I was in prison - that was fighting, playing cards or scheming, someone out of something.

I then begin to think to myself that I was only half way through doing my time, and I still had not found the Devil.

I will get him if it's the last thing that I do.

CHAPTER 9:
I LOST A TRUE FRIEND

Only one week of hole time to do. I had gotten bigger and stronger. My hair grew long, and my muscles were toned up. I was standing on the top floor looking down on the first floor with my shirt off. The captain and a sergeant walked in.

"Lowe, are you ready?" the captain asked me.

"Yes, send them in!" I responded, while flexing my muscles.

"The tours are coming across the compound now with a group of teenagers. Do not touch them, but I want you to make their asses so afraid until they will run from trouble when it comes their way. I want you to make it so that they don't want to see a jail!" the captain said, giving me the green light to cut up.

Before they walked into the dorm I dropped down and did about 200 pushups to buff myself up. With nothing but my chest and my six-pack showing when they walked in, I had them intimidated. With my dark sunglasses on my eyes, they couldn't tell who I was looking at. Some of them had a fearful look in their eyes as if they were already afraid. The big kids with smiles on their face were the ones that I was after. Still standing up top now looking out of the window with my back turned.

"Ahhhhhhh, I can't take it on more!" I yelled to the top of my voice getting everyone's attention. I then hung from the top rail and jumped down to the first floor, while making my chest bounce like basketballs.

"What in the hell are you all doing in my house!" I yelled out while watching the kids running trying to hide behind to grow folks.

Two officers were pretending as if they were trying to hold me back from getting to the kids. Every now and then, they would let me go just enough to almost grab the kids' clothes. I caught a hold of one of the taller kids by his shirt tail.

"You sassy ass boy; come here. I'm going to put a dress on you and make you my girl!" I yelled at taller kid, and he cried like a baby.

"I'll will spank you on your…" I said while faking at one of the girl's hind part.

She took off running and yelling to the top of her voice. I then walked up to another taller teen while the officer was holding me back and said. "Boy I'll break you down like an old rusted shotgun; I'll hit you in the top of your head and break both of your ankles!"

He looked down at his ankles and started crying. Behind that, I broke a loose from the officers and started running his way. He fell trying to get away from me. All of the other kids took off running with him. They made it out of the door, but he fell again while crying and yelling to the top of his voice.

When it was all over, I felt really good on the inside. It looked like that I was hurting someone, but at the same time I was helping someone.

I felt that I had done a good deed. I walked back to my cell with a smile on my face. Later on that day, the captain gave me an extra tray of food.

"You did good, I like that. You did a good job. I will see if I can cut some of your hole time," the captain said and walked off.

"You know by you doing that, some of the kids may never come to jail in their life. We sure thank you a lot," the sergeant said before leaving out with his officers.

When I was released out of the hole, the sun hurt my eyes while I was walking across the Horse Shoe to 8-building. I was housed in the 8-building C dorm.

I noticed some familiar faces, and I wasn't too quick to converse with inmates or a convict unless they would come to me. Some were my home boys, and some was just inmates I knew from 201. There was this convict name Big Body. He was the realest and most down to earth man that I ran into. He kept it real to the end of our departing. From this day, may peace be with him and love.

"What's up? Are you Danny's brother?" Big Body asked me while reaching for my hand to shake it.

"Yeah, you know me?" I asked.

"Yeah, I'm from the hood, and I knew your whole family."

"That's what's up."

"Yeah, they call me Big Body."

From that day on Big body and I were tight. This was a good dorm that we were in and no violence was going on. As time began to roll, it was a little gambling going on along with cards and dominos.

I never shot dice, but I played the hell out of some cards and dominos. I stayed in that dorm longer that I did anywhere else. I stayed in it so long that when I laid on my bed, I could tell almost everyone that walked past my bed without looking, by the sound of their footsteps.

There was a basketball tournament going on, and I played point guard on the team for our building. This was one game where I cut up, and we won the trophy and sat it in the window of the building.

A few weeks after that an officer realized how good that the inmates could rap, sing and dance. He had it set up so that we could do a concert for the compound and the officers. I rapped two songs. One was called "MY NAME IS COCAINE" and "LOWE DOWN."

The crowd was amazed by the lyrics that I was rapping. It was as if they hadn't heard the words in a way that I laid them down. Because of the way that drugs and violence had taken over our city, the rap songs gave everyone an eye opener on life.

Behind that everyone gave me a standing ovation, and the show was over.

The next morning while we were getting ready to eat, one of the lady officers was sitting on the dining table. She was one of the nicest looking ladies that worked at S.C.C.C. Before I could take a seat, there were a sergeant, and said to her. "Get off the table so they can eat."

She sat there a while as if she was in a daze.

"Ok, she is ok, she can sit there. I'm a country boy. I'll eat anything. If she sits there long enough she will be eaten along with my food!" I said, and everyone laughed. She also laughed while she was getting up.

She must have understood that doing time was getting a hold on me because, she asked me, "Lowe, how much time you have to do?"

"I have done 88 months, and I have 72 more to go."

Behind that everyone laughed again. It was just a normal day in the chow hall.

While back in the dorm, Big Body smoked a joint with me; it had me high as a kite.

"Lowe, that's your phone, and this is my phone, if anyone try and violate, we will deal with them, bet." Big Body said.

"Bet!" I said while both shook on it.

From there I had everyone that was going to use my phone to put their name on a list. I ran the phone until about 10 pm. That gave me until 12 midnight to do whatever I wanted to with the two hours. Sometime inmates would give me commissary to let me use my time. It was an inmate named Booie, who was the biggest and tallest in the dorm.

"Hi Lowe, I've been watching you for a while and I can tell no one will violate. I know you don't take any mess. Can I pay you to be my bodyguard?" Booie asked me.

"Man, what the fuck are you watching me for?" I yelled out with my dog on my face.

"Naw, no, it's not like that it's not like you think it is," he tried to explain.

"Then what in the fuck are you talking about?" I asked.

"Man, I will pay you commissary and something to smoke if you get me on the phone and be my bodyguard," Booie said, standing there looking like George Foreman.

"Ok, deal. Pay up now," I said, knowing I had a duck.

Booie walked out and came back with four packs of Kool's cigarettes and a pillow case of commissary. This was one big scared man. He needed security in a dorm where it wasn't too much going on. He must have been still shaking from being in 201.

A few weeks passed, and there wasn't anyone messing with Booie. I had to get someone to make it look as if they were going to do something to him. I got two of my home boys to act as if one was going to attack and the other was holding him back.

"Lowe, Lowe help, help," Booie yelled out to me.

I ran in and acted as if that I was going to make an attack on my home boy.

"You better not ever put your hands on this man. I will kill you!" I yelled out as if I meant business.

"Ok Lowe, my bag. I didn't know!" my home boys said as he looked fearful.

'The next time, it's going to be on like a pot of neck bones!" I yelled out, and Booie got on the phone peacefully.

For doing that, it was a heavy charge on Booie, and he paid up. A month later, Booie got out and told my sister, Dorothy, that I was his bodyguard.

When she saw him, she told him, "big as you are, you should be his bodyguard."

That following weekend, my sister, Brenda, bought my son to visit me. By her doing so, that opened my heart up to her, and brought me closer to her than my other family members. It also was a way of showing me that someone still loved me.

I hadn't seen my son since he was born. Four years had passed, and he had grown. It was as if I was looking at myself walking around. I hugged him so and didn't want to let him go.

"Daddy, I need to use the bathroom," Lorenzo Jr. asked me, and I took him to use it.

At that time, I wanted to cry, but I had too much pride to cry. Deep in my heart, I was crying knowing that I couldn't be there for him. It was as if my whole world had crashed and left me under the rubble. Knowing that I was in too deep but looking at my son was giving me a reason to pull myself out. I never felt so hurt in my life.

God knows I will get Satan for this, he will pay, I thought to myself.

"Lorenzo, Lorenzo are you ok?" Brenda asked me, while I was looking at my son and at the same time I was angry at Satan.

"Yes, I'm alright."

"Lowe, Mama want you to call her. She needs to talk to you," Brenda said to me in a concerned way. At the same time, she was looking as if she had lost her best friend by seeing me locked up.

"Ok, I will call her," I responded, wondering what she wanted.

At this time, my son was the most precious thing in my life. He meant the world to me. I was seeing myself all over again. I recognized that because of the son that Denise had given me, I will love her in the same way that I love my mother, and that is for the rest of my life. When my son and sister walked out, a big part of me walked out also.

While back in the dorm, I began to think about some of the things that my sister said. She was showing me love and giving me a word of hope. But at the same time, it was going in one ear and going out the other. One piece of advice that I took from her was to call my mother.

"Hello," My mother answered the phone.

"Hi Mama."

"How is my son doing?"

"I'm ok."

"How are they treating you out there?"

"I'm alright, Mama. I love you," I said trying to end the conversation, because I didn't want to tell the truth. But all the time a mother can tell when something is not right. There is not too much that you can hide from your mother.

"When are they going you let you come home?" Mama asked with a crying voice.

"Mama, to tell you the truth, I don't care if I come home or not. I really don't have a home to come to; I have lost everything that I had."

"Son, you do have a home to come to. As long as I have a home, you will have a place to stay. Please come, home, son. You know Mama loves you."

"I love you too, Mama, but I'm doing time, and I can't come home until my time is up."

"Baby if you stop all of that fighting maybe they will let you come home. Your brothers and sisters miss you. They all told me to tell you hello, and they love you."

"Mama they don't love me! How can they say that they love me, and they won't do anything for me? I have been locked up all this time and they haven't put $5.00 dollars on my books. What kind of love is that? I haven't got any sisters or brothers. If Cleveland wasn't messed up, he probably would be the only one that would do something for me. I can understand the situation that he's in but the rest of them I just can't see why they won't help me. A bunch of sisters and brothers...no! If this is what you call family, then I don't want one!"

"Lorenzo, just make me a promise that you will stop fighting and come home. Administration and a captain called me the other day and asked me can I talk some sense into your head. You are out there cutting up, and you need to stop it."

"Mama, that's not the truth. The devil is at me, and I'm not backing down for on one. I will get him before he get me. I love you, but I have to let you go. I have to let someone else get on the phone. Goodbye, Mama. I love you. I will call you back some other time."

"I love you too, baby, and I will be praying for you. Bye."

Before my mother hung up the phone I could hear her say, "That boy done lost his mind."

I hung up the phone but called back. "Hello, Mama, this is me again, I heard when you said that I have lost my mind. If anything, I have found it. Mama, how can someone say that they love me? If I have lost my mind it is because my family has left me for dead. No one will come to see me, and I'm just out here hungry, and no one will do anything for me. I have never done anything to anyone in the family and they can't help me? There is not love in my heart for anyone in my family. I'm beating everyone out here who tries to do me wrong. Or say anything to me!"

"Lorenzo, you listen to me. You better make a change. I didn't raise you like that, and it hurts me to see you in a place like this. Do they have a church out there?"

"Yes, Mama."

"Well you need to go to church and stop that fighting. God gas a special calling on your life. He has shown this to me, and nothing is going to go right until you change. I believe every fight that you have been in. At the same time, you were fighting, I was praying for you. I'm telling you know God is calling you. He is trying to use you, but you keep running."

"Why is God not letting anyone put money on my books, or coming to see me?"

"Did Brenda and your son come to see you?"

"Yes, but…" I tried to talk.

"Well that's a start. Just stop what you are doing, and you will see God will help you."

"Mama have got to go now. I have a pot on the stove. I love you."

"I love you too, Mama," I said and hung up the phone.

Behind that, things got worse, I began walking around looking for a fight, but I just couldn't find one. Inmates and convicts were asking me, "Are you alright?" I would respond with. "What the fuck you mean, are you alright?"

After a while, I walked to my bed and laid it down. While lying in my bed, I felt deep in my heart my mother was praying for me. All the time, it was God showing me mercy through my mother's prayers.

A few weeks later my oldest sister was in town and my mother sent her to see me. I could tell that my mother told her to see if she could talk some sense into my head.

We both were glad to see each other, and she had a long talk with me, but it didn't help. She put $50.00 dollars on my books, and I loved her for that.

After that visit I didn't see anyone else, but she gave me her daughter's phone number, because she wanted to talk to me. I called her, because she is my favorite niece. Cookie turns out to be one of the most loving family members that I had.

Every time that I would call her if she didn't have time to talk she would put one of her daughters on the phone so that I would have someone to talk to. *That was what I call real family love.*

As time rolled on, everyone else went home, but Big Body and me. We were surrounded by a lot of new faces. Most of them were my home boys from Orange Mound. They all looked up to me, and before I knew it, they were about 20 deep.

They gave us a name called, The Orange Mound Posse. They all were young and looking for someone to lead them in the right way. But at this time in my life I couldn't lead myself in the right direction. By them being new to the system, no matter what I would say they would believe it.

At the same time an officer entered the dorm and posted a memo on the window that said, 'The Government will be taking all tobacco out of the jails and out of the Tennessee prisons system. A month later it took place.

When it did, it caused some inmates to get beaten down to the point of death. Some were badly hurt over one cigarette. At this time, a piece of cigarette would cost about $2.00 on the street. But in jail they would cost an inmate $5.00 dollars.

Some inmates began to do almost anything for a rollup or a cigarette. I've seen it all. I have heard them saying, "some ladies would do anything strange for a small piece of change."

During this same time, some of my home boys were smashing the hip hop Billboard with a song called, Lyrics of a Pimp. They helped put Memphis on the map, one behind another hit after hit.

When we would go out to eat, the young Orange Mound Posse would walk across the compound doing the new Memphis Gangster Walk.

At the same time, they would be listening to their headphone radios while throwing up the Orange Mound hand sign.

They were singing, 'Niggers, Niggers, Niggers, Orange Mound Nigger's strapped with them things strapped with them things.'

They would walk behind me every day while saying this. They were getting a little out of hand with it until the captain told us that we couldn't bring our radios out of the of dorm any longer, but that didn't stop them. It was as if they were getting worse with it. The captain could do nothing but look at them while saying, "Them fools gone crazy!"

One day, we were at the front of the dorm getting ready to change clothes.

"Lowe, look you see that sucker ass boy? He caught your brother off guard and slammed him to the floor. Here, take this and stick the shit out of his ass," Big Body told me, while giving me a long shank.

"Here Body, I don't need this I'm going to beat him with my bare hands." It was as if could see my brother, Cleveland, getting slammed to the floor.

At the same time my eyes were filling up with blood. I felt as if I was hurt myself. When I made it up to him to get my clothes that was all it took. I was close enough to make my move. When he passed them to me, I caught him off guard.

"FIGHT # 8"

The next night I was laid back on my bed and fell asleep.

"Lorenzo, son wake up." My mother appeared in my dream, waking me out of my sleep. It was as if I really had wakened up out of a dream, and I didn't know that I was still asleep.

"Here, take this seat, sit down here and eat. When you are done, read this Bible. I have told you that the only way that you will make it in life is to stop fighting and running from God. God has a calling on your life, and you need to obey Him, so your life won't be so hard. I have told you that you're going to have some stormy days, and rainy days, some up's and down's but if you only read this and obey God, the sun will shine again."

While I sat at my mother's dining table, I took the Bible that she had given me, put it under the chair that I was sitting in and began to eat.

"Chow, time; Chow, time;" an officer yelled out through my door just when I was about to bite on some of my mama's cooking.

"Here, get your tray," he told me while the rock man gave me a tray that looked like slop.

All I could do was think about my mother's cooking and wish that I was there with her to eat some of her down-home food. But I choose to be in jail instead.

After I sat down the cold tray of food, I had to rub the back of my hands, because they were so sore and out of place.

About two weeks had gone by and I talk to my sister, Brenda, on the phone. I got some of the worst and tragic news of my life. She told me that my nephew had got hit by a car and was killed.

This made my hole-time the hardest time that I had ever done in my life. He was closer to me then some of my brothers. First, it was my grandmother, then my step-father, now my favorite nephew, Sarell Spencer. My mother gave him a nickname Hump. I knew without a shadow of a doubt that he was an angel down here on earth. He didn't even like the food that was here on the earth. He would always ask me, "why do people talk bad and do bad things?"

I will always thank God for my mother for showing him the way to God. A part of my mother rubbed off on Hump. No matter who he would come in contact with, he would talk to them about the Word of God.

Being around him was like being around an angel here on earth. Behind Sarell passing away, it took a toll on my mother, because of the relationship that they had. Not, only that, with my brother and I being locked up, also had my mother worried as well. She ended back up in the hospital, while I was out of my cell on my rock time. I called and talked to my mother; she sounded so weak when she talked until I begin to cry in silence. It was as if I was in pain also.

"FIGHT#9"

"Come on, get off the phone, your rock time is up; get your ass off the phone!" an officer yelled out at me in a disrespectful way.

Not only did I get rushed off the phone early, but also my mother was sick, and this officer was really disrespectful.

"Officer, look Sir, my mother is in the hospital and very sick. Can I talk to her a little while longer," I tried to explain.

"Hell no," he stated, and behind that he snatched the phone out of my hand and hung it up in my mother's face.

"What the fuck you think you're doing, you bitch ass, you hoe ass boy!" I didn't waste any time.

Behind, that he caught a quick left, and a fast right to the chain that took him down to the floor. Seeing this officer lying out, I backed up in fear knowing that I had knocked out an officer. In the back of my mind, I was saying,' damn, I have dropped and officer, they are going to beat my ass.'

He laid there for a while, and then shook while getting up off the floor. This man out weighted me two-to-one. He began coming my way with his guard up, while moving in slow motion.

"Man, you shouldn't have hung the phone up in my mother's face. This is not what you want," I tried to warn him.

But he just wouldn't listen. He kept coming my way. I did what was called a step away, moving around him before he could turn around, and at the same time giving him about six quick ones to the face. He then backed off and rushed to the control both to call for backup.

I then walked up the stairs to my cell and got prepared to be jumped by the officers. I took my locker off my locker box and looped it to the end of my belt. I took some magazines that I had, ran strings through them, then tied them around my body to make a body pad to stop the licks.

While I stood at my door looking out of the window, I began to rub my hands again. They were sorer than they had ever been. The officer began coming in alone with the captain. They came up the stairs and posted up at my cell door.

"That's Lowe. You all go back down the stairs; I will talk to him," the captain told his officers, and they walked off.

"Lowe, put down your lock; I know you will use it. But you won't like what will come behind it, if you do. So, put it down. I'm coming in to talk to you," the captain talked me down in a cool way, and then called to control to open my door.

"You are not going to let the officers in on me?"

"No, now put that away."

I put down the lock with the belt tied to it, and the captain came all the way into the cell, and we had a talk. I explained my situation to him about my sick mother, and how disrespectful his officer was to me. He understood and told me, "I will go easy on you by sending you to Administration Segregation lock down. You hurt that officer pretty bad. I can't let you get away with that."

Behind that I was giving 30 more days for assaulting an officer. When I was moved to Segregation, it looked like real animal cages. In order for me to just see anything, I had to look out of some little holes that were on the cage.

It was so hot in the cell until I breathed in hot air every time that I inhaled. I couldn't do anything but workout. When I got out of the hole, the Orange Mound Posse was glad to see me.

I was housed back in the same dorm. They began to sing our favorite song. "Niggers, Niggers, Orange Mound Niggers strapped with them things."

My sister, Brenda, mailed me some money; I got my hair curled and something to eat. I also bought two pack of cigarettes. By doing so, I was able to sell some, that helped me fill my box with food.

Every time I would get ready to smoke a cigarette there was an inmate who would come over to my corner and ask me for a hit. I had gotten to the point that I had gotten tired of him, so I made plans to stop him. I took some paper that we rolled tobacco into make it look like a real cigarette. I then pulled some lint off my sleeping blanket and put it in the paper to puff it up. I then sprinkled salt and pepper in it and roll it up.

As soon as I was about to light it, Ron came walking into my corner. I lit it and passed it to Ron. He was so anxious to get some nicotine in his lungs until he inhaled it very hard. I thought that he was going to stop after the first time that he inhaled but he took a second puff.

Tears began to run out of his eyes, mucus ran out of his nose, and at the same time he was coughing. He also was spitting the nasty taste of pepper out of his mouth. He passed it back to me. I took it, opened it up and showed him what he was smoking.

Everyone was laughing out loud. That taught him a lesson not to run into my corner every time that he saw a cigarette being smoked.

"That's what you get for begging, now stay the hell out of my corner!"

That very same night, it was a white boy that we called, Dirty White Boy. He would always make store calls and by cigarettes from me. He owed me for two cigarettes, and they were $5.00 dollars each. But he had missed a week of paying me. He went to the store but lied to me as if he didn't make it. I was going to wait until the next week for him to pay me. One of my homies and I were smoking, and Dirty White Boy walked in my corner and asked me, "Can I hit that cigarette?"

"Hell no, bro you owe me. You need to be trying to pay me my commissary!" I said while he was about to walk off.

"Lowe, he owes you?" My home boy asked me.

"Yes."

"He went to the store!"

"Hell no, this fool is trying to play me!" I said, and my blood began to boil.

"FIGHT # 10"

"Come here, Dirty White boy," I called him to see was this true?

"What's up Lowe?" he asked.

"Did you go to the store?"

"Hell no, that bitch ass boy is lying!" When he called my home boy a bitch and knowing that he wouldn't lie to me, before anyone could blink, I slapped Dirty White Boy so hard he on each side of his face it really sounded like a 12-gage shotgun.

"Damn!" my home boy yelled out while holding his hand over the both side of his ears.

"What the hell was that!" someone else hollered out.

Dirty tried to draw back to hit me but only made me drop him like a hot potato. With some hard blows to his face, he went down to the floor but jumped back up and took off running.

"Well, I know he wasn't the Devil," I said, and every-one looked at me like I was crazy.

I then walked over to Dirty White Boy's locker and took everything that he had. The next day while in the bathroom area brushing my teeth, Dirty White Boy was coming out of the bathroom. He walked past me without turning his back. At the same time, he kept his eyes on me at all times. He looked so afraid looking like he was going to use the bathroom on himself. I got a good look at his face. It made me feel kind of bad to see him looking like that. He looked like Pinocchio by the nose, a raccoon by the eyes, and he had my fingerprints on each side of his face.

You could actually see black marks on his face that looked like my fingers. Come to think of it, I didn't feel so bad after all, he brought it on himself.

When it was time to go and eat, Dirty stuck out like a sore thumb. My home boys knew if Administrative found out about this, I would go back to the hole. They didn't want to see me go so they tried to help. They told Dirty to walk with another white boy and some of the Orange Mound Posse, would walk around them and camouflage them in the middle.

"Dirty, what were fuck you were thinking about?" one of my home-boy asked and everyone start laughing.

"Man, look like dirty cigars on your face, oh you steal-ing cigars now!" The jokes just kept coming and laughing didn't stop. While in the chow hall, the camouflage plan didn't work. By the sergeant being tall, he was able to see Dirty's face and pick him off the top.

"Hey, you, come here," the sergeant called Dirty out of the line.

"Who in the hell slapped you like that?" The Sergeant laughed at the same time while asking, and officers laugh also.

"No body." Immediately Dirty White Boy responded. Knowing that if he snitched, chances were he might have it coming again. One the sergeants saw that he couldn't get anything out of Dirty White, so he asked the other white boys.

"Do you know who done this?"

"No, sir. I don't."

That was the end of that conversation. When we were coming out of the chow hall, the sergeant had some of the officers to look at everyone hands to see if they were busted up.

"Hey, sergeant, I think we have him," one of the offic-ers said, while looking at my hands.

"Step aside," another officer said to me.

"No, I don't think he did it. He just got out of the hole for fighting. His hands were already busted up. Let him go," the sergeant said, and I walked out.

'That was close.' I said to myself while rubbing my very sore hands.

When I was walking across the compound, the OM posse and others were waiting on me, so they could see the outcome. Someone began to beat on a window that was in another dorm. When I got closer look, it was some of our Orange Mound homeys.

"Lowe will you beat his ass?" One of the homeys yelled out of the window to me while pointing at one of the inmates that was walking in the front of us.

I'm not going to put my hands on no one for someone else. Especially, when I don't know what it's all about. I'm not anyone's hit-man. The only one I want is the Devil, this man don't look like he has done anything. But the way they were trying to get me to beat him, he had done something.

"That's Toe to Toe, Lorenzo. Don't know one want to see him one-on-one," someone yelled out of the window.

When we were back in the dorm, I was about to wash my hands. I looked around and at the face bowl and they were so nasty, until I didn't wash my hands. I walked over to the toilet to use it and it was nasty all around it also. I wanted to snap, but I kept my cool.

Later on that night, we were sitting in my corner smoking, when one of my home boys said. "There is an inmate name Tim that won't get into the shower."

That's it, I thought to myself. Knowing that I had to live around this and stand in line with these inmates.

"Hey where is he at?" I asked. When one of my homeys showed him to me, I walked over to him, to get a look of who I was facing. It was very dark in the dorm, only night lights were on.

"That's him right there; he said no one in here can make him get in the shower," one of my home-boys said to me.

"Yep, he played ball in the gym for two days and still hasn't got in there!" another homie said.

Knowing that he was nasty, I didn't want to put my hands on him. So, I walked back to my bed and grabbed a shank that I called the monster. It was a small hand shovel with all the edges sharpened like a razor. I had four shanks in all. One was a long skinny rod with a hole in the end of it. I ran a small rope through it to tie around my hand so when I swung it, it would not slip out of my hand. I called it King Kong. I had another one; it was the third one that I would always keep with me at all times. It was a real pocket knife about six inches long. I would always wear some briefs whenever I had it on me. Because, they had pockets in the bottom of them. I called it Godzilla. The last one was an icepick. I called it the picker.

"FIGHT # 11"

Wasting no time, I walked over to his bed and put Monster in his face. I could see fear in his eyes.

"Man, you are going to get your ass into the shower!" I said while talking through my teeth.

"No! No! Lowe, put Monster back up. You will kill him with that. Let him slide. He's ok. I will talk to him," one of my older homies said, pleading with me.

I was waiting on Tim to say anything or make any kind of move. If he would have, I was going to give it to him. He didn't, so I walked off and put Monster back up. While I was doing so, Tim said to my homies, "I'll whip his ass one-on-one."

I heard it.

"Oh, it's going down!" I yelled out while running Tim's way. My homies tried to stop me by grabbling me. *But if a man really wants to fight, can't anyone stop him.*

"I'm warning you, if you touch me I'm going to knock you the fuck out!" I said to my home boys who were trying to stop me.

While Tim was still sitting on his bed talking smart at the same time, I kicked him in the face. His head and upper body went backwards on the bed. I then backed up giving him room to stand up off the bed. He stood up and came my way.

I knew then I had a fight.

By it being dark, I could hardly make out his face. But it looked as if he had horns flashing on and off of his head. At the same time, it was as if I could see my mother on her knees praying for me.

As I danced around, I gave Tim time enough to pull off his shirt, not only was he taller than me but he was also more cut and muscular than I was.

"Oh!" I let out from a cheap shot that Tim got in on me.

While brushing it off, and dancing as if I was in the ring, I saw the horns on his head again. "Yeah, the real Devil, I have finally found him," I said while looking at Tim.

Tim kept looking behind himself as if I was talking to someone else. He thought someone was going to jump him from behind. He didn't know that I was seeing him as if he was the Devil himself. I don't know if it was the statement that I made or if it was my lazy eyes that caused him to look back. But it gave me time enough to move in on the Devil with a right, left, right, left and Tim was toothless.

Now, just knowing that I was fighting the Devil, I had to come with everything that I had. While I was giving him some rib shots, I took some blows to the face that wasn't effective, at all.

One thing a real fighter must learn, and that's not to hit his opponent with a flat fist. His licks only sounded half way good. When I heard the Devil cough from the rib shots, I knew that I had cracked his ribs. Behind that it was nothing but fast lightning licks. Everyone in the dorm was hyped and yelling to the top of their voices.

"Damn, this is some TV ass shit!" Someone yelled out after seeing a good fight.

At the same time, Tim when down to the floor, as I stood over him as tall as a giant.

"I have finally got him," I said just knowing that I had downed the Devil.

Someone ran up to Tim and doused him with a cup of water in order to get him awake.

"Come on, Lowe, that's enough. Calm down. You fucked him up," one of my older homies said while pulling me away.

After that I had to go and get into the shower to wash Tim's blood off of my hands and hands. When I got out of the shower and laid back on my bed, Tim was headed to the shower with his towels.

"He said no one can make him get into the shower, I see that ass whipping made him get in there!" someone yelled out.

Behind that, everyone laugh. Before I fell off to sleep, I wondered why I saw a vision of my mother on her knees praying while I was fighting.

That very morning, when I got up to wash up and use the bathroom, the filthy smell took my breath away. It was tissue paper left on the toilet seats and floor. Also spit in the face bowls. I just couldn't take it, my mind snapped.

"Ahhhh; Fuck this shit!" I yelled out to the top of my voice.

"Orange Mound, post up at the front door!" I said giving commands.

I rushed over to my bed and got all my shanks. I put two in my waistband and one in each one of my hands I then walked over to my bed. There wasn't anyone sleeping over the top of me. I then took my shank, King Kong, and hit the empty bed with it to wake everyone up.

"Get up, you bitches; get your nasty asses up!" I yelled to the top of my voice, at the same time hitting on some of the beds where inmates were asleep.

Some of the inmates began to talk under their voices, cowardly to speak their peace. All I was trying to do was get our dorm in order but going about it in the wrong way. I guess being around convicts had taken a toll on me.

"Hey man, let me tell y'all something! Some of you need to get into the shower, you all are some nasty mother-fucker's up in here! You hoes are reaching for my cigarettes when you need to be reaching for that shower. Then what makes it so bad, you won't even clean up behind your selves!"

It was as if I stirred up a beehive. They began walking around, while some was talking in their own groups. A few inmates got their soap and towels and got into the shower. While some of them walked into the dayroom and started watching TV. I had the wrong mentality about trying to make a grown man take a shower. Little did I know, I was putting more responsibility on myself than I could bear?

While I was talking, I kept hitting the beds with King Kong giving everyone a bell ringer. It was one inmate that always bragging on himself. At the same time, he had other inmates calling him, Penitentiary. He was one of the first ones that walked into the day room, ignoring me by turning on the TV. He was also one of the one's that wasn't getting into the shower. He was my first target.

But the Devil had me so blind, till I had made it up in my mind that I was going to stick half of the inmates that were in the dorm. I walked into the dayroom and cut off the TV. The so-called Penitentiary was in the front of it watching on. Along with him were about five inmates that I had zeroed in on, who were going to be my victims that I was about to stick on.

I swung King Kong at the heads of two inmates, but they blocked the locks with their arms. The lick cut their arms. They took off running to the other side, while crying like babies.

"You around here calling yourself Penitentiary. Bitch as hoe ass boy! You don't clean your ass; how can you say you been to the pen? You never been to the Pen a day in your life, you filthy dick sucking ass boy!"

Behind me saying that, I hit one of the tables while headed Penitentiary's way.

"Lowe, bold up! Hold up, man you're going to kill somebody. Man, you won't ever get out of here; they will hide you in here!" my old school home boy said to me with a fearful look in his eyes as if he was about to cry.

"I don't give a fuck; these bitches need killing. What are you looking at, you nasty son-of-a-bitch?" I said to the so-called Penitentiary, while he was slowly making his way to the other side.

"Chow time! Chow time!" an officer yelled out while entering into the dorm stopping the uproar. Everyone ran out to the chow hall.

"Lowe put that shit up, here come an officer, the little guy that our homies were trying to get you to whip was watching you the whole time that you were cutting up. But we were watching him. It looked like he was trying to ease up on you, as if he was going to stick you," my old school homies said.

But at the same time, he was more focused on where I was putting the shanks than anything. He then walked out in a quick pace ahead of me. I put all my shanks up and walked to the chow hall.

"Lowe, old school homies was talking to the sergeant before you came in," one of my little homies told me.

When we made it back from eating, it was quiet as a church mouse. I sat on my bed looking around at the fearful faces. As soon as I was about to open the empty drawer that was at the end of my bed and start part two of my rampage, the Sergeant walked straight up to me.

He then took a pair of my boxers that was hanging on the end of my bed drying out. He saw the name Lowe on them. He opened the drawer that I had the shanks in and put my boxers on the top of the shanks.

"Who drawer is this?" he asked me.

"I don't know!" I answered.

"Well, those boxers have your name on them. Pack your shit! You're going to the hole."

"Man, that's not mine!"

"Man, I said pack your shit! Can I get some back up in B-building?" He stood there until I was done packing along with his back-up officers.

"Just look at his hands! They busted up bad as hell, and they all dislocated," an officer said, while they were taking me to the hole.

This time while in the hole a few days had passed. Later on that night, I fell off to sleep and had a dream of my mother. I could hear her voice saying to me, "Son wake up, wake up."

I couldn't see her, but I could see her hands coming out of the clouds with a Bible in them.

"Here, take this Bible; pray before you read it, and you will get help. And when you learn it, teach it to others. There is a calling on your life."

I took the Bible and behind that everything went away.

"I don't want this," I said while trying to give the Bible back. The hands came back and took the Bible out of my hands. But this time I didn't hear my mother.

"Mama, Mama," I called out to her, but I got no answer.

I then shook my head, because it seemed so real. As I was waking up, I was still shaking my head. Later on that morning, there was a cool breeze that came into the dorm. I could feel it coming up under the cell door. I could feel cool air blowing on me as if there was a window open.

It had to be death himself coming to get someone, because at the same time there was a man in one of the cells hanging himself. This all took place upstairs in E-building. They took the dead man out; where, I don't know. One of my little homies was talking out loud in the dorm telling everyone.

"Lowe is on his way out of the hole, and he is going to kill whoever snitched on him!"

Dirty White Boy thought that I thought that he was the one who snitched. So, he was looking for a way to get out. He asked the officers to put him on PC. He couldn't give them a reason, so they didn't. He began walking around asking inmates what he must do. They gave him all kind of ideas, but they did it work. Later on that night, he began to talk to the other white boy that was in the dorm. Then both of them slept in the same area and were always talking.

"Man, you have tried everything, all I could tell you know is break bad."

"What does that mean?" Dirty White asked the other white boy.

"That means, if you got some rabbit in you, and then get somewhere." The other white-boy told Dirty White.

"What? Escape?"

"Yeah, fool!"

"How?"

"I'm not for sure, but we can think of something." The other white boy said.

"I know what I can do, come on." Dirty White Boy said as he headed to his drawer. When he took the lock off his drawer, his entire commissary had been stolen. He pushed the drawer back up as if he opened the wrong one. He then opened it back up and realized that what he was seeing was real. He then put his hands on the other side of his head and said, "Oh my god." He couldn't believe what he was seeing. His box was empty.

Someone had put their hands in his drawer from the back and pulled all his commissary out.

"Man, I was going to pay someone my entire commissary to help us to escape."

"I have some, I will pay them man." The other white boy said and did so.

Dirty White was so terrified of me doing something to him, that he was willing to escape. They paid inmates to help them to stack beds on the top of each other; the beds were high enough for them to reach the skylight. They took the broom and busted it, then climbed out. From there, the inmates took the bed down and felt off to sleep. All of this was done because Dirty White thought that he was going to have to face me.

Then next time that I saw Dirty White, he was on the news being caught, and that was after I was out of the hole. I wasn't housed in the same building. I was placed in D-Building;

Someone gave me a letter that stated, "My name is Tony Spencer; I'm your brother that you have never seen. Come to church tonight, I want to meet you. My daddy name is Alonzo Spencer Jr."

In a way could say.' God has his way,'

While at church, I asked an officer that was named Officer Tony if could he help me find my brother that I never seen. He said yes. Once I gave him his name, he got on the microphone and called for him, but no one came forward.

"There is another building that has got to come in. Have a seat until they get here, then I will call for him again."

By then the preacher began to preach his message. The only seat that was available was on the front row. It was like I had to hear what this Preacher was talking about if I wanted to see my brother. When I got a close look at this preacher, it was as if I was looking at myself. This man looked just like me, but if I was about 20 years older. It was like me talking to me.

Then at the same time, his message was, "You can run, but you can't hide." The preacher sat and was looking directly at me. I tried to look back to ignore him by looking over my shoulder for my brother, but it didn't work. It was like God had me locked head straight forward to the seat. I couldn't turn if I wanted to.

"Some of you shouldn't be alive, but because of your mother's prayer, God has allowed you to be here. You have been running long enough. It's like you're running without legs. You keep running and falling. Every time you get up

God has a way of knocking you right back down. When some of you were in the free world, you didn't have time to go to church and hear the Word of God. You were like Jonah, called himself running from God. Jonah ran, but he couldn't hide. You can't hide from God, so stop running. Some of you ran in here, because you know you need God. Well let me be the first to tell you, don't stop. Keep coming, and he will see you through. But for you who trying to run from God, you need to stop. The word said, 'Resist the devil and he will flee.' Run from the devil, stop looking for Satan and start searching for the Lord. You need to surrender before your time is up. You need to stop running from Him and start running with God. He will show you that one makes a difference. When you do find the Lord, don't give up the fight, fight to the end."

It was as if my mind was somewhere else. At the same time, I was trying to hear the preacher.

"God is trying to tell you something. You are too busy running and doing everything but the right thing. You are looking for God in all of the wrong places. While you are rejecting the Bible and reading other books, you need to pick up the Bible and read it. You probably can whip man, but your arms are too short to box with God," the Preacher said, while looking directly at me, and then he walked out.

This was one of the scariest days of my life. This preacher didn't know me and had never seen me. I could hear God tell me I had to make up my mind now.

"Lowe. Lowe. Your brother is in my office," Officer Tony said, calling me twice to get my attention, because I was shocked not only from hearing the Word of God but looking at myself preaching to myself.

This was my first night out of the hole, and it was like I had seen my whole life flash before me in 30 minutes.

While we were in Officer Tony's office, my brother and I were so glad to see each other. We hugged and talked about how he looked just like one of my other brother and daddy.

"I knew he was your brother when I first saw him. You look just alike," Office Tony said while also stating that it couldn't be a better place to meet than in the church.

My brother, Tony, gave me our sister's phone number while saying, 'This is your sister's number. I have told her about you, and she said call her." Her name is Marie. When I made it back to the dorm, I called her, and we had a long talk.

When I got off the phone and walked over to the TV, I saw an inmate that I hadn't seen since he was a little boy. It was one of my brother-in laws. His name is Rell. He began talking to me about an inmate that was hogging the phone.

"That's him on the phone now; he has been on there all day and won't let anyone get it," Rell said with a sad look on his face. There were three phones in the dorm but one of them was out of order.

"Before he came in here I was getting on the phone at 8 o'clock. Now I can hardly get the phone," Rell told me.

"Look, brother-in-law, I'm going to get you on the phone at 8 o'clock, and I'm going get the time that I have got for every dorm that I go in."

"What time is that, Lowe?"

"That's 10 till 11," I said to Rell with confidence.

We began to watch the news, and this time they were showing the other white boy, Little Tommy and Dirty White Boy getting into a police car. I told him about everything that happened in the building that I came from.

After that, it was time to get the phone from the phone hog. I really want to talk to my sister also.

"FIGHT#12"

"What's his name?" I asked Rell while walking up to him.

'They call him Lee." I then walked up to Lee asking him, "Hey, look bro, I need that phone!"

"Ok, I will be off in a minute," Lee said and turned his head. After about five-minute passed by, I was out of patience with this disrespectful man.

"Lee! Come on down, phone check!" I said, in a high-pitched voice.

"Hold on!"

"Hold my ass! Hoe get your ass off the phone!"

Behind me saying that, Lee still didn't hang up the phone. He left the phone hanging and walked to the other side. I then walked up to the phone and hung it up in Lee's party's face.''

"Rell, get the phone. Bum that joint for about two hours. Here, call my sister." I gave Rell Marie's number, but her daughter, Vickie, answered, and they talked. When Lee walked back into the dayroom, I did waste any time when I notice he had put his shoes on.

"Come on in here you motherfucker. I have hung up the phone, now I'm going to hang up your ass! When tell you to drop that phone off, you do what I tell you. Now I'm going to make it rain down body pieces!" I yelled out to Lee while walking out into the middle of the floor and dancing.

This man was every bit of 6 '4" tall, so I rushed in on him with about four blows to his face. When I backed up and looked around, we were surrounded by inmates who were looking on. Lee shook my blows off, but at the same time he kept backing off. Little did he know that gave him an advantage; I knew I had to stay up on him because he was tall, but that's all. I made another move in on him and took two licks to my face. But me, myself, I could accept it better than I could dish it.

But I could dish it damn good.

"Oh boy, you got some fight in you," I said while setting up my next target. "I'm going to make a bitch out of you. I'm going to make you put your thumb in your booty and bounce on it!"

After I said that, I realized I had him in a corner, and I made my move. He tried to come out, but I just wasn't going. I went in on him like white on rice. God knows I put a combination on him that too many men wouldn't have taken. He almost went down, but almost wasn't good enough. He was getting a few licks in on me, but it was like I couldn't feel them.

But for some reason, he kept letting me in on him and I had it made up in my mind, this time I was going to knock him out. I ran in on him with everything that I had. From there I just knew it was over when I saw Lee go down like a melted candle. He laid there for a good minute.

"Lee, Lee, get up!" Someone tried to wake him up.

"Is he dead?" Someone then threw water on him.

When he got up, he spent around in a circle as if he was looking for me. I was still standing in his face. Everyone started laughing. In a bloody mess, he rushed out of the dayroom as if he was running crazy.

"Lowe, your niece is on the phone!" Rell yelled out to me. I got on the phone and talked to my niece that I never seen.

"I have got to let you go!" I told her after Rell yelled out.

"Lowe, he's coming back!"

Lee ran up to me with about four bars of soap in a sock and swung it at me. By me dodging, it missed me. He swung the second time, aiming for my head. I threw up my four-arm and blocked it. When I did, the sock busted, and soap flew in the air. I then bomb-rushed him again with a quick open can of a double six-pack, with follow up of five blows to Lee's ribs.

The only thing he got out of that round was more blood running down his face. I got a knot on my arm from blocking the soap from hitting me in the head. He took off running again to the sleeping dorm.

This convict was like Chucky, he just kept coming,

"Come on you motherfucker. You got to be the Devil, you won't die. I'm going to kill you this time!" I told him while he was sizing me up with three ink pens in his hand.

After he swung at me about five times, I made my mind up. I wasn't going to kill him with my hands. I pulled out a close friend of mind, my six-inch pocket knife that I kept in my briefs.

While I was reaching into my briefs, Lee made a move on me, sticking me in the right side with the ink pins. After doing so, the pens broke into pieces. By then I was coming his way, moving in for the kill. I made it in on him with his back in a comer and gave him two sticks to his side.

"Oh! Woo!" he yelled out.

"Lowe, don't kill him. Drop the knife and kick it to Rell."

I had him posted up in the corner again were he could not get out. Not only was he bloody, but my arms were bloody from his blood.

"So, you Lucifer, huh, tell me," I asked him, but he wouldn't answer me. I was now posted up on defense trying to slick get some rest.

"Lowe, do that boy!" Rell said to me looking like a dark and older version of my nephew, Hump. I never feared this man at all I smiled, but he didn't. He had more wind than I did. He just wouldn't give up. I made it up in my mind; I was going to take him out with my bare hands.

I got back in on him, giving him some of the same thing that I gave the others and more. 'Fight to the end.'

I could hear the preacher's voice. This time he tried his best to fight back, but his best wasn't good enough. I was like thunder and lightning on him with some powerful licks.

Where I got the power and wind, I don't know. It was almost like someone was fighting for me. He hit the floor but some kind of way he got up and ran to the other side.

Only this time, I was on his heels.

The worst thing that you can do while you are fighting is run from your opponent.

By Lee running, he gave me all the advantage that I needed to do whatever I wanted. When I caught him, he was almost between two beds, at the same time, the crowd followed on. I could feel a small burn in my side, knowing that this guy stuck me, which only made me more upset about that then I was about the phone.

I could hear something in the back of my head saying, 'I'm going to catch a murder charge.' I grabbed him and pulled him to me. At the same time, I hit him in the side about five times. I then turned him around and went to work. I gave him more licks then it took to lick a Lollipop.

The inmates were fascinated; they must have gone wild. I then had him in a bent over position with his head locked in one of my hands. While I was beating him with my right fist, he took a big deep bite into my left arm. At the same time, he had a hold of my nut-sack, and I couldn't shake him a loose.

"Ohhh," I yelled out in pain, "if you don't let me go, I'm going to bite your ear off!"

I continued, and at the same time hitting him in the face. But every time I would hit him, he would bite deeper into my arm. He still didn't let go and believe me; I had his ear in my mouth, pulling if off his head.

When it came off he blanked out and hit the floor. I then spit his ear on him while saying, "About time, I have finally got him."

The inmates were on the loudest up roar I have ever heard since my incarceration. This was the longest and deadliest fight I had ever been in, in my life. We started fighting at 8 pm and fought until the officers came in to do their 10 o'clock count at 10:30.

When a lady sergeant came in to do a count, she saw me standing over Lee with his blood all over me. I was also bleeding from my arm and a little from the ink-pen holes. She called for backup, and Sergeant Holmes came in. She could tell that I was willing to go without resisting. So, she grabbed me by the arm and escorted me out to medical.

On our way out, I was so thirsty. "Can I have some water?" I asked her, and she let me drink.

When I was done, "Are you ok?" she asked me.

"Yes, I'm all right," I responded with a smile on my face still thinking that I had killed the Devil himself.

Sgt. Homes walked out of the dorm before we left the building and said, "We are going to need an ambulance. That man is fucked up in there!"

While in I-building medical, the paramedics were taking Lee out on a stretcher. I got a good look at the job I did. He was in such of a mess. They had his whole head wrapped up, and I could see blood coming through the bandages. I then really thought that he was dead, until he rose up and said, "It's not over," before passing right back out.

"It looks like it's over to me!" Sergeant Homes said, and they laughed.

When I was done in medical, I was taken right back to the cage, Administrative Segregation lock down. This time in the hole, I didn't dream about my mother. Out of the hole, 30 days that I had to do, I dreamt about my grandmother and my nephew, Hump. In the dream, God was showing me that they were in Heaven. I saw their faces on the clouds.

Weeks later, "Sign here," the lawyer said.

I was so hurt from hearing that. After, I was done getting my time in court. I was told that I had to go to the big house and from there to the Federal Pen. Not only that, I still had a pending charge. So, I had to come back to 201 and back to S.C.C.C.

That night while I was lying on my bed, my mind began to reflect on what the preacher was saying. It was like he was in the cell with me. No matter what way I turned in the bed, I could hear his voice as if he was in the cell with me. It was clear as day, telling me to stop running from God. But I wasn't trying to hear it.

CHAPTER 10:
FORT PILLOW

While getting off the bus at Fort Pillow, on our way to intake, convicts were mugging us as if they had beef with all of us.

"What's up with these boys, why are they looking at us like that with their dog on their face?" I asked One Day.

"Ah, you're all good, home boy. That's just a part of a prison mentality of acting tougher than you are. Then again, some have a bone to pick with each other."

While in intake, the convicts that work in intake were checking us in. They already knew everyone's charges. They knew who we were before we got there. Some of the same so-called staff members that were cutting up at 201 were looking so afraid. They were looking as if the world was about to end. They must have known it was time to reap what they had sown. They were shaking like a leaf on a tree. One of them was shaking so bad until he was dropping his property.

"Boy, I hope your hole is deep, because there is going to be a lot of pipe-laying in your ass," a convict named Larry stated to an inmate who rolled in with us. His name was Chester, and he had a double-rape charge. One of his charges was on a 12-year-old-girl. The little girl's uncle was locked up in Fort Pillow. There were other inmates that were told, "You better watch your backs."

This was told to the inmates who were cutting up when they were at 201.

"For all of you tough motherfuckers that was riding on folks downtown. Don't think any of you got away with that shit. Every dog has his day. There's a hit out on all of you hoes. You got by, but you won't get away," Larry said, and then called all of them out by their names.

"And if that's not good enough, I'll tell you where you and your mammy stay. Oh Lowe, your cousin, Big Ike, said what's up. He's doing time out here."

"That's what's up. If you see his tell him to come to see me," I said.

"Ok, I will," he said to me before turning his attention. "Back to you, buster. I have 100 years to do. I have me a boy in my cell, so I don't need you. Some of you sugar hoe's never been tampered with. You are like virgins never been touched. They're going to put a dress on you and make boys out of you."

After that saying, it was really quiet.

There were about four inmates that he was talking about besides Chester. They were some of the most lowdown and violent convicts that had come through 201. *Or you could say,* through the dirty south. Now, they are not making a sound. So soon things changed, and the tables turned.

We were giving a pouch with tobacco in it along with our indigent packs. I was housed in B-3 and was given a job working making license plates. This wasn't like other institutes. Convicts were getting their money as if they were on the street, in all kind of ways.

This was a world with in a world.

While in B-3 housing, there was so much animosity in the air until you could almost see it. Not only that, but convicts were looking at each other like they were killing with their eyes.

A few convicts that had been waiting on their enemy to arrive were walking around like a ticking time bomb waiting to go off.

I was bypassing Larry's cell.

"Lowe, Big Ike been here looking for you. He said he will be back in about an hour."

"Ok, Larry, thanks a lot. King, is that you?" I asked.

"Yeah, what's up?" He responded in a shameful way.

"Take that base out of your voice and tell Lowe your new name!" Larry said, while giving King a slap upside his head. In a ladylike voice King said, "Queen," and turned back around washing clothes.

From there I kept walking around with my hand over my mouth, trying not to laugh. The next day while out on yard, One Day, and I were sitting on a bench that was close by the gate. I rolled up my tobacco before I came out.

One Day was rolling his while we were talking.

"Look! A Deer;" I yelled out.

Besides in the zoo, this was my first time seeing one up close. The deer was standing up on his back legs, hitting on the gate like he was knocking trying to get in. All of a sudden, the gate open and the deer that they called Buck came running in. He ran straight up to One Day and stood up on his back legs.

I turned and looked to see a hand full of inmates were looking on with smiles on their faces. I then got up and stood with the in crowd while looking on. One Day and Buck were reaching for One Day's tobacco pouch at the same time. This deer was known on the compound. He could smell the tobacco a half of a mile away and would fight for it.

As One Day grabbed the tobacco and headed our way, we had to move a distance off. While One Day was running, he looked back only to see Buck on his back.

"Aghhh somebody help me!" he yelled, but no one came to his rescue.

Buck swung and knocked One Day down to the ground. One Day stood up and the deer stood upright with him. The both of them begin to box each other as if they were in a ring.

Buck stood up on his hind legs in One Day's face and boxed him like he was a man. One Day still had his tobacco in his hand while he was going down to the ground. Buck then took the tobacco out of One Day's hand and began to eat, while he had one of his legs holding One Day down on the ground.

"Damn that's all you wanted. I would have given you that shit if that what it took from getting my ass kicked by a Deer!" One Day said while rubbing Buck on the bead.

From that day forward, One Day was the only one that Buck would let get close to him, besides a lady that would feed Buck tobacco from out of her breast.

On the next day, while back in B-3, I was walking past Chester while, he was sitting on his bed.

"I have got to find a way out. They are going to kill me," he was saying to himself out loud. I was about to say something to him, because I thought he was talking to me. He sat there with a fearful look on his face, like he knew that he was going to die.

"Come on, Chester. It's time to go to work," an officer said as he walked in to gather the workers.

"Yes, Sir" Chester said as he slowly walked out.

While Chester was on a work line cleaning up around the compound, he saw his chance to get away, and he took it.

While they were picking up paper off the yard near the front gate, it opened so that a lady could come in. Everyone's eyes were so focused on her that if the other inmates weren't looking they all could have all gotten away.

Chester was bent over near the opening, picking up paper. When the woman walked past the officers, their heads turned. At that moment, Chester took off running like a rabbit, running and jumping. The officers didn't see him until all officers were alerted on their walkie-talkies; they took off running behind him like flies. One officer had a hound dog that they called Roscoe. Every time that Roscoe would catch someone that was trying to run, the Warden would give him a gold tooth. This was the quickest catch that Roscoe ever made. Chester was the cause of Roscoe getting another gold tooth. Chester was taken to the hole and given 30 days for and an attempt to escape.

While hack in B-3, there was two beat downs on the way. Before they started, Larry and Uncle Joe were the overseers' over them all. They had about ten convicts working with them in all. The main hit-man that they had to lead their crew was the Birdman. He now had jumped on the other side to keep himself from getting killed.

OG and Tedd were now cell mates. While Tedd was standing up at the face bowl washing his clothes, he was listening to the radio with his head phones on. OG was laid back on his bed looking out of the cell door as if he knew that something was about to happen.

"Put your radio on playing the 'Big Payback by James!" Tedd said to OG.

Larry and Uncle Joe would pay an inmate named Sharkey to turn his radio up real loud. So, whenever they would get ready to kill or beat someone, the officers couldn't hear it. All anyone could hear was the song 'The Big Payback,' while Sharkey was doing his dance called the James Brown.

Barse was also in his cell. He must have known that his enemies were coming. He put baby oil all over his body and was prepared. He was standing up in his cell when five convicts came in on him. He was posted up with his back up against the wall throwing hay-makers trying to defend himself. But they were too deep for him, and he couldn't hold up. They threw baby powder on him to dry up the baby oil. *Things weren't slipper anymore.*

"Bbbbbblllleeppp, Bbblliippp!" The Birdman ran in and began his sticking with an ice pick, as if he was picking ice.

From the beat down and the sticking, all Barse could do was lay still and lifeless as if he was dead. Only God knows how he survived.

Regarding the beating of OG and Tedd, they couldn't hear it coming because of the plugs in their ears. OG was now lying flat on his back looking up at the ceiling.

While Tedd was still washing clothes, the crew moved in on them with shanks, beating and sticking them every bit of a hundred times. After they were bloody as a hog... "Bbbbbiippphh," that funny sound that the Birdman made was audible again.

He went in for the final sticking. When he came out he had so much blood on him, it looked like he had been stuck.

Tedd was killed, but some kind of way OG made it through. After the blood bath, the compound remained on lock down for about 30 days.

A week after we were off lock down, things heated right back up. However, after seeing the bloodiest murder and beat down I had ever witnessed, I didn't want to fight anymore. I was done looking for Satan and ready to go home.

But I had a long road ahead of me.

Once Chester was released out of the hole, he didn't waste any time. In a fast pace, he headed to the captain's office. A Lieutenant was also present.

"Hey, don't you just bust in my office like that!" the captain said to Chester as he entered into his office without knocking.

"Will you please, please, put me in protective custody? If you don't, they will kill me!"

"Who will kill you?" the Lieutenant responded.

"They will!"

"Who is *they*? You have to give us a name and a reason!" the captain said.

"If you don't give us a reason then we can't put you in PC!" the Lieutenant said.

"I don't have a name, and I don't know the reason. All I know is they are going to kill me!"

"Where are you housed?" the lieutenant asked.

"B-3. They put me back in B-3!"

"Well, you go on to your house, and we will be over there to look things over," the lieutenant said while almost forcing Chester out.

After Chester was out of the door, the captain said, "Maybe, we need to look into this matter. You know that's probably the reason that he tried to escape."

"Maybe, but we can't just put someone in protective custody every time that they want to go," the lieutenant said, as if he wasn't concerned.

"He's doing time on some rape charge, and one of them was on a little girl," the Captain said.

"Oh, he will be alright," the Lieutenant said and walked out with a sneaky look on his face like he knew what was going to happen.

Later on that night, Chester sat up in his bed and stayed awake long as he could. At the same time, Mike, the guy that had raped the inmates in 201, was in the shower.

As soon as Chester fell off asleep, the watch-out man for Larry and Uncle Joe began to make his move. He gathered everyone up, half were with Larry and the other half were with Uncle Joe. This was another one of their double hits.

"Sharkey, turn your radio on, and up loud," the watch man said.

Sharkey started dancing and everyone made their move. That same old song was playing by James Brown, 'Big Payback.'

Chester must have been dreaming about some of the little girls that he had raped. It must have been the rape he had done that we saw on the news, where the little girl gave a testimony that Chester chased her into the woods, and she was pleaded for him to stop, but he continually molesting her.

Chester's cell mate was pretending like he was asleep. As soon as he heard Chester snoring, he got up and gave them the cue to move in after he walked out.

As the Big Pay Back played on the radio, the other half went to work in the shower on Mike.

"Bliiip;" Birdman was about to make his funny sound.

"Shut up, you crazy mother fucker," Larry said, stopping Birdman while they moved in.

It was as if everyone wanted in on the tall giant. They all had locks in socks but two. Two had pocket knives. When they went in on Mike, he tried to fight back, but he didn't stand a chance.

While in Chester's cell, someone put a pillow over his face so that his hollering couldn't be heard. The five went in to beat him with locks in the socks while Uncle Joe would never know and then stuck him with a shank.

Uncle Joe had a broken broom in one of his hands, but never used it. Back in the shower, the blood was running out of Mike from all directions. After Mike was laid out with no movement in his body, Larry pulled out his manhood, and entered it into Mike's back-hole.

"Yell, how does it feel now you piece of shit. Does it hurt, because it feels good to me?" Larry said while pumping into Mike.

"He must have dropped his soap, I want some of that!" another one said.

After Chester was beaten to death, Uncle Joe took the piece of broken broom that he had and forced it deep into Chester's back-hole.

When it was all over, the captain and the lieutenant walked in. Chester's cellmate told the captain that he saw Birdman coming out of their cell with a shank in his hand.

"He also had blood all over him."

When the captain and officer are walked into Birdman's cell, he was lying under his covers on his back. He had blood all over him, and the shank still in his hand, when they pulled the covers from over him.

"Bbbblliiippppippp!" he said while laughing.

"Bird, give me that shank," the Lieutenant asked him afraid, while putting gloves on his hands.

Bird gave up the shank with no problem.

"I didn't do it; I didn't do anything!" Bird said while he was being cuffed and taken out.

"We'll see you, Bird!" the crew said.

"Bbbiiillpppp;" Bird said and it was over for him.

"He must have gone on a killing spree, because some-one is laid out in the shower!" Chester's cell mate said with a lying look on his face, while putting everything on the Birdman.

While in the shower, the captain asked, "Is he dead too?"

"No, get the paramedics in here. He is still alive!" the lieutenant said, while checking Mike's pulse for a beat.

"We need to put Bird in mental health, that fool has gone crazy," the Lieutenant said, knowing that Bird didn't do all of this blood bath himself.

I hadn't seen that much blood being shed in my life. I see now, Satan doesn't come alone. When he comes, he has demons with him. After seeing this it made me not want to look for Satan any longer. Although I have never raped anyone, I thought to myself, *it could have been me lying out dead.*

After these two incidents, Administration locked down the whole compound for two months, then put us under investigation. Behind that, things slowed down for a while.

Before I left, the only big thing that happened was the two white boys escaped. We were then back on lock down for about two weeks. When it was all over, I was extradited to the Feds.

CHAPTER 11:
I'M NOT A HITMAN

While being extradited to Mason, TN to be sentenced on two Federal charges. Riding on long back roads, I began to get paranoid. I thought that the two Federal Marshals were mafia sent to take me somewhere to kill me. The whole time that we were on the road, it was very quiet. When we pulled into the institute, I was relieved.

While I was being processed into intake, I looked up and saw a sign that read, ' If you have a friend, why do ten! At that time, I didn't understand what it meant so I over-looked it. Doing time began to change my lifestyle. I began to fall back and wise up a bit. But at the same time, I began to move faster in other ways.

I was housed in H-unit, and there was a lady officer, for some reason, who dug my style. When she first came on, she would let me out to clean up. Then, she would talk to me all night long. One day she saw me play basketball, and she was very impressed. She began to talk to me about how she always wanted to be a cheerleader when she was in high school. She got down on the floor and did a split, trying to impress me. That was something exciting for a man who had been locked up. It was like she opened the door for me, and quickly I stepped in.

"Help me up!" she said while trying to get up out of a split.

I grabbed her arm and pulled her up. While she was coming up off the floor, she was close to my face. Things got little heated, and I could tell that she had some liking for me. But all I wanted out of her, being locked up, was something that every other convict wanted, and that was sex.

But I knew I had to wait till the right time. Not too many things happened while I was at CCA. I found out, right before I came in, North Carolina and the DC boys had a riot and cut up.

One night I was laid back on my bed when someone knocked at the door.

"Come in" I said.

"What's up Lowe?" One of my home boys that I had heard a lot about walked into my cell. We didn't know each other at all. This was my first time seeing him in my life.

"May I help you?" I asked

"Yeah, I'm going to get right down to the point. I know that you don't know me, but my name is Donny. Some of our home boys have told me how good you can fight. I don't want any problems," he said as I rose up off my bed, because he mentioned the word *fight*.

"It's a boy in here from another country, and he crossed me out. Here, this is a lock and a sock. If you take him out for good, I will pay you big time. He's in cell 13 down stairs."

"Man look, I'm NOT A HIT MAN, and furthermore, I don't know you. I don't have anything to do with that. You have got to work that out yourself," I said while almost forcing him out of my cell.

After that I laid, back down on my bed and fell off to sleep. The next day, my brother, Cleveland, and his wife, Peaches, bought my mother to visit me.

My mother was looking so good and doing fine. I was glad to see them all, and this was one of the happiest days of my prison time. My mother was also so glad to see me all she could do was smile, and what a beautiful smile she has.

We had a long talk about the good old days. I told her that I went to church and got a chance to meet my brother, Tony. I also told her that the Preacher told me to stop running from God.

She asked me was I going to stop, and I told her yes.

When the visit was over with I felt so good just to see my mother, I had a smile on my face that whole day. My family left me some money on the books; I was lying on my top bed looking at it.

At the same time, I was glad that I had money on my books. My cellmate was lying on his bed listening to his radio. I dropped my money receipt down on his bed on purpose. I call myself trying to get him to see that I had money on my books. The first time I dropped it, he gave it right back to me without looking at it.

The second time that I dropped it he looked at it while saying. "Man, you don't have to flog with me." He then got up and got one of his money receipts while continuing. "Look, I have over $500,000.00 on my books."

I really was doing it, because I wanted to get something to eat from him. But behind that embarrassment I laid down and fell off to sleep.

There were white-collar crime inmates that were in here with money long as a choo-choo train. I felt one foot tall.

While my cell mate was down stairs watching TV, about four of my home boys came back into my cell. I thought that they were coming to jump me.

Once I let them all in, "Look, Lowe, I was told that you can beat a man to death with your bare hands. If you do what I asked you, I will put 10,000.00 on your books today," Donny said with a serious look on his face.

"Yeah man, we will look out for you; I know that you can do it. I have seen you fight. You're toe to toe Lowe; you're flat foot jacking!" Another one of them said.

"Look man, I have told you once, y'all can get the hell up out of my cell. I'm not a damn HITMAN!"

Behind that, they all rushed out, and I had no more problems with them asking me again. Afterward, another one of my home boys knocked at my cell door.

"What in the hell do you want?"

I opened the door and he said, "Bro, I just want to talk to you about teaching me how to fight."

"Man, look, I'm not fighting for no one, and I'm not teaching no one how to fight. Y'all can stay the fuck up off my door!" I yelled out while Terry was shaking in his pants.

"Well look, can I just holler at you."

"Yeah, come on in," I said, and we began to converse.

"Look, uh what's your name?"

"Lowe." I said, while shaking Terry's reached out hand

"Lowe, don't let them play you out of pocket. That boy they are trying to get you to kill, he ratted them out, 5-K-l on them, if you know what I mean."

"No what does 5-K-l mean?"

"It means to snitch on someone, or turn someone in. All of them are charge partners, and Terry sold all of them out."

"Man, I would have to be the craziest man in the world to do something like that."

"Yeah, Lowe, if you kill him you won't ever get out. That's would be stupid, because you would catch a charge on a federal inmate."

After that conversation, Terry and I became very close. While talking we found out that we grew up on the same street. I also found out that his brother, Bull, was the guy that my brother, Cleveland, whipped back in 1969.

My brother was being toted around the hood while everyone cheered him on. One day, we were outside, and I called myself singing. An inmate heard me and asked if I would sing with them in Washington DC and North Carolina at a GED Graduation. Two other brothers along with him talked me into it, and I did so.

It was recorder and put on film. I was told if I wanted, I could come back up there when I got out to get a copy of me singing.

From hearing the time that the homies were getting, I began to get butterflies. I didn't know what I was facing, so I took my mother's advice and went to church.

The preacher preached a good message that was called, 'STAY IN THE SHIP.' There were a lot of things that I didn't understand. But I understood some of the same words that my mother told me. And that was, I will have some cloudy days, some rainy days, and some dark days, but *Stay in the Ship*.

After the service was over, they talked me into coming forward and singing. I sang a song that I wrote called *It's A God Up Yonder!* I realize I was singing about someone that I didn't even know, but at the same time the words also touched me. It was as if a change started to come over me slowly. It was as if I didn't write the song, and God was trying to tell me something through the song.

But I was hearing and wasn't hearing.

About a month later, I saw one of the funniest things that I had seen in a while. It was an inmate that looked like Chong, from the actors, Cheech and Chong. Not only did they look alike, but they also talked a like.

There was a poker game going on, and they were playing for $100 a game. Chong wanted to play but didn't know how. Everyone wanted him to play, because they knew that he had a lot of money. They didn't waste any time on teaching him how to play.

Within ten minutes, Chong was playing while talking really slow with big eyeglasses on his face. At the same time, you could see smirks one everyone else's face, because they knew that they were about to win some easy money. They must have played for about two days in a row.

When I woke up the next morning, I heard Chong on the phone making a call to Jerusalem. The way that he talked was so funny.

"Honey, honey, I need more money now right away," Chong said to his wife over the phone. Everyone laughed behind that phone conversation. He was their duck and they did pluck for $10,000.00.

After that we played some softball and some basketball games. Behind that I was sentenced and was waiting to be extradited.

I was awakened out of my sleep early one morning and put in shackles.

From there, I was taken to Millington Naval Base. When I got off the van, I was surrounded by Federal Officers with all kinds of guns. We were put on an airplane that had a hole in the wing. This was a plane that was confiscated in a drug bust.

Once we were about 24,000 feet in the air and had been flying about two hours, the plane began to make some weird sounds.

I was sitting in a window seat where I could see over the wing. There was a door in front of the seat where I was sitting. There was a lady lieutenant standing in the front of my seat wearing a parachute.

When I looked around all of the officers had on parachutes. All of a sudden, the plane shut off and it made a funny noise. Everyone got very silent, and the captain made an announcement.

'This is your captain speaking, brace for emergency landing. If this plane crashes and you survive, you will get time served!"

Immediately after that announcement, I wasn't worry about an oxygen mask or anything. I was zeroed in on the lady that was standing in the front of me. All though I was shackles, I place myself in a jumping position. I was going to jump on her like a pit-bull, and lock to her with my claws, legs and teeth. I had it made up in my mind; she wasn't going out that door without me. I was going to be on her back. I also was going to be the one that pulled the string on the parachute.

For some reason, it flashed across my mind when my brother, Calvin, and I were in his car. We were sliding down a steep ice bank headed into a large icy creek. Calvin yelled out loud, 'Jesus!' and the car stopped in its tracks. He then put the car in reverse and backed it up.

"Jesus!" I yelled out, and the plane came back on.

After that, we made a safe emergency landing in Atlanta, Georgia. We stayed there for about a week until the plane was repaired. From there, we took back off flying to

Oklahoma. While pulling in, I had never seen so much barbed wire around an institution in my life.

When we were taken in and done with classification, I was housed on the 3rd level. Once some of the inmates found out that l was from Memphis, they wanted to know about 201 and the 1991 riot.

"We heard a lot about 201 on TV, but you have been there. I know that you can give it straight from the horse's mouth," one of the inmates said.

I told them a lot about the riot down to the end, and they all were very impressed.

"Clothes exchange! Clothes exchange!" an officer yelled out, and we all lined up.

While we were in the laundry building changing clothes, one of the inmates said, "Look, there is John Gotti!"

I couldn't believe my eyes. He was standing there before me. A man whom not only the world, but gangsters, drug dealers, rappers and the Mob looked up to. It was the real John Gotti, and he had bodyguards standing on each side of him. They both were inmates as well and were very tall.

"What's up, Mr. Gotti?" I said, while walking up to him with my hand out for him to shake it.

"What in the hell you think you are doing?" One of the 'Italian stallion' looking bodyguards said to me while holding his hand out for me to stop. Immediately, he came between Gotti and me.

"It's ok; it's alright." Gotti said, and the big guy backed off. I shook Gotti's hand and the other bodyguard gave me my clothes.

"It was nice to meet you." I said to Gotti and walked out.

When I made it back to my cell, there was a convict in my cell from Memphis. His name was CJ. He was tall, laid back and cool. That's why they called him AC-CJ.

While in the middle of our conversation I was still excited about seeing Gotti.

"Guess what, man," I said.

"What?" CJ responded back to me.

"I just saw Gotti in the laundry room, and he shook my hand."

"YOU lying!!!

"I'm not lying, he's down there now."

Before I could end my conversation, CJ took off in a sprint, headed to the laundry building. Moments later, one of the men that was asking me about Memphis came back into my cell. He had five brothers and all of them were known as heavy drug dealers. He told me that he would like to move to Memphis and start a new life. I told him, "Memphis is a good place to live as long as you stay out of the hood."

"Memphis." He called me.

"Don't call me Memphis, my name is Lowe."

"Well, Lowe, you want some pussy?"

"What the fuck are you talking about?" I responded in an aggressive way, while looking at him as if he was a pussy.

"No, no, I'm talking about some real pussy!"

"Where," I asked, and he began to tell me about a lady counselor, that one of his brothers hipped, him to. After he was done giving me the rundown, he told me to walk with him to chow. He then walked out while CJ was walking back in.

"Man, you got me clotheslined!" CJ told me, while rubbing his neck with one hand and holding his back with the other.

"What you mean, I got you clotheslined?" I asked.

"You were right. I saw John Gotti, but you didn't tell me he had two bodyguards. I ran up to him and one of his bodyguards clotheslined me."

"Man, you shouldn't have run up to him," I said laughing at CJ.

After that we talked until it was chow time. Once we were done eating chow, the man that I called Texas that was from Texas, told me to walk back with him. I did just that and we lagged behind a bit.

I just knew that we were about to get in trouble. This would have been a write up for being out of place. We walked into one of the units where mostly counselors' offices were.

Once we entered the building, her office was near the entrance door. When we walked up to her door, she was sitting behind her desk, looking over some paperwork.

"Don't come in yet, I will go first and when I'm done, you do the same thing that I do. Look out for me, and I will look out for you," Texas said to me then walked up on the lady while pulling his manhood out.

"Oh no, oh what are you doing?" she said with a shivering voice. But at the same time, she was participating. Texas pulled up her dress, and she had no under clothes on. For some reason she kept saying, "Oh, oh, what are you doing." While at the same time she was bent over while Texas entered his manhood in her from the back.

I couldn't take just standing there looking on. I walked in and put my manhood in her mouth, and at the same time it stopped her from saying, "Oh, oh what are you doing."

Before I could release my load, Texas was done and began to look out.

Once I was done, and she swallowed all that I released. She just laid there with her legs open trying to get me to come inside of her. There wasn't any way I was going.

I had never been the kind of man that went behind sloppy seconds. She was still rolling her body as if someone was still on the top of her, at the same time licking her lips with her tongue, while playing with her womanhood. Although, my manhood was still hard as a steel pole, I wasn't going.

"Is someone else out there?" The counselor asked while still in heat.

I looked at her with a look on my face letting her know that she was nasty.

"You want some of this good pussy?" she asked me.

"No. I'm good."

Before she could say another word, we walked out quickly.

The next day, "Put your Jordan's on, it's time to ball," CJ said to me while I was lying back on my bed reminiscing on my family.

While in the gym, it was more of a crowd than I expected. Before the game began, we were warming up doing some shoot arounds.

"Lowe, why didn't tell me you could jump that damn high? If you jump any higher you're going to get an escape charge," CJ complimented me after he saw me pull down a rebound to shoot for a team.

After I hit, I picked three other Memphians along with CJ and myself to run a five-man whole court.

The other team had players from different states. They were also bigger and taller than us, but it made no difference. Our team was from Memphis, and we shined.

I ran point, and CJ stood tall at the center. When it was all over the crowd applauded us, and it was a good feeling.

"This that Memphis shit," I yelled out to the crowd as our team walked out.

After we were done taking showers, it was chow time. We ate some of the best food that a convict could eat while in the penitentiary. On the dinner tray was a whole deep-fried chicken along with side dish and dessert.

We sat and ate like we were in a restaurant. That next morning, I got my tray and sat down to eat, I had everything that I wasn't getting at home anymore more. After I took my first bite, two officers walked up to me.

"Your time is up, get up!" One of the very big and tall officers said to me in a heavy voice.

"Sir, I just sat down!" I replied.

"I said get up now!" an officer yelled back. After being disrespected, I sat there and continued to eat as if I didn't hear them.

This food is too good to give up, and besides, I'm at breakfast man, I thought to myself.

"Man, you all got life fucked up, I'm going to eat. You'll better not put your hands on me!" I said while still eating.

The officers didn't waste any time on calling for back up. Before I knew anything, I was surrounded by ten officers. One of the officers was holding a camera pointed directly at me.

"We will ask you one more time to get up."

"Man, y'all ain't shit. Y'all some weak ass boy scouts!" After saying my piece, I stood up and was cuffed. All of the officers escorted me to a room, three sides of it was glass. I was stripped of all my clothes.

An officer walked up to the window, looked at me and stated, "Oh, we have a tough guy." All of the officers were white.

"Your mammie is tough! What in the hell are you looking at, Bitch ass boy? Cum licking ass, dick eating ass dog!" I yelled out in anger.

I knew I was in the mud, and it was if he was getting a kick out of seeing me lose my mind. If I wouldn't have responded to their negative foolishness, I probably would have been sent back to my cell.

"You see the holes covered on these walls?" the officer asked while I looked around at them. "If you disrespect me or one more of my officers again, I will push a button and gas your ass up until you go to sleep."

After that, I only looked tough. After about four hours I was given back my clothes and taking to the hole. This was my first time going to the hole without getting into a fight.

For some reason I felt as if I had defeated Satan. I could feel the respect that convicts were giving me as though I was not to be violated. They knew that when it came down to fighting, they would have to bring it.

I felt like time was downhill and no more fights. Looking out of my window in the hole, I could see inmates walking across the compound.

Being locked down in a one-man cell, it seemed as if they were free. To help keep my mind off moments of sadness, I did push-ups until I got tired, after that I fell to sleep. The next day was the 4th of July. That whole morning everything was going smooth, while standing at my cell door.

"What's up, where are you from?" a convict asked me that was at his cell door across from me.

"Memphis!" Everyone else yelled out.

"Tell us about Memphis. Tell us about the riot!" They shouted out.

I gave them a full run-down on the 1991 riot, the streets of Memphis and how good of a tourist sight Memphis was. I didn't have to worry about cigarettes or marijuana. The convicts were giving me it all.

"Chow time; chow time," an officer yelled out loud.

Once we received our trays, it was like a nightmare. It was only a little food, mostly coleslaw. Also, a very small chicken wing with barbeque sauce poured on it.

"Ahh hell no! On the 4 of July in the hole or not I'm not going for this shit. No one eat. Believe me, I know how the system works. If one of us eats, then they have the right not to feed all of us. Just hold to your trays. I will try to get the warden in here!"

Behind that, everyone held their trays until I spoke to the lieutenant.

"Wait until you'll get back from recreation, I will get him in here."

While outside, I was locked in a 6x8-foot cave. I was only able to do push-ups and run around in circles. After that we took showers and waited on the warden.

Moments later he arrived, and we all complained about the food.

"You all are going to eat what you have or nothing at all," the warden stated in a way that indicated he meant what he said.

Before he could make his way around to hear everyone who were complaining, I had my blanket rolled up and stuffed into my toilet. I flushed, and then held the bottom on the toilet until was ran out into the hall.

The sergeant walked up to my cell and said, "Look stop! Why are you doing this?"

"Go get me some Bar-B-Q ribs, and I will stop!"

"There is no more food. It's all gone!"

"Well then, you go cook some, you hoe ass boy. Then I will stop!"

"You're going to be in big trouble for this. Warden! Warden!" the sergeant yelled out while standing at my cell door.

"Trick; I'm already in trouble. I'm in prison, you punk!" I stated.

"There isn't any more food. If you don't stop flooding my building, I will get my cowboys in here on you!" the warden yelled out in irritation.

"Fuck you, bitch!" I yelled back with the highest authority. I then threw the cole slaw and other food in his direction from off my tray.

"Here, you eat this shit."

The other convicts began to follow my lead by flooding out their cells and throwing food at the sergeant and the warden.

"Memphis! Memphis!" Everyone yelled out calling me 'Memphis'. This gave them a small taste of 201 and the 1991 Riot.

Moments later, the convicts across from me yelled out, "They are coming! They are coming!"

I saw the cowboys coming by looking out of the window. Quickly, I flushed my contraband down the toilet, before I could flush the second time everyone's water was cut off.

"Everyone, get naked and put your backs against the gates!" a cowboy lieutenant yelled out loud.

It was about 50 cowboys dressed in armor with guns and shields on their faces. By now water was ankle high and food was flooding in it. Four of the officers were targeting right in on me. But everyone else had only two officers at their cell door. Knowing that I did not want to be stuck in the hole, in every way that I was commanded, I obeyed.

"Get on your knees!" the Lieutenant yelled at me with a look in his eyes that said, *make my day.*

"I have already heard about you. Let me see you cut up now." He bent over and spoke to me through his teeth, as if he was going to bite me.

All I was thinking about was how long I was going to be on my knees in the water. With three guns around me, I didn't make a sound. Once everyone was strip-searched and violated by another man looking up in our back hole, we were put back into our cells.

The whole time that I was entering into my cell, the officers were waiting on me to say one word or make the wrong move. When I looked around, I could tell I was getting a different treatment than the others convicts. I was being roughed up a bit, but I played around them.

"This fool has grease all over him!" one of the officers said.

"I wonder what in the hell is it for?" Another officer asked.

"It's for…"

"Shut up it doesn't matter!" the Lieutenant cut my words short when I was about to explain why.

The next day, the lieutenant walked in with two additional officers, while I was being shackled and readied to be extradited to my final destination.

"Do you know what these print outs are?" the Lieutenant asked me.

"No," I replied.

"It's a print out of your background. We don't want you around here. You do anything but fight. *You* are a troublemaker."

From there, I was taken out of the prison and put on an airplane. This time the plane sounded safe while flying. It looked like the engineers fixed the hole in the wing with duct tape.

While entering the compound at Seagoville FCI, a low security facility in Texas, I noticed that it looked like a college campus. I saw all kinds of men from all over the world in street clothes. There was a gazebo that was situated in the center of the compound were loud music was corning from. However, it wasn't American music; it was Spanish. There were tables that everyone sat around in their own groups.

I walked to Warden's office that was located over the hole. As I was going in, some convicts nodded their heads at me. I nodded back but with an unfriendly look on my face. It must have been a dark cloud over my head.

As soon as I entered the entrance of the unit, it began to rain very hard. While I was looking back across the compound, everyone began to run into the units for shelter.

Once I checked in and was given my room all alone, I couldn't do anything but lie down and go to sleep.

CHAPTER 12:
A DOUBLE VISION

While I was asleep, I had a vision of me standing at a window of a house looking inside. I heard a woman yelling out for help, pleading for her life. I could see a man beating her, but I couldn't catch a glance of his face. It was as if the windows began to fog up. As the woman and I made eye contact, I could see tears rolling down her face. The man continued to beat on her, and I tried to go in to help, but it was as if the fog was stopping me from getting in. I could tell that the man was white, and she was a red-skinned black woman. She was beaten until she passed out. It was like I was trying to go in to help my baby sister.

"Spencer! Spencer!" An officer walked into my cell, stood over me, and handed me a trash bag.

"Here, take this bag. Go out on the compound and pick up trash. This is a duty that everyone has to do on the first day here."

The whole time that he was talking, I had my mug on my face. I didn't want anyone waking me up at 4 AM, talking about picking up trash. I did not want to, but I got up, got dressed and headed out the door.

When I open it, the rain was pouring down so hard until I couldn't see two feet in the front of me. I walked back to the officer's booth looking for him, but I didn't see him. I then walked back to my room, laid down and fell back to sleep with the trash bag on the floor.

I must to have been asleep about 15 minutes before the officer came back into my room.

"Spencer! I'm not going to tell you again to go out on the compound and pick up trash!"

"Man, it's raining like hell out there. I'm not going anywhere. Who you think you scaring with all that hollering? I'm not your child. You got me fucked up!" I yelled back to the officer, while standing up from my bed.

He rushed out, and I laid back down. About five minutes later, the officer showed up with a sergeant and four officers.

"Get up! You're going to the hole for refusing to obey a direct order!" the sergeant commanded boldly.

"What? What the fuck are you talking about? I'm not going out there in all of that rain!" I yelled back while looking at them standing over me in their rain clothes.

They wasted no time putting cuffs on me and taking me to the hole. After I was put into a cell, moments later, I heard a loud squeaky voice with a high-pitched tone saying, "Man, you all got this shit fucked up out here! You all think I'm going out in the rain and pick up some trash. You're got to be out of your rabbit ass minds!" CJ yelled out while he was being place in the hole also.

"CJ, what's up?" I said.

"What's up Lowe? They got this Memphis-shit fucked up. They are going to learn to respect Memphis!" We both were in the hole for the same reason. CJ and I talked for a while about how tough the officer tried to act, but when his bluff was called, he ran for help. After that we laid it down.

The next day, "Memphis; Memphis!" someone yelled up to my cell window from the ground level. This hole was underground.

"What's up?" I yelled back.

"How many of you are from Memphis that they have in the hole?"

"Two," I answered back while looking out of my window seeing about twenty Memphians standing there.

"Why? What's up?" I asked.

"We just checking on y'all. Is everything ok?"

"Yes," I responded.

We talked a little while longer; the Memphians told me that the officer who had us put in the hole went by the name Al Green. They also told me that they would be hard on him.

After they walked off, I read a sign that said, 'OUT OF PLACE DO NOT CROSS.' But my Memphian home boys crossed just to talk to me. The next day, we were called to a board hearing that was called the Team Unit. The team consisted of a counselor, a social worker and a unit manager.

"You have been here one day, and you are already in the hole. What do you have to say for yourself?" I was asked by one of the team leaders.

"I was asked to go out into the rain at 4 AM without clothes. It was raining so hard until I couldn't see. Tell me, would you have walked out there when it was raining so hard that you couldn't see?"

After I asked that question, the room was silent, and I got no response. They look at me as if the officer lied to them or didn't give them the full story.

CJ stood 6'5", 210 pounds. When he came in the room and gave the same story that I did that really put the team on our side. That same day we were let out of the hole. This let me know that I stood up for my rights. The word must have gotten out on the compound quickly that we were getting out, because when we walked out of the front door, it was a crowd of Memphians waiting to greet us.

Later on that day, we had to go into the team office again. They told me that I had to pick a job, or they would pick one for me. I wasted no time picking to work in food services.

At this time, the little money that I had before had run out. There was no money coming in from my family. My sister-in-law, Aiddie, sent me $10.00. That was all I received the entire time I was in Seagoville, TX.

By working in the kitchen, not only would I be able to eat, but I would be able to steal food to get money. Time was rolling on, and I was granted a small settlement for getting hurt on the job in Memphis before I was locked up.

I tried to call all my family members to get them to pick up my money. Not one of them answered the phone, after I tried to call for a week. I was told that I had to get someone to pick up my checks, or they would be sent back. I then called my sister-in-law; she was the only one who answered the phone. She talked as if she was going to handle the business for me. Once I called my old job and had the money released into her hands, I then learned, I was deceived. I called her phone for about two weeks straight and got no answer. By the time I got my sister to call her on three-way and she answered the phone, she was broke.

"Hello and what's up with the money?" I asked.

"I spent it all. When you get out, I will pay you back. I will be home. I messed it off."

"What in the hell do you mean you *messed it off*? How could you mess off $26,000.00? I told you to get the boys some beds, and you were to take $300.00 for yourself, but you spent it all?" Needless to say, the conversation didn't end well at all.

"You better have my money when I get out!" Behind that, I told my sister to hang up the phone in her face.

"If someone would have answered the phone in the family, I could have given them the money. No one would pick up. NO ONE," I sadly told my sister.

"Okay, Lorenzo. I love you, but I have got to go to work."

"Bye," I said.

"Bye," she replied.

The next day I was put to work in the kitchen working in food services. When the convicts found out that I was from Memphis, I could feel that sense of respect.

As I looked around, I could tell there was a division. Everyone sat at their own tables. The Blacks, Whites, Jamaicans, Indians, Cubans, Africans, and so on. Some convicts would tell funny jokes, while others would watch TV until we were all accounted for. From there, we began preparing lunch and dinner.

"Sir, I don't have a duty." I said to one of the supervisors.

"Where are you from?" he asked me.

"Memphis."

"So, you should be a good cook. I will put you on the grills."

I was then locked in the fence with three other convicts. That made three cooks and one floor man, which kept the floors clean.

It was grade one, two, and three levels of cooks. I was a grade-three. After about three months had passed, I was ready to move up to a grade-one cook. I talked to a lady supervisor, who I felt had some liking for me. I told her I needed more money, and I wanted to move up.

She told me if I got my GED, she will move me up. After failing twice in 12 months I finally completed my GED. The two head cooks were in my way. They were stopping me from moving up.

That night after work, I was talking to my roommate. He told me that I could get a job in UNICOR making $5.00 an hour. It would be better than working in the kitchen making only $.50 an hour. The next week when it was time for me to get my GED certificate, a new teacher was sent in. When I walked into the classroom, all the students were in their seats. Some of them used to stand up while the teacher was talking.

"Have a seat everyone!" the teacher said, while walking to the front of the classroom.

I had a front row seat.

"My name is Mrs. Hightower," she introduces herself. When I saw her face 'Ah,' I slightly moaned aloud while covering my mouth, trying to catch my words.

"Sir, you have something to say?" she asked me with an angry look on her face.

"No, no, I have nothing to say," I responded while all eyes were on me.

I didn't waste any time. I began writing the vision I had on a piece of paper. This was the lady I saw getting beaten by a white man in my dream. I wrote everything down just the way I saw it. It was as if I was dreaming, but it was a vision.

I wanted to explain it to her, but I felt she would understand it only if I put it on paper. At the end of our session, I gave her the note and said, "Mrs. Hightower, will you read this? And my God bless you."

Behind that I walked out.

I felt that I had given her a warning and advice. I was only trying to be helpful. That was some night. While in my room, I was feeling good. I smoked me a joint after I showered and read while listening to my radio.

Convicts were coming by buying food that was given to me from the kitchen. I made a little money, stamps and cigarettes. I would say, it was a good day.

The next day, before I could go to work, two officers walked into my room with bags.

"Here, Spencer, pack your things. You are going to the hole," one of the officers said.

"For what? I've done nothing!" I tried to explain out of anger and in a shock, not knowing what I was going to the hole for.

It was read aloud to me from the write-up. The GED teacher, Mrs. Hightower, alleged that I had harassed her.

"Could I see a lieutenant?" I asked.

"No, not now. We have the captain's order to take you to the hole. The lady feels threatened. You will see some-one tomorrow. Let's go," one of the officers said.

I packed my things and was cuffed, then taken to the hole. While in the hole, one end was for the innocent until proven guilty. That was the end I was on. We could smoke cigarettes on that end. Once you were found guilty you were sent to the other end. On that end all rights and privileges were taken away.

A few days later, I was found guilty for harassment and disturbing Mrs. Hightower. The board gave me thirty days for giving a worker a letter. I found myself back in the old routine of doing push-ups. When I was done, I laid down to fall asleep. There was a Bible on the table beside my bed. I took it, put it under the bed and fell off to sleep.

It was as if I was asleep, but I wasn't. It was if I was led away from where I was, but I wasn't. Suddenly, I was standing in the front of 14 doors. I walked through them; it appeared as if it was in dark thick clouds.

A coffin rolled out of the clouds in the front of me. When the coffin opened, I could see myself lying in it dead. My arms were folded with a Bible under them. A great fear came upon me like never before.

"Lorenzo, Lorenzo, take this book open it, and read it. This is my last time telling you."

I turned to see the heavy voice that was speaking to me, but I saw nothing but clouds.

When I turned back to the coffin seeing myself, tears began rolling down my face. I then tried to pull the Bible from my dead self, but I couldn't. It was as if death had a hold on it. I then heard another voice, but more wicked saying, "It's too late! It's too late! Hah! Hah! Hah."

"Let go! Let go!" I yelled out loud, while pulling the Bible away from my own dead hands.

Pulling it away caused me to fall backwards out of the doors, floating and spinning. At the same time, I held on to the Bible.

"Aghhh;" I yelled out, awakening. I was still lying back on my bed with a Bible in my hands. How it got there, I cannot remember. I then yelled out again while I was awake and covered in sweat. I threw the Bible upside of wall. I was looking at the Bible as if I had seen a ghost.

My heart was beating fast like I had been running. I know I put the Bible under the bed before I fell off to sleep.

As I laid there for a while, all I could come up with was that the spirit within myself guided my hand to pull the Bible from under the bed.

All I could do was shake my head, because at the time, I just didn't understand. I then got out of the bed, picked up the Bible and laid back on the bed.

I opened the Bible to Matthew 7:7. I sounded like a third grader reading. I only read that one verse. It said, 'Ask, and it shall be given, seek and you shall find, knock and it shall be open.'

I then laid the Bible down on my bed, got down on my knees and began to pray. In my prayer, I asked God to give me spiritual wisdom, knowledge and understanding of His every word of the Bible.

When I got up and re-opened the Bible, I opened to John 14:26, "But the Comforter, which is the Holy Ghost, whom the Father will send in my name, he shall teach you all things, and bring all things to your remembrance, whatsoever I have said unto you."

From there, I slept in peace.

CHAPTER 13:
ONE MAKES A DIFFERENCE

On my way out of the hole, I heard someone from the other end calling my name. "Spencer, Spencer." One of the cooks called me, letting me know that he was in the hole for fighting with the other grade-A cook.

"I'm on my way out!" I yelled back to him.

"Spencer, Spencer! Let's go." An officer called for me to go.

When I made it on the compound, I began to talk to everyone about the Bible. But no one wanted to hear me. Because I found God, I thought it was time for everyone to find him. It seemed as if I was in a world all alone.

So after about a month, I laid the Bible down on my table in my room. This time, I didn't put it under the bed.

It was a Battle of the Bands concert. I was in one of the bands playing the drums and singing. Everyone could only play two songs. But I also played the drums behind a Rapper called Little Yoo.

It was like a concert in the free world. Ladies were there mixed with us as well. We all had a good time. I was put back into the kitchen working as the grade-A cook, because the grade one and two were in the hole.

Cooking a Christmas dinner was one of the best times of my life in jail. It was only three of us in the fence, the kitchen supervisor's name was Miss Pam. She was a jet-black sister with a nice body shape. And God knows I don't have anything against a red-skinned sister, but I'm so crazy about a jet-black sister.

She did things that hadn't ever been done since I was there. The radio was playing she began to dance with me. She would let me get a little close to her and then back up. It was the joy dancing with a woman while being locked up. We cooked a big meal, had fun and ate well.

For New Year's I made some of my Memphis hooch. This time, I had the chance to let it set longer. It was a hole over the top of our shower across from one area in our building. I had a Mexican looking over it.

Every two hours, I had him to let the pressure and heat out of it. It would get to the point it would cry like a baby with sound that it made when the heat built up in it.

On New Year's night, it was ready to be sold and drank. Everyone bought it until it was all gone. The Mexican that looked over it for me was named Lamberto. He slept in the dorm alone with two other Mexicans. The Memphis whoosh had convicts drunk all over the compound.

When court time came, Lamberto couldn't stand up on his own. The two Mexicans who were in the dorm with him stood on each side of him to hold him up.

"Let him go. What are you all doing? Stand by your own beds!" one court officer said to them.

When they let him go and walked to their beds for the 10 o'clock stand up court, Lamberto fell flat on his face and busted his head. He had to be taken to the hospital to get stitched up. It wasn't funny when it happened, but it was so funny the way he fell in a drunken way.

The next day during visitation, it was CJ's lucky day. It was a Saturday. While an officer was walking around from inside visitation to outside visitation, CJ and his lady saw a chance to have sex, and they took it. They were around picnic table with a tree in the center of it. CJ timed the officers walk from the inside to the out. It was two-and-a-half-minute walk that gave CJ two minutes to take care of his business Memphis-style.

"Why did you wear panties?" CJ asked.

"I don't know anything about these people here!" his lady Lisa said.

"'Damn, these people pull your panties off now?" CJ said, while the officer was about to walk back on the inside. CJ's lady took them off, and he didn't waste any time on pulling her dress up from the back.

"I gotta lick it before I stick it," CJ said, while bending forward while she was standing up and took a lick on the back of Lisa's womanhood.

"Man, it's sweet," CJ moaned, while pulling her down in his lap on top of his manhood. Lisa began to grunt, because of the tightness of her womanhood. She had not had sex in over a year, before CJ was locked up. But from holding back the pressure from years of being incarcerated, CJ began to go to work on Lisa's womanhood. She tried to hold back and tried to stop her groove.

The officer would be back in just a few minutes.

"Close your eyes. I'm going to watch out, I got this," CJ told Lisa, while he was just about to get in the mood.

When she closed her eyes, she let go knowing she had only a moment of pleasure to get her pleasing off. She opened up and pounded down on the top of CJ's manhood until she began to release her sweetness.

"Oh, oh yes, God its good." She released out, while CJ pressed upward into the deep back of her womanhood until he released.

We could stand up and look over the gates from where we played basketball.

"Damn, your homey got my dick hard as hell," Someone said, while we stayed to the end just looking on.

"Here he come. Get up," CJ told his lady, and she got up, talking to CJ like nothing happen.

While we were still standing there, a black bag came over the top of the visitation gate. Suddenly, a Cuban ran out from nowhere as if he was running track, picked up the bag and ran into the building. The bag was full of drugs.

The next day, while in the kitchen, I was sitting at a table eating alone with some other workers, before it was time to feed the compound. When I looked closely, it was Carlos sitting at the table with us. He was the Black Cuban that my home boys tried to get me to take out with the lock and sock. He had grown a head full of hair. It was in something like an afro. Some said that he was facing 70 years, but from the 5-K-1, on a lot of convicts, he got this time cut down to only 20 years.

No matter what, I wasn't the one to take him out; I'm not a hit man.

"Carlos!" I spoke out, almost not recognizing him.

"What's up Lowe?" He spoke back, realizing who I was.

There was a Spanish convict that kept walking back and forth past the table, where we were sitting. He was looking for Carlos from the corner of his eyes. He was seen earlier crawling on his knees coming out of the fence where we cooked. He got a knife without anyone seeing him, and we didn't do a knife count until after we were finished feeding everyone. It had to be a hit, because at the same time that this was going down, Castro was out on the compound trying to escape by a helicopter that was flying over the compound.

But it didn't work because the officers stopped him and took Castro to the hole.

The white Cuban walked up from behind Carlos grabbed him by the back of his hair pulling his head backward while Carlos was still sitting down eating.

I was sitting across on the other side of the table. He had a firm grip on Carlos's hair until nothing was showing but his neck. He then pulled the knife from out of his waist line and quickly stuck it into Carlos's neck pulling the knife from one side to the other side, splitting Carlos's neck open like a watermelon.

"Dirty rat! Rats don't live!" the Cuban hit man said, carrying out his hit. It was the same Cuban that ran up to the gate and picked up the black bag that had a half of pound of pot in it. When the officers walked up to Carlos, he threw the knife down saying, "I told him to stop fucking with me!"

One of the officers football-tackled him and about three others helped cuffed him, and he was never seen again. Things were back to normal in the kitchen. I was back to selling food and getting my groove on.

Summer rolled in and things were heating up. I had a home boy from Memphis that slept in one of the units that had no AC in there, so they had to use fans. He was telling some of the convicts that he knew me from the town and I bar none.

"Oh, that don't mean he can fight."

"Shit, I don't know what you're talking about. My little homey is jacking out of from, he's a flat-foot jacking fool." Walter was telling some of the convicts that were in the dorm with him about me.

It turned out to be a five-minute conversation about me. At the same time, everyone in there that didn't have a fan was sweating and fanning with cardboard. I was getting off work on my way in. Walter walked up to me asking me could I get a fan for him, and he would pay me half of the cost in commissary. I had an associate with me, whose name was Rock.

We walked into another building where it was mostly Mexican. It didn't take long at all to spot a fan. It seemed to be no one's bed. So, I grabbed the fan off a table.

"What's up, hom, home, homes?" A Mexican that talked really slow and stuttered his words ask me.

"Motherfucker you better close your eyes, you haven't seen nothing. You tell and I'm going to kick the tacos out of your ass?" He was lying on a bottom bed under a sheet.

When I told him that he put the sheet over his head. I walked out while Rock was standing at the door looking out for me. Usually, when I did something like this I didn't feel remorse, but later that night I felt really bad deep inside. I picked up the Bible and began to read it. The more I read the more it applied to my everyday life. I found myself at church that next day. It shocked the hold compound.

"The world must be getting ready to end, if you are going to church," someone told me when they saw me coming from church with the Bible in my hand.

I met this brother in church who told me how he found God, and a change came over his life. He told me about a class he was taking at night called Editors and the instructor was a convict named James Jenkins.

The Christian brother invited me to the class, and I went. I began to go every night, and when I talked with this man one-on-one, I dug his style. He was giving me all the keys to writing a book. I spent the whole summer in his class. When I was done with my first project called 'The Wide Side,' he told me it wasn't going anywhere. He told me I could redo it or throw it away, because it was nothing but trash. I got so mad at him I took my 400-page novel from him and gave him a few bad words. He told me he wouldn't lie to me and if it was any good he would have told me. He said he did not want to lie to me by telling me it was good, and it wasn't. But I put so much time into it until I didn't want to hear it.

I did a lot of typing and writing.

"Listen, Lorenzo, the best advice I can give you is, write about something you experienced in life, something you have been through. Lay it out day for day."

I walked off with my dog on my face as if I was going to do something to that man, while looking back. Before I walked out the door I stated to him, "The only the I've been through was jail, and it was like hell."

"Then write about that," he replied back, "because that's no good what I read, nothing but straight garbage," he said to himself after I walked out.

"FIGHT 13"

Everyone was paying me good for the food, all but one inmate. I guess because he stood 6'3" he felt like he could take something. He got jalapeno pepper along with bell pepper for him and some of his friends to cook with it. We call it when an officer allowed us to have a weekend, get-together cookout. He was called Lowdown White Boy, he always hung out in the weight room. I walked over to the weight shack to pay him a visit about paying me. He told me he would pay me tonight, and he was coming over to my building.

It had been over a month, and I hadn't got paid. I was on my lunch break, so I had to get back to work. When I got off that night, I saw Lowdown White Boy in my building, but he wasn't supposed to be there, except on the weekends. He was with some of his friends and he showed out.

"What's up dirty? Are you going to pay me?" I asked him.

"Man, I'm not paying your lazy eye ass anything!"

He responded, and his friends laughed out loud. I didn't say a word, I rushed to my room to take off my work boots, then put on my Jordan Flights 23. I rushed to the stairs behind them. I knew this man was taller than I was, so I sat at the top of the stairway and waited until he came out. My mind was made up, he wasn't going out without a fight.

"Now, what you say, boy? You think you took something? You're not taking anything but this ass whipping!" I told him, with an angry look on my face as if I was about to fight with the devil himself. By me standing on the flight of stairs, I was standing face to face-with-him. He tried to go around me.

"Let me go; it's about to be count time. I'm out of place," he repeated, as if I cared.

"Fuck that. You're going to pay me or that's your ass!"

"Ohh, I'll whooo!" Lowdown White Boy yelled out as I dropped a quick six pack on his face and every lick landed in the right spots. He came up off his feet backwards landing on the floor-out cold.

"Don't let up!" As I quickly looked around hearing that voice I knew, it was Ty from H-Town.

We dug each other's style off the top. He stood behind me watching my back, because he knew the white boys were clicked up.

This time, I didn't give a damn. I didn't let up. Low-down white boy was lying on the floor out for the count. I followed up on my six packs with about four more left blows. I hit him and woke him up. I hit him two more times and put him back to sleep.

"Damn, what in the hell was that!" an officer yelled out, and everyone took off running, but Ty and me.

"What happened to him?"

"I knocked his ass out; he was over here fucking with me."

"Spencer, you know you're going to the hole," the officer told me while putting cuffs on me and then calling for Med and back up.

While in the hole, I was found guilty, given 90 days and sent to the other end.

It was this big officer that kind of admired my style of jailing. He would sometimes let me stay out a little while longer and talk to me about Memphis. He would also give me extra food. When he smelled smoke, he wouldn't come to my cell. His name was Officer Williams. Every time someone would come to the hole to do short time, they would yell out my name from the other end or leave me something.

One day my friend Rock was in the hole on the other end.

"What's up Lowe?" Rock said.

"What's cracking?" I responded.

I then told Rock to put me some cigarettes and match-es in a little cereal box. I then told him to put toothpaste in it for weight and threw him a long string from the end I was on to the end he was on with a shower shoe attached to it.

I tore the sheets from my bed the day before when we changed out for clean ones, so the officer couldn't charge me for destroying government property.

When I threw it to his end, I told him to tie the box to the string. It had to be about 30 feet in distance.

The officers on all shifts tried to figure out how I was getting my smokes in my cell. I would get only enough to smoke for one day. I would always smoke one as soon as I got them and put two in the pocket of my briefs.

On shake down days they would always say to themselves, "How, is he getting smokes in here, and where in the hell are they?"

But they could never find them until one day, I was pulling the line back to my cell that Rock loaded up for me, and Officer Williams saw the line and began chasing it. It was so funny. Every time, he would bend down to try and pick up the box, he couldn't get it. I would reel it in closer until I got it to the cell door, and then he grabbed it. I was laughing, and so was he. He didn't write me up, but he told the other officers, so they would be on the lookout. And that stopped my smoking.

They all gathered at my cell door, and asked me, what's did I call this.

"We called it fishing in Memphis," I told them, and they all laughed.

After a month past, I began to read the Bible more every night, and when my eyes would get tired of reading, I would write on my novel.

I took Mr. James Jenkins' advice. I began to write about my prison life. The next day Lowdown White Boy walked past my cell, and I got a close look at my after work on him. It was an ugly sight. He looked like a raccoon around the eyes with bubble lips. I know that God began to change my heart, because I felt guilty. I really felt sorry.

The officer took me outside to get my recreation on. It was a little cool outside.

When I took my coat off he said, "It's not funny, but look at the way you move playing basketball and your body, or you look like you can fight. What in the hell was he thinking wanting to fight you?"

"I don't know," I answered as I kept playing basketball.

"He has got to be crazy," the officer said, to himself while looking at me showing out on the court.

I had been in the hole about 60 days, and the warden was walking through making his rounds. I asked him to let me out of the hole.

"For what? I have you on the shipping list, we already have you going to Alaska, and we are not going to have that on my compound. You have a record of fighting and it's not going on here."

The warden pulled one of the officers to the side and asked him how I was acting. He told the warden that I had been ok, and the warden walked out.

Later that night, I fell into one of my deep sleeps. It was like I'm sleeping, but I wasn't sleep. It was like I could see my brother and his children, but I never saw his wife. All of a sudden, some clouds appeared, and a dove came out of the clouds and sat there.

Then I looked at my brother, Calvin. We were loading music equipment. It was as if I could see the children and a voice said, "For these are my children, and you have a job to do. Take care of them."

When I looked up, I could see the dove as if it was talking in a lady's voice saying, 'one makes a difference.' I never saw my brother's wife, Addie.

I then looked at my brother and said, "Calvin, we have a job to do."

Behind that I woke up, still hearing a voice saying one makes a difference, and you will make a difference.

A week later I wrote a letter to Calvin and told him about the dream just the way it happened. That next day, I was let out of the hole. While I was walking down the hall coming out, I saw my name really on a shipping board under Alaska.

"Yes, that's your name. They are about to send you underground under the snow where you won't be able to fight," An officer told me on my way out.

Two days later, I got my brother Calvin on the phone and before I could start talking, he told me to wait, he had something to tell me.

"You know you had vision. That letter you mailed me wasn't a dream, it was a vision. You know you have a gift. Don't take this hard; everything is ok. That dove you saw was Addie. That was God's way of showing you that she's in Heaven. She is no longer with us, she has gone on to see God."

I had a vision a few years prior to this about Michigan winning the playoff game by one point. I was on the phone with Brenda, my sister, at the same time the game aired. I told her I already dreamed Michigan won by one point. As soon as I told her that the game ended. Michigan won by one point.

Why would God allowed me to have a vision about basketball, I don't know?

Behind this vision, I really began to make a change in my life. In a way, it was as if the world was really closing in on me. I had no friends and no one to talk to. But I could always go to God in prayer, and things would be ok. Everyone was saying I just wasn't the same any more.

One day, in the kitchen someone was sitting directly behind me saying, "Every, since he beat Lowdown White Boy, he hasn't been the same anymore."

"Yeah it's something that came over him," someone else said.

Before I left, I talked to James Jenkins. He told me the book I wrote this time was a number one seller.

The next day I went to church. A preacher as was there and asked if anyone who was going home or leaving soon had anything to say that might encourage the convicts.

"Yes!" I responded, not meaning to say anything, but I don't know what opened my mouth to say yes.

"Come up!" the preacher called me.

When I looked around, I could see some of the same convicts that did want to hear me talking about God. I once was a convict. The only reason that we would come to church was to pass money or drugs, or gang members would come and have meeting. Anything but hearing the Word of God. All of this was going on here and more.

When I began to speak, it was still like someone was using my mouth to talk. I even gave a topic on the message. "One Makes A Difference."

When it was all over, about 50 convicts came up and gave their lives to God. I let the entire church know that with one man sin was brought into the world, and one man came and took away our sins. By saying that, one can make a difference.

My time ended there, and I was put on a plane back to Memphis to get the remaining of my time at 201.

The song was playing while I was on the plane by Jerry Butlers, "Only the Strong Survive."

A lot of convicts didn't make it back or got stuck to the point of death. By the Grace of God, I'm strong, and I survived through it all.

CHAPTER 14:
FIGHT TO THE END

While on the lower level, I could truly tell a change had come over me. Flying in the airplane, I had a closer encounter with God. Things just weren't the same with me. I could tell that I was a totally different man. I could tell God took the stony heart out of me. I was no longer thinking the same. I was no longer looking the same. I was no longer feeling the same. My name was no longer Lowe; it was Brother Lorenzo.

Also, I could tell 201 wasn't the same, not only had the acts changed but the names had changed also. Usually the names were *Big* this and *Big* that. Now, all I was hearing was Little *this* and Little *that*. Everyone was putting *Little* in the front of their names. Not only that, but they were more wicked than ever.

"GYG;" I heard one of the young inmates yell out up front.

It means guard your grill. He pulled his manhood out around other men inmates, just to flash it before a lady. It's not comfortable to use the bathroom around another man who is gay. Inmates began covering their eyes. Some of them wanted to lust on the lady by looking at her. Some of them didn't put their hand over their eyes but stood there and lusted at the lady, while some flashed their manhood.

After she walked out, the young inmates bragged to each other saying, "I gun that hoe down."

All I could say was, *this is a perverted generation.*

Standing by my cell door looking around, I never saw so many young black men in jail.

"No! You don't suppose to do that," a lady officer said to an inmate, while walking in the pod. At the same time, she didn't stop looking at the inmate, who pulled out his manhood as she was about to walk off.

"No! Wait look, look at that man! Give me all eyeballs. That's all I need is your eyes to watch this man throw up!" the perverted inmate yelled out to her in a harsh voice.

It was like his yelling had her under control. She stopped in her tracks and looked on as if she was hypnotized. When he was done, she walked off as if she was pleased. The entire time while standing at my cell door, I could see the lady. I could only hear the voice of the inmate. After it was all over, this let me know what kind of generation I was facing. That next morning right after I just got off my knees from praying, an office let us out for feeding.

"Did you feel that?" I asked the lady officer.

"No," she responded and looked at me like I was crazy.

"What are you talking about?" she continued.

I felt a cold breeze feeling blow pass me.

"It was cold air like," I told her.

"No, I felt nothing," she said.

Seconds later, "Aghhh! Help, help someone please help me. It's my daddy. He's dead! Please help, why, why, why!" A white inmate cried out in tears, while holding his dead father in his arms. "Help, Help, someone please help me!" he continued, as the cold and stiff body hardened.

At the same time that I was asking the officer did she feel that, she was rubbing her arms as if she was cold? That coldness I felt was death himself.

Rev. 6:8 says, Death rides a pale horse and hell follows.

After the dead man was taken away, and things calmed down, and I was finished serving. It was quiet as a church mouse. Looking at the officer and inmates faces, I could see fear on them.

After God changed my life, I was at peace. I was able to read my Bible and hear God's spirit like never before. I prayed and read all night asking God to give me spiritual wisdom, spiritual knowledge, and spiritual understanding of His every word. It was as if God himself was there with me in my cell. That let me know that John 20:26 was true. There are no gates or doors closed too tight for Jesus to come through.

That next morning, one of Memphis' famous rappers was on lower level. Inmates and officers were getting his autograph as if he was a dead man. All I could say to myself was, if we were after God in that way we wouldn't be in jail.

Once the word got out that he was in jail, inmates were sending for his autograph from all over the jail. Officers were giving him paper to sign and taking it back to the inmates on every floor. It was an uproar on the entire lower level. I couldn't hold back any longer.

"If we look for God in that way, this jail would be closed down!"

After I spoke that out, all eyes were on me. It was if officers and inmates were looking for me to say something behind that. That was all God gave me to say at, that time. Some kind of way, it was God's way of showing me, with him, all come under submission.

Later on, when the officer came to get me for food, the inmates, some old school convicts, and offices bragged on me and spread rumors saying, "That fool flat foot jacking, don't mess with him you or you will get your ass torn out the frame."

While the inmates and officers were talking, I paid them no mind. Now that God has changed my life, I did like the jacket on my back.

Convicts would try me, just to try and get a name for themselves. I could hear God's Word telling me, 'to be wise as a serpent and harmless as a dove.'

Now that I have a better understanding of life, it's not the man himself that's after me. It's the adversary that work through an unclean man or woman. For the remainder of this mission that I on, God showed me the adversary was going to try and take me out.

Later on that night after I was done reading my Bible and praying, I laid down. The old saying came to mind, when you lie on your stomach and fall off to sleep, the devil will ride your back. When I fell off to sleep I was laying on my stomach. While I was asleep I could hardly breathe. I struggled trying to wake myself up. I awakened in my sleep but at the same time I was still asleep. I then could see a demon on the top of me while I was lying down.

Some kind of way, God must have opened my eyes. I began to wrestle with the two-foot demon. He had on a black hoody. All I could see under his hoody was his red eyes. I looked for his face but couldn't see it, only darkness, and an awful smell.

Some kind of way while wrestling with him, I turned over. He then began putting my cover over my face so that I couldn't breathe. At the same time, he was choking me.

All of a sudden, I over powered him and got him off the top of me. I threw him to the floor at the same time tryed to stump him. Every time I would stump him, some kind of way he would pop from under of my foot. I looked around the cell for my Bible to hit him over the head with it. While the cell door was closed, he ran out of it before I could hit him. I ran out behind him. Before he ran out of the pod, he wasn't close enough for me to hit him with the Bible. Before he could turn the corner running at full speed, I kicked him so hard until he disappeared in a black ash of smoke. From there, I awakened realizing this was something my spiritual man had really gone through.

I rose up in my bed trying to put it all together. I then stood at my cell door looking for the demon as if he were still there. I set back on my bed and shook my head knowing that this was real. At this time, I realized I was sweating and breathing hard. I could tell I was really fighting for my life. I then began praying the 23rd Psalm. After that I open my Bible to Ephesians, 6; 11-18. That opened my eyes to what I was up against.

The next morning, I looked under my bed for that demon but didn't see him. I then remembered what I read, that they sit in high places. I then began looking up in the corners of my cell! I sat on the bed and thought. I had a spiritual encounter with a demon.

When the officer let me out of my cell to eat, I began looking in other cells for the demon. Inmates were looking at me as if l was crazy. I then remembered, I kicked him out into a cloud of dust. When I was done eating, I was tired. I wanted to take a shower and lay down. I could hear God's same voice that call me in 1984 saying, "Preach my Word. Cry out and spare not!"

I then asked God, "What is it you want me to do?" I could hear Him say 'Preach.'

I was tired of running. I got on my knees while crying. When I got up, I walked out of my cell with the Bible in my hand opened to Isaiah, SS; 1

It was as if God was moving my mouth and speaking out of it. I didn't sound like myself. I was also reading words that I had never read before. From hearing the inmates talking about the wicked crimes that they had committed; the Word of God was cutting like a sharp sword with two edges.

When I was done, not only were inmates convinced and converted while crying but some officers were also. All I could say was, *What a Mighty God.* Officers began coming to me sharing their personal problems and asking me to pray for them, and asking, *what must I do to be saved?*

The next day, I did the exact same thing with another message called, 'How can you escape The Death Penalty of Hell.' I guess, the reason God gave me that message was because some were saying among themselves that they were going to keep doing what they were doing, and they were still going to Heaven.

That message ended with Peter 2; 4-6. If God had not spared the angels who were in Heaven and kicked them out when they sinned, what makes us think that sin will enter back up there?

Later that day, a lieutenant lady officer came to my cell door. "I heard every word you preached. God is truly with you. How long have you been down here on lower level?"

"Almost two months." I responded.

"Well that lets you know the jail is overcrowded. We have no room on the floors to put anymore inmates. If you like, I can make some room for you to go into a pod. Will you help them to make a change and stop all the fighting? I remember how you use to fight. Maybe they will listen to you. Do you want to go?"

"Yes, I will go."

"I'm telling you now, they are cutting up, up there."

"I will go."

"Ok, pack your things."

About 9:15, before shift change the lieutenant was standing at my door asking me, "Are you ready to go?"

"Yes," I responded.

While we were going up the escalators, "How I'm telling you, I been getting bad reports on this pod. They have been fighting every day. I hope you can make a difference," she said with a serious look on her face.

"I can't change the pod but with God, one makes a difference," I responded.

While walking down the rock before entering the pod, "Was that Spencer?" an officer asked another officer?

"No, that could have been," another officer responded.

I must have had a different look about me. God changed me from inside and out.

When I entered into the pod, everyone was locked in their cells. Everything had changed; there were no OB beds in the pods. I saw food trays stacked up outside of the pod. That let me know that they were eating in the pod also.

"Who's the pod man?" I asked the lieutenant before she put me in the cell.

"There's no longer a pod man; it is everyman for himself There are two men in a cell, but I gave you a cell to yourself."

Once I was in my cell, the TV was no longer turned to the front of the pod; it was now facing the back. From my cell, I could watch it. That next morning when the cell doors opened, a sound awakened me, but I laid there for a while. I heard loud yelling and fighting words. When I got up to see what was going on there were two inmates at the foot of my cell door fighting. There were inmates in the front and back of the pod fighting.

There was an inmate chasing another inmate around the pod with a shank in his hand. The pod was in a complete uproar. It was just like the lieutenant said but worse.

When all the commotion was over, my name was called for a visit. It was a true friend of mine named Sharon. While standing in the front of the control exit, waiting to go into the visitation, there was a lady officer in the control booth who made all men's heads turn. Inmates were asked to move on because they were holding up the foot traffic trying to get a look at her. She had gold hair, gold ear rings, gold nails, and gold glasses. Her skin was so smooth that it looked gold. I gave her the name, the Golden Girl.

She made the control booth look gold. For some reason, they kept her in the control both for years. *However, sometimes, looks can be deceiving.*

If she had a good heart it would have been like finding gold in the ghetto. Being a single man, I don't think God minded me looking at her in admiration, along as I did not lust. I said to myself, *201 has gold and does not recognize it.*

When they open the visitation door for me, I was glad to see Sharon. She was also happy to see me. We had good conversations and said our goodbyes.

When I entered back into the pod, "What's up Lowe?" One of my orange mound homeys said to me.

"My name is no longer Lowe, its Brother Lorenzo."

"I will respect that," he said.

Then, he began to tell me about something that was going on in the pod. I was listening but not hearing it. My focus was more on the inmates who were walking around with their puppies in their faces. I overlooked it all and walked into my cell. I remember reading what God said, 'Don't worry about their disfigured faces.'

I got up and walked to my cell. Another one of my homeys that I knew from the old school stood beside my door. He knew how I would take up for my homeys. He then began to talk out loud saying, "Look man, I'm tired of you weak boys hogging the phone!"

By me being in the pod, he felt like he had some help, but I was now a changed man. God had me on another mission. I was not back in this place to debate about the phone.

He noticed me walking up to my cell door. He then began to walk up to the inmate that was on the phone while talking with disrespectful words.

"If you want the phone come take it!" the inmate that was on the phone yelled back.

My home boy name was Decker. He walked up to the inmate who was on the phone and grabbed him. While Decker had Little Pimp wrapped up with his left arm, he was beating him with his right fist. As they wrestled into the corner were the phone was left hanging, Decker grabbed the phone, while still having little Pimp wrapped up by his neck and beat him over the head with the phone.

"Help! Help!" Little Pimp called out for his gang members.

All though they were in the pod, they were nowhere to be found. After Little Pimp realized that they weren't coming to his rescue he yelled out, "Officer! Officer!"

No one ever came to rescue Little Pimp. When it was over, Little Pimp had knots all over his head and face. He slowly walked into his cell and laid it down. I then walked over to sit in the front of the TV, an heard an inmate talking to himself. He sat beside me and began running off at the mouth.

"Man, I have made some good stings before I was locked up. On one of them was where my brother worked. He worked at a place called Off the Top. It's a beauty salon. My brother set it up so good I had no problem breaking in and get the whole stereo system. He told me how to get in and out."

I then got up, walked to the phone and called my brother Danny. "Was your place broken into?"

"Yes." He responded.

"Well guess what?"

"What?"

"This guy is in here with me is who broke in!"

"How do you know?" Danny asked me, and I explained the hold situation to him. He fired his worker. I was so angry, until I set it up for my home boys to jump the brother that was in jail with me.

Before I gave them the go ahead, God stopped me. I could hear His voice saying, "This is not what you are here for." I looked around.

"What are your looking for?" an inmate asked me while I was looking for that voice. '

"Nothing, nothing," I responded. I then walked into the cell where my homeys were gathered and waiting on me to give the word.

"Don't touch him; I'm going to let God deal with him."

"Ah Lowe, you done softened up on us!"

It was about five of them in all, and they all agreed with each other that I had softened up.

"But God said His way is easy. If that is what you want to call soft."

I then called the inmate into my cell. I let him know that I was Danny's brother. His eyes got big as a bow dollar.

"Don't hurt me!" he said.

"I'm not. I want to talk to you about God." I responded.

When I was done talking to him, he asked me, "What must I do to be saved?"

I opened my Bible to Romans 10: 9-11, and he did confess. That was all it took to be saved. That same night while I was asleep, I had a vision of one of my brother's employees that had him set up to be robbed.

The next day I called him back and told him. When I gave him the lady's name, he didn't want to believe me, only because she was an old friend of the family.

As the week passed, inmates and convicts were getting more wicked than ever. The gangs were taking over the jail, and it was very little that the officers were doing. Sometimes it took death to bring people together.

Just when a fight was about to erupt, breaking news came on. It was being announced that Officer Paylor was killed by gang members. They said there was a hit out on him because of his treatment of inmates. All of the inmates began clapping and giving each other high fives.

God's Word says that we are supposed to be happy when one leaves out of the world and cry when one is born into the world. We have it all backwards.

On this occasion, everyone had it right, only because of his lifestyle. Behind that, the news began to flash faces and charges of some of the inmates that were standing there with us.

From the looks on their faces, they were embarrassed. They had some of the most serious charges that I have ever seen. From some of the gang member charges being exposed, the other gang members were putting them in violation.

Like God's Word says, *it's your own who persecute you.*

The ones who carried out the acts of violation took their own gang member into a cell and beat him. They flushed the toilets to drown out the sound of the beatings. The ones who were doing the beating would have the violator to take his shirt off. Then about two or three of them would beat him over his body so that the nurses would not see. I also saw gang members taken into the showers and given the pumpkin head.

On this, day fights were breaking out all over the jail and in the pod that I was in. I went on a three-day fast, asking God to remove the things out of me that were not pleasing unto Him.

All of a sudden, it was as if God Himself was in my cell talking to me.

"Now it's your time. Preach the word!" I heard.

I walked out of my cell and cut the TV off while inmates were watching it.

"Church Call! Church Call!" I yelled out loud with the Bible in my hand.

I began to preach out against all sin, wickedness and disobedience. This time, I wasn't trying to disobey God. I was at the point where I was going to do what God told me no matter what.

I remember being on my knees crying out to God in tears asking him, "What is it you want me to do?"

I was so fed up with sin, until I was sin sick. Some of the inmates began walking around with dismayed faces. They could walk around like a roaring lion. They could not bite; they only roared.

When I was done about 20 inmates gave their lives to God. Some of the ones didn't give their lives to God, however, complained against me in silence.

Once I went into my cell, I reflected on some of the words that I said in the message. I found myself trying to use an excuse, so that I would not have to preach the Word of God. Because of my tied tongue I didn't feel that God could use me, but He did. I tried to make excuses like Moses did, but it didn't work. I began to do this every night making myself a living sacrifice, and God did the rest.

I was reading, and words began to come out of my mouth like never before. It was the gospel uncut with no sugar.

On this night, about 20 inmates gave their lives to God. Officers stood in the sally port listening on. I didn't know it until I was done.

Little Otis begin to sing, 'Wake up Everybody' by Teddy Pendergrass. All the gang members began hugging each other and shaking hands. At the same time, I could hear them telling each other, "God bless you, and I love you."

The lieutenant heard how good of a change that was made in the pod. She then moved me to another violent pod where inmates were cutting up. I made a difference in it also. Another 30 inmates gave their lives to God.

It was one pod that I was put in, I could feel the presence of evil spirits. It was cold as ice. This pod had half gang members and half Muslins.

I walked to my cell saying, "Lord what am I'm in?"

I'm here with you, He answered back.

Three different gangs were clicked up together against one gang. I see one gang member fighting three gang members about the phone. It was hard for them to get in on him. He held them back with a shank.

When it was over, the one that they were fighting put one of his gang members in violation for not helping him.

About a week later, it was an inmate who called himself a thug guy. He stood 6' 4" about 300 pounds in muscle. He began making threats against some of the young gang members. He was about to go to a visit, and he wanted his hair cut. He went to one of the same young guys that he threated saying, "I got chee-chees for a haircut. I am going to a visit, and I need my head cut."

They called this muscle man, Black. He was so black until his eyes looked blue.

"I got you, I got you," the young gang member said.

He went into the cell where there was about five other young gang members. They plotted up on a quick plan on the muscle-bound bully

Black sat in the chair to get his hair cut. "Here, I got my own razor," he said, giving the youngster a razor. At that time, we would take the razor out of the disposable razor shell and put it in a comb.

"Man, take care of me good," Black said.

"I got you, I got that," the youngster said.

Black was sitting there at ease, as if he was at home. The young man put a towel around Black to catch loose hair. He then pulled Black head's back and cut him from his neck down to his throat. The towel caught was the running blood from his neck.

"Aghhh!" Black yelled out while holding the towel around his bloody neck.

He ran up to the sally port gate calling for an officer.

"You won't threaten no one else, you stupid boy!" Someone yelled out, while everyone laughed.

An officer let Black out to go to the Med. When they brought Black back, to point the youngster out and identify him, he couldn't pick him out.

I began to preach in the pod every night after that event. Gang members were giving up the gang life and giving their lives to God.

A few gang members didn't like that brothers were changing their lives. At the time, those who were unhappy about my preaching wanted to come against me, but God said, 'Touch not my anointed one. Do my prophet no harm."

All I was doing was taking care of God's business. Some of the brothers didn't want to give up some things. God said to give it all up. I ran it down to them like this.

"If you keep doing what you are doing, what's the purpose of giving your life to God? No, you not going to stop everything in one day, but allow your help to come from the Lord."

"Is there a Heaven for a gangster?" one brother asked me. I told him yes. If a gangster was willing to give his life to God, his life would change. If God tells you to do one thing and a gangster tells you to do another, who will you obey? God says if you love Him, you will keep his commandments. He all so says; how can you say you know Him and you don't keep His commandments? So yes, there is a Heaven for a gangster.

You can't take sin into the kingdom of Heaven. If that gangster is living in sin, then no, he will not get in. Be a gangster for God. He accepts all kind of sinners, but they all must change.

"You can't serve God and the Devil."

After that, even more gang members were giving up the gangs. They knew only God could help them with the charges and situations that they were facing.

While I was in my cell, a brother asked me could he come in.

I invited him with tears was rolling down his face like rain. At the same time, he was shaking like a leaf on a tree. He was holding a picture in his hand of a young lady holding a new-born baby. He explained to me about the drug charges that he had. I explained to him, he had to give something up. He had to give up the main strong hold that was keeping him from God.

"I will stop selling drugs, if that's what God wants me to do. If God lets me go tomorrow when I go to court, I will get a job and take care of my wife and my little baby. I will do anything that God wants me to do. Will you pray for me? I don't know how to pray? I know God will hear you."

"Do you know how to talk to me?" I asked the brother.

"Yes," He responded.

"Well, you know how to pray. Prayer is a sincere conversation with God from your heart. I will pray for you and your family."

We then got on our knees and knelt by my bed.

"What is your name?" I asked the brother.

"Rico," he responded.

I like to call names while I pray. I prayed, and Rico cried. Once I felt that God had answered *yes* to my prayer, and Rico's faith and request, we got up from our kneeled position.

While Rico was walking out of my cell, he said, "All I want to do is take care of my baby." While he was still crying, Rico had earlier gave his life to God and admitted, that he was giving up the gang. Now, he admitted that he would stop selling drugs and start taking care of his family the right way by getting a job.

God knows the heart.

God was showing me that because of the little baby, He would answer the prayer to be released.

I called my brother and asked him if they were hiring. He told me not at the time and asked why I wanted to know. I told him I was going to send a brother there that gave his life to God. My brother told me to tell him that he could come in and fill out an application. I told Rico and gave him the address and phone number.

"You know what? They dropped all charges against me," Rico told me.

The next day when Rico returned from court, he stood in the sally port and said, "Preacher, God answered our prayers. I'm going home today."

Everyone was glad for him. They began to clap and cheer. *Sometimes God will allow things to happen just to prove His power.*

This miracle of God's doing showed others that sometimes you have to give something up to receive something. Some people want God's blessing, but they don't want to do what it takes to get God's blessing.

Two weeks later, Rico was standing in the sally port looking down at the floor with a sad look on his face.

"What are you doing back?" I asked him with a disappointed look on my face.

I called Rico into my cell, and we had a talk. He told me the truth. He said not only did he let his family down, but he also let God down and lied to Him. He then told me, as soon as he got home, he kissed and hugged his little baby girl. He made love to his wife. The next day he got back with his drug supplier. He got a sack of rocks, stood on a corner by the church that he was planning on going to and sold rocks. He said the next night someone walked up to him; put a gun in his face and tried to rob him. He said they wrestled over the gun. Rico ended up with the gun in his hand, shot the robber and killed him.

I told Rico, "You can't play with God. You only play with yourself."

During this time, there were so many babies in Christ who had given their lives to God, and I wanted to help them to grow. There were also five Muslims who moved in the pod and were causing problems. Two of them would come to me asking me for some of my pork sausage.

Some of the men told me they were using the Muslims as a gang, and they knew the Muslims would fight for them otherwise

Later, there were five more Muslims who moved into the pod. Three of them were trouble makers and after hearing what the Christian was saying would try to find fault in the Word, so that they would have a reason to pick on the young Christians.

At the time, not only did I had to defend the Word of God, but I also found myself defending the Christians.

The next night, I preached a message called, "One Way." It explained that there was only one way to enter into Heaven and that way IS through Jesus Christ.

My message stirred the Muslims up to the point that they disagreed on God's every word. They did their thing, and I had to do like God's Word says.

Every man has the right to choose the faith that they want to believe in. There is one thing that God won't do, that is stop you from doing what you want to do. If God won't stop you, who is man to try and stop you?

Not only were they picking on the young Christians, but they were picking at me also. By me being an overseer or you can say a shepherd over the Christians, I found myself at times putting my life on the line.

At the same time, I was being wise as a serpent and humble as a dove.

When I was out of the pod or asleep, they would try to convert the Christian brothers who had given their lives to God. However, there was only one that I knew who turned to the Muslim faith. It hurt me, but like I said, every man has his own choices. I tried to win him back, but he had a strong hold.

I preached every night with a different message. One night, I preached a message called, "Be careful Who You Entertain."

In the message, it told about the life of Elijah and the life of John the Baptist lived. Not only did they talk about us eating pork and the way that we prayed, they built up enough of guts to ask me, "Could we see you in your cell?"

"Yes." I said boldly.

By now I was fed up with their foolishness. Three of them walked in.

"Look man, you don't have the right to use the name of Elijah when you preach. We are the only ones who can use the name," the one who was supposed to be head muslins said, while holding a shank.

"Man look, let me tell you all something. I'm going to use any name that is in the Bible. I'm going to say whatever God gives me to say. I remember God's Word. No weapon formed against me shall prosper. It took three of you and a shank to tell me that! Man, look, in the name of Jesus, all of you get out of my cell!" I yelled boldly.

"That man is crazy. Let's go," one man said, and they rushed out.

The next day one of them said, "Man I was just trying to see what was going on."

"Yeah, that's what I assumed," I replied.

The next day one of my so-called home boys plotted with the Muslims. He tried to tell him that he couldn't whip me one-on-one.

"I don't believe that he is going to fight from the way he preaches," the Muslim said.

"Man, you are going to need a shank; you might get him like that. Toe-to-toe, you won't win."

Afterwards, my home boy gave his Muslim brother a shank to stick me with. Because the brothers had been talking and picking on me for two months and hadn't done anything, I was caught a bit off guard. Aikey built up enough guts to try a steal on me.

While I was in one of my Christian brother's cell standing up, I was breaking down some Bible scriptures that he didn't understand.

"FIGHT #14"

While still standing with the Bible in one of my hands, I felt a sting on the right side of my face. This was the Muslim brother that all the other Muslims were afraid of. They would listen and do whatever he said.

"You hit the preacher! Please don't fight!" my Christian brother yelled out.

I could tell he did not want to see anything happen to me. While my so-called home boy stepped in the face of the door, "Let them fight, it's one-on-one!" he yelled out to my Christian brother.

Quickly, I laid my Bible on the top bunk while keeping my eye on the send out. He must have dropped whatever it was that he hit me with. He was looking down on the floor. This must have been God's way of giving me the upper hand on my enemy. Before anyone could say another word, Aikey was hit by one of my fast closed-fists to his right eye.

He grabbed it and at the same time tried to run out of the cell. I pulled him back into the cell and began to go to work on him.

"Ohhh! Howw! Ohhh!" Aikey yelled out as if he was going to get some help.

"Man, preacher is flat-foot jacking!" someone yelled out, while everyone stood at the outer facing of the cell door.

"Someone stop it! He's going to kill Aikey!" Someone else yelled out.

"I'm not going in there, he might get me!" Another one yelled out.

From seeing Aikey's eyes roll back his head, I could tell that he couldn't take too many more licks. While I was over the top of him and had beaten him down, an officer yelled out through the catwalk window.

I knew from there I only had a minute to put his lights all the way out.

"Let me go! Let me go! Here come the police!" Aikey yelled out.

"You weren't worry about the police when you hit me!" I said while continuing beating on his head.

The officer rushed in and pulled me off of Aikey.

Aikey was taken out to the Med and from there, he was glad to be removed out of the pod.

After it was over, I wanted to let loose on my so-called home boy. God had to give me a heart to hold my peace.

I had some home boys who would never cross you. However, he was going against the grain and was headed to a dead end. With these kinds of people, all you need to do is sit back and watch them reap what they sow.

I then walk to my cell, thinking to myself, "This man didn't get but one lick and the weapon didn't proposer."

Everyone could tell that Aikey was embarrassed by knots on his head, face and swollen his eyes.

As I sat m my cell, I felt a little bad after the way the brother's face reflected back through my memory. At the same time, I gave this man no reason to hit me. It was all because of the Word of God. I was only hit because I was a child of God and had been defending the Word. Because I knew that Jesus went through something worse, tears began to roll down my face.

Later on that week, things went back to normal. I was on a three-day fast. I felt light as a feather. When I would walk, it felt like I was floating on clouds. It was as if I was in the flesh but walking in the spirit.

I heard the sally port door open. It was two very dark-skinned men walking in. One of them was an old-school homey that played football with me. The both of them were some very big men. Emmanuel was about 5'6', 320 pounds, all muscle. Williams, who played football with me, was 6'2", 245 pounds.

I didn't let up on preaching the Word of God none cut. Williams would stand there from the beginning of God's Word, until I was done.

Emmanuel would listen as well but from a distance. For some reason, it was as if he was a big angel in the human-form.

The next day while in my cell reading the Word of God, I opened the Bible to Matthew 1:23. God was with me. At this time, it was the last day of my three-day fast. I got on my knees and asked God to show me that he was with me.

I told God that I had faith and no doubt. I just wanted to see a miracle. Later on that morning, the doctor came up to the bars and gave out pills. Williams walked out of his cell taking baby steps in a bent over way. I could tell that he was in pain.

"Doctor, doctor," Williams sadly called out for help.

"What's the problem?" The doctor asked.

"I have a hernia, and I am losing lots of blood, when I use the bathroom."

By me caring for my homeboy, I walked closer to hear what the problem was. At the same time, Williams pulled the upper part of his pants down, and a hernia popped out big as a soft ball. It looked like a human fist was hanging off his lower stomach.

"Put that back up. Take this and fill out a sick call slip!" The doctor said, as he passed Williams two Tylenol pills and walked off in a fast pace.

While I was still standing there, Williams gave me a phone number and asked me to get someone from that number on the phone.

"Let them know that, this is it. I know I'm about to die," he said and took his baby steps back to his cell.

I made the call and gave his family the message. When I gave Williams the message that his family gave me, I walked to my cell.

About five minutes later, "Preacher! Preacher! Williams want you," one of the Christian brothers told me.

"Lorenzo, will you pray for me, I'm about to die," Williams said as he laid there in the floor hardly breathing.

When I walked into the cell, I could feel a cold spirit. It was very cold in his cell. When I looked into his eyes, they were red like blood.

I told two of the Christian brothers to hang a sheet up at the door. I then walked back to my cell, got the Bible and some Holy oil that I had to fast and prayed over myself.

I had two of the brothers to stand on the outside of the door. I took one of the Christian brothers in with me.

I put the oil around the post of the door and then oiled up my hands and head. I anointed and prayed over my Christian brother. I then told him to say Amen to every word that I said and put his hand on my shoulder while I prayed. I then anointed Williams's head with oil while saying, "God bless you, anoint you, and heal you in the name of the Father, the Son, and the Holy Spirit."

I then began to pray words of healing from the Bible over Williams. When I laid one of my hands on Williams' head, it felt like cold ice.

I prayed for 40 minutes using every Bible scriptural that I knew had something to do with healing.

I could hear Jesus say, "This don't only come out by praying but by fasting and praying."

Williams then stood up saying, "Lorenzo, I feel better."

The whole time that I was praying, I was glancing at the fist-like knot. It was going down slowly.

Knowing that Williams called on me, I told him, "It's our faith in God that healed you."

I remember Jesus said to those that he healed," It's your faith that made you whole."

I had the brothers to take down the sheet, and I walked to my cell.

"Man, I'm scared of him!" one of the Muslim brothers said. "I don't believe he is human."

From that day on, I had no problems out of the Muslims. It was God's way of showing them that He was with me. He got the entire cell to see Williams stand in the back of the pod smoking a cigarette.

I was glad to see him up and doing well but not smoking.

The more Williams showed the inmates where the hernia had been, but was now gone, the more the inmates stated that they were afraid of me.

Behind that, it was ten more brothers who gave their lives to God.

As weeks rolled on, I began to pay Emmanuel close attention. Every time I would call prayer, he would turn the TV off. He then would go from cell to cell telling everyone to hold down the noise, because it was prayer call.

There were times some of the inmates didn't respect prayer call unless they were going to court the next day. That showed me how some want God's blessings, but they don't want to do what it takes to get God's blessings.

God is so merciful; however, he would sometimes still give them blessings.

Before and after I did prayer call, Emmanuel would do his work out and pushups. A few weeks passed and some of the Christian brothers were having problems with the gang members over the phones.

Emmanuel heard Christian brothers asking me to talk to them. However, before I could, "I'm tired of you gang bangers trying to take advantage of the phones. From now on this is the Christian brothers' phone. If that's a problem, you all can take it up with me. All of you, can bring it on."

While Emmanuel was saying that he snatched the phone out of one of the gang member's hand and hung it up.

"Man!" the gang member yelled.

"Man what?" Emmanuel said while giving the gang member a quick loose fist, knocking him down to the floor.

"Help, help!" the gang banger yelled out for his bangers to help him.

About five of them ran to his rescue. Nothing they tried worked. Emmanuel was just too big. He was knocking them around like rag dolls. It was funny but not funny. They all were being hit with some powerful blows and getting tossed like a French salad.

Before long, an officer walked passed and saw the commotion. He then called for the Direct Reinforce Team (DRT). The fight was on one side of the pod. I was standing alone on other side. I knew that this man knew me when we were young. His name was Sgt. Davis.

He zeroed in on the fight, then looked at me without saying a word and sprayed me in the eyes with pepper gas.

What point he tried to prove, I would never know.

Like it says in God's Word, you reap what you sow, and revenge is the Lord's.

Deep in my heart, I believed that the girl that he liked, she had liking for me when we were young. The officer didn't have to ask the gangers to move out. When the gates opened, they ran out. When it was all over, I could see a relief on the faces of the Christian brothers.

About a month later, I felt that my job was done in this pod.

"Spencer! Come here," the lieutenant called me to the bars with a smile on her face.

"I heard how good of a job you have done in this pod. Do you want to go to the Trustees Houses?"

"Yes!" I answered with a smile on my face.

"Pack your things," she replied.

The brothers were glad to see me go to Trustees Houses, but at the same time, they were sad. The next day while in the Trustees House, I was given a job to cook in the main kitchen. Only days later, after the chef found out how well I could cook, he moved me to the main dining room.

Not only did I had to serve the officers, but I had to cook their food. Officers began to brag about my cooking. They began to pay me to cook special plates for them. They were really crazy about my Mc BLT' s.

I was giving a key to all the meats. I was allowed to put all of the extra food in a food cart and take it to any pod of my choice. I had a chance to feed all my Christian brothers and some of my enemies.

"Thank you, preacher," they would say to me.

"You 're welcome," I responded.

A month later, I got a message from one of the convicts who worked in the kitchen with me. He told me that two of my brothers were in the jail, and they wanted to see me. I was pleased to see my brothers, but not in jail.

After I was done for that night, I took all the extra Bar-B-Q and left overs that I had cooked and put it in the food cart.

I looked on the count sheet and found out where my brothers were in the same pod. I pushed the food cart to their pod and called their names.

I got the officer to let Cleveland out. We had a talk and were glad to see each other. The officer could only let one of them out. I only spoke to Tony. I was allowed to feed them, and we said we loved each other and gave good-byes.

The next day while in the kitchen, the food that I was cooking had everyone's noses in the air. There was one inmate who always gave cooks a problem. He would try to take the cooked food and it all would have to be accounted for. I noticed how he had been watching me the whole time that I was cooking.

No matter how hard I would try to do right, wrong would find its way to find me.

This inmate was called Green Eyes. When I was done cooking, he asked me, "Can I have one of your sandwiches?"

"No, they are accounted for, and they are for the officers," I told him.

"Man, you're not talking about nothing; I'm going to get me one of them burgers!"

"So, you're going to take something?"

"If that's what you want to call it!"

I gathered all my food and locked it in the hot box. I had been around long enough to look into the eyes of a convict and the eyes of a coward and tell the difference.

I knew I supposed to fight my situation with the Word of God, but I took it upon myself. I made it up in my mind that I was going to scare the heck out of him.

Poncho was a heavy drug dealer that supplied the whole jail. Also, he would pay the officers to look out for him. There was a saying, *scratch my back and I'll scratch yours.*

Poncho was over canned goods. I would give him perishable food, and he would give me canned goods. He also was over the butcher's knives that were kept in the warehouse.

Green Eyes had been on a spree all day, and I knew that he was coming my way.

"Poncho, give me one of the butcher's knives," I asked him.

"Lowe, I can tell you' re not the same man. If you want to take care of some business, I will give it to you. I just can't see it in you anymore," Poncho said in a respectful way.

He then gave me a long butcher knife and I put it in the waistband of my pants and walked back into the kitchen. I took the sandwiches back out.

While Green Eyes looked on, he began to walk my way just knowing he was about to eat.

"Let me see you take something!" I said, talking through my teeth while swinging the long butcher knife.

Green Eyes backed up. All I could hear was him hollering in the air and the sound coming from the butcher knife.

"Come here boy, don't run now!" I yelled out.

"Ok, Preacher, I don't won't none. I don't want no problem!" he yelled out.

"Lowe, Lowe, please don't kill him." Poncho said.

"You can easily wipe him. I told your brother how good you can fight." Poncho continued.

There was no away out of the kitchen. We were locking in. Green Eyes was in a corner shaking like a leaf on a tree.

Once I gave the knife back, I talked to Green Eye about God. He listened to every word. He must have seen death, because he gave his life to God.

I never told him I was only trying to scare him. On the other hand, what if Green Eyes tried to fight back and Satan would have got the best of me? Then I would have had to really defend myself.

I could have caught a murder charge. But I thank God that wasn't the case.

That night while lying on my bed, I was glad that Green Eyes gave his life to God. But I felt bad that I attacked him. That let me know that I had to be careful about everything.

The next day, we went to the gym. There was an inmate there who had a nasty charge of shooting innocent people. Little children were killed also.

He couldn't hold me for nothing on the court.

"Hold the old man!" they yelled out.

It only frustrated him more. He began to call me all kinds of names, which I over looked. It only made me play harder. Once we were back in the pod, he kept talking about me like a dog. Then he got into the shower.

The Word of God says, 'Be angry and sin not,' But I did both. An officer was looking on the whole time. As if he was waiting on me to retaliate.

I didn't say a word.

When the officer walked off, I thought, "This young man killed some little children, then talking to me like that?"

I walk into the shower area, pulled the curtain open and said, "Say one more word to me, and I will kill you dead! Say another word!"

His eyes got big as a bow dollar, and he froze like a piece of ice. He didn't say one word, but I sinned. Not only did I threaten a man, but I disobeyed God.

Not only did this man cool off, but he stopped going to the gym.

Again, I took food back to some of the pods that I preached in. The inmates were locked down.

All I could hear was "Preacher, Preacher!"

It reminded me how God said that He let it rain on the just as well as the unjust. I got a chance to look in some of the cells that brought back memories. I could see scars on the walls where we had been sharping our shanks.

One day some brothers came to me telling me about one of the chaplains. They asked me to come hear how he conducted God's house.

'You have got to come,' they convinced me.

So, I paid him a visit.

When I walked in, I liked the fact that he had everyone to sit up front. But he had one of the quickest and most insincere prayers that I had ever heard. I really couldn't understand what he was saying.

"Any questions before I get started?" he asked.

"Yes, Chaplain, my teeth are killing me. I have been trying to go to the dentist. Can you help me?" a brother asked.

"Yes, if it is killing you, why don't you go on and diem and it won't kill you," the chaplain responded. "Any more questions?"

"Yes, Chaplin, I want to know if you commit suicide, will God forgive you?" another brother asked.

"I don't know I never tried it. Try it and you will find out," the chaplain responded.

If he was talking like this, I wasn't going to sit and hear what he had to preach about. I got up and walked out.

The next day I paid the chaplain a visit. After I apologize for walking out, he gave me the opportunity to preach in the chapel. He looked at me in an amazing but shocking way. Not only did I have him on his toes, but I could hear him say a word.

"A man like this is locked up?"

The message was, 'Deliverance' and believe me, about 40 inmates were crying from their hearts and gave their lives to God.

The next day, I signed for the remaining of my time and was bused back to S.C.C.C.

When we were riding out, a song was playing on the radio by Dennis Edward called, I've Been to Paradise. I made some noise with some good old boys, and we rocked the southern jail.

While back at the penal farm, I enrolled in carpentry, metal studs, and brick mason classes. I completed all three and received my certificates. I was also placed in the kitchen and given a job over all of the cooks.

When my time was winding down, and it was less than a month for me to go home, I pretty much stayed to myself, unless God lead me to someone whose life could be changed.

I got a chance to preach in the main chapel. I gave a testimony on how I had overcome the world and gave my life to God.

After I was done preaching a message, "Stay In the Ship" the church was in an uproar.

When the Holy Spirit came down, Big Mike gave his testimony on how he was reaping what he sowed. A lot of the things, this ex-convict had done are not mentioned in this book. He lifted his shirt up and showed 100 cuts and a hole in his body were he had been stuck with a shank and told how God spared his life.

The next day, gang members were looking at me as if I had committed a sin, because I preached the gospel uncut.

For about two days while, I was testifying to gang members and they were giving up the gang. Some were looking at me as if they were the devil himself.

The next day, while getting ready to watch a movie, one of them picked at me. Knowing that I was a different man and on my way home, I over looked them.

"Someone better sleep in their shoes!" one of them yelled out while looking at me.

I never checked out or ran from a man. I decided that I'd get the officer to move me down the hall. An officer was sitting in the hall, and I knocked on the door. He opened the door, and I spoke with him saying, "Officer, will you move me to the other end? I'm trying to go home."

"What? You have a problem in here?"

"No, I don't have a problem. Someone else is the problem."

"I know you from the old school, and I know you are a fighter. I know out of all people, you are not trying to check out."

Before I could say another word, he closed the door and walked off. I then walked over to my bed and laid it down.

A little later that night, "You might as well put your shoes on. You around here turning our brother against us. We heard about how you jacking; let's see if God is with you now?"

I had my shoes on the whole time. I could tell Satan was at work. I walked back to the door and pushed the button.

"Officer, I want to move out. They are about to jump me in there," I told the officer that answered the intercom.

"Look man, we are not going to move you this time of night. You can lay it down," the officer said and shut off the button.

I pushed the button again.

"Look man, stay off the button, or I'm going to write you up!"

While walking from the door, I was approached by one of the big gang members. My back was now against the wall, and I had no choice but to fight for my life. We ended up in the day room. I thought I had a crowd around us, but it was only gang members. I knew that I had to take this man out quick, while I was watching my back.

It was dark; the only light that we had was the light coming from the hall. Not only was this coward slow, but he was just big and tall, that was all.

With about five licks, I dropped him like a hot potato. He was out for the count.

"Man, what is he hitting with; he got something in his hand!" one of the cowards yelled out.

They all were zeroing in on my hands, looking for something, but it wasn't anything but bare knuckles.

"You have messed up, come on with your lazy ass eye!" an even bigger gang-banger said out of anger, because I had knocked his brother out.

"I'm telling you man! Dude got something in his hand!" another one said, still looking for something that wasn't there.

This gang banger made it easier. He kept looking back for help, and no one was making a move but me. He caught a left right to both eyes.

When he bent over, I began to hit him with everything that I had.

With my back to the wall, it made it hard for them to rush me. Suddenly, one of them called a code, and the remaining eight of them rushed me.

While I was still standing throwing blows like flash, I was going down to the floor. I couldn't feel anything but fists connecting to my face, head and body.

The way that I was being kicked and hit, the sound was like baby bombs. My lights were all the way out. They must have kicked me for five to ten minutes. I laid out on the floor all most dead.

Minutes later when I awakened, I could see one of them standing at the front door still looking out with his back turned to me.

All I could do was ask God to give me strength to make it to him. As I slowly in walked pain, through the door up on him, I couldn't get but two noneffective licks upside of his head.

"He is back up!" one of them shouted.

"I thought he was dead!" another one said, while another one called the code again and about ten of them quickly surrounded me.

I was beaten, stumped and kick in the head so hard till I had no more feelings.

All I could see was a big bright light.

"You 're going to make it," a soft voice said.

When I came to, I had no shirt on and the paramedics were pumping my heart with a machine.

"He's back!" one of the paramedics said when God sent me back to life.

The same officer, who told me that he knew that I wasn't trying to move out because he knew that I could fight, was standing over me putting cuffs on me.

Now, in my right mind, I thought that I was still being jumped. I tried to attack the officer, but I was too weak. He wrestled me down to the floor and continued to cuff me.

"My God, who did this to him? I know this man, ain't no one or two men could do this. This man can fight," the head of administration said, while I was being taken out on the stretcher.

I was taken to the hospital where I stayed for about two weeks in a coma. I didn't know my own name or that I was in the world.

One of my brother's friends worked as an officer at the penal form. She called my brother, Danny, and told him how badly I had been beaten up.

A month later, administration put me in the hole on one side, and the gang bangers on the other side.

In J-Building it was only a glass wall that separated us. The gang members were pleading, begging for me to forgive them.

Another one of their gang leaders who was over all of them knew me from the old school. He had them put in violation and beaten down, because of jumping on me.

A week later after God had restored and healed me, in the court room, the judge saw the pictures of me that were taking from the beating.

"I can't believe this is you," she stated.

From there, I was sent home where I continued to heal and preach the gospel of Jesus Christ.

God told us to watch as well as pray. So, I will always be looking out for the Devil. Not to fight him with my hands, but to fight him with the Word of God.

That is the only way that we can defeat him. I learned trying to fight Satan on your own, or without God, you will never win.

Although I was winning every fight physically, I was still losing spiritual. Now that I have acquired a lot of spiritual knowledge in my life, I have learned I would rather fight someone that I can see, than try to fight against Satan, someone that I can't see.

God's Word tells us, we wrestle daily not against flesh and blood, but against principalities, against power, against the rulers of darkness of this world, against spiritual wickedness in high places.

Like the Bible says, "We will sit in Heavenly places here on earth."

And I will say," If you go through hell here on earth, don't stop."

Now that tells me just because that I'm a new man, my fight doesn't stop. It is now a spiritual fight, and I must fight to the end.

I'm fighting a good fight; I'm running the race; I will not give up; I will keep the faith; and I will endure to the end.

THE END

ABOUT THE AUTHOR

L orenzo Spencer was born in Memphis, Tennessee in the year 1962 during a time of depression. He came from a very large family of twenty-one sisters and brothers. His father passed on when Spencer was only seven years old. With twelve children at home at that time, his mother found a way to provide for them all. Due to the trouble his mother had keeping a job, it was difficult for them to stay in a regular home. They would move around the city, causing Lorenzo to fall behind on his education. When Lorenzo did try to learn, because of his good sports ability, coaches would come into his classroom and tell the teachers to pass him. The teachers would give him a C-average because the coaches needed him to play. Lorenzo tried to hustle in the wrong way, and he learned that crime does not pay. As of now, Lorenzo is a free, single man living for God and looking for the love of his life. He still lives in Memphis.

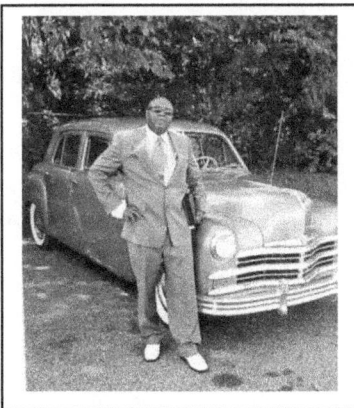

Lorenzo was called to preach in 1984 at the age of 22 but, avoided it and ran instead. After God wiped him with many stripes, he accepted his calling while in prison in 1997 but yet straddled the fence. During this walk, he went under teaching of

Pastor Ernie Smith, the pastor of Independent Christian Church, where he received several commemoration awards for sharing the Lord's Word. Over 200 inmate's lives were converted through his preaching of the gospel of Jesus.

On August 13, 2002, the Salvation Army of Atlanta, Georgia, presented Lorenzo a certificate for completing the Bible Correspondence study courses at the Life of Christ, The Christian Life, The Early Church, Early Beginnings, History of a Nation and Survey Course.

On May 28, 2011, he received a Participation "Real Talk" from Officer's C. Reynolds and A. Taylor.

On June 17, 2012 He was presented a certificate of Achievement for the G-pod program from S. Anderson.

In 2012, the Shelby County Jail presenter Lorenzo several certificates of completion including the Life Skills, Domestic Violence, MET, and Anger Management Programs.

On March 13, 2003, he received a Certificate of Recognition from the World Bible School for the completion of the course.

On April 11, 2013, he completed the intensive study on Beginning Steps from Chaplain Ronnie Osborne.

November 20, 2013, he was presented a Certificate of Completion for NCWX PRO SOCIAL LIFE SKILLS from THERAPEUTIC COMMUNITY, Program Manager Vivian Windsor.

He is now the Assistant Pastor at the Church of the Living God, Unser Pastor Thompson also the Assistant Pastor here at The Temple of Love under Pastor Danny Spencer.